The Founding of New Societies

Books by Louis Hartz

Economic Policy and Democratic Thought:
Pennsylvania, 1776-1860
The Liberal Tradition in America
The Founding of New Societies

The Founding of

Studies in the History of the United States,

With contributions by

Kenneth D. McRae, Richard M. Morse,

Richard N. Rosecrance, Leonard M. Thompson

New Societies

Latin America, South Africa, Canada, and Australia

by LOUIS HARTZ

Harcourt, Brace & World, Inc.
New York

© 1964 by Louis Hartz

C.9.67

Library of Congress Catalog Card Number: 64-11535

Printed in the United States of America

Preface

I attempt in this study, on the basis of an earlier analysis of American history from the angle of Europe, to present a general theory of five societies created by European migration in modern times. In the course of developing the larger view I arranged a conference among the contributors to the volume in Cambridge, Massachusetts, in January, 1961. Since that time, however, the essays have evolved independently, and no effort has been made to organize them in a single pattern, save in one or two instances, mainly for purposes of terminology. They include diverse points of view and represent the individual responsibility of the authors. I should add that the materials in Chapter Four were originally delivered as the Commonwealth Lectures in American History at the University of London in 1962. I am happy to express here my thanks for the fine hospitality accorded to me at that time.

Louis Hartz

August, 1964

Contents

Contents

Chapter Eight
The Radical Culture of Australia   275
by Richard N. Rosecrance

Part One

A Theory of the Development of the New Societies

by Louis Hartz

Chapter One

The Fragmentation of
European Culture and Ideology

1 The Fragment

There is a problem of traditionalism and change common to the societies studied in this book, and it derives from the fact that all of them are fragments of the larger whole of Europe struck off in the course of the revolution which brought the West into the modern world. For when a part of a European nation is detached from the whole of it, and hurled outward onto new soil, it loses the stimulus toward change that the whole provides. It lapses into a kind of immobility. Nor does it matter what stage of European history the part embodies, whether it is feudal, as in Latin America and French Canada, bourgeois, as in the United States, Dutch South Africa, and English Canada, or actually radical, charged with the proletarian turmoil of the Industrial Revolution, as in Australia and British South Africa. The fragments reflect every phase of the European revolution, but they evince alike the immobilities of fragmentation. Moreover they are involved alike, because of this, in one of the strangest issues of change that the world impact of the modern era has produced. For it is the irony of that impact that it has hurled back at the fragments, after centuries and from wholly unexpected angles, the very Western revolution they originally fled. Their escape

3

has turned out to be an illusion, and they are forced now to transcend the conservatism to which it gave birth.

All of this is to say that these societies, in the midst of the variations they contain, are governed by the ultimate experience of the American liberal tradition.* That tradition arose as a result of the extrication of a bourgeois fragment from the turmoil of seventeenth-century England, and it gave to the United States over three hundred years of liberal immobility, but it now confronts on the world plane, thrust back at it from places as distant as Russia and China, the very alien ideologies it managed to escape. On the surface it might seem, precisely because the content of many of the other fragment cultures differs so widely from our own, that there could be no possible connection. What could the hacienda culture of Peru have to do with the bourgeois farming of Wisconsin, the socialism of Sydney with the almost hysterical antiradicalism of Nebraska? But if we focus on the element of sheer traditionalism that all of these cultures contain, and on the loss of the European challenges out of which it arose, these differences recede into the background. Nor does this happen only in connection with the feudal world of Latin America, or French Canada, a milieu where one might expect conservatism to flourish. It happens also in connection with the radical setting of Australia which enshrines, no less passionately than the United States enshrines Locke, the spirit of the Chartists and of Cobbett. The paradox of a liberal conservatism is proof enough of the traditionalizing impact of fragmentation, but surely the paradox of a radical conservatism places the matter beyond any doubt at all.

When a fragment of Europe becomes the whole of a new nation, it becomes unrecognizable in European terms. We must not assume, because the fragment cultures do not shout out at us the European terms feudal or liberal, that the European ideologies are not there: they have lost the need for shouting, which is proof of the new conservative power that fragmentation has given them. Of course there is some intrinsic com-

* Cf. my *The Liberal Tradition in America* (New York, 1955). I have dealt on pp. 20-21 of that volume with the comparative study of the new societies in light of the partial embodiment of the European ideological complex for which I here use the term "fragment."

plexity here. None of the new societies is exhausted by an ideological category, whatever it is. Not only are there always "imperfections" in this respect, as when feudal remnants cling to the American fragment or capitalist Whiggery to the Australian, but there are a wide variety of factors alien to ideology which can twist it out of shape. Some of these are to be found in the peculiar stamp of the European homeland, the nature of the colonial relationship, and the sort of contact the fragment has with African and aboriginal peoples. Latin America, which might have had as a feudal fragment a quiet, French-Canadian kind of history, was actually streaked with revolution as a result of these forces. Iberian feudalism was anarchic to begin with,[1] the imperial discrimination against the Spanish creole drove him toward the Enlightenment, and the absorption of non-Western peoples at the lower grades of the feudal order inflamed the usual hierarchical relationships.

But after these complexities have been noticed, it remains a fact that the very triumph of the European ideology in the fragment traditions makes it unrecognizable in the old sense. We know the European ideology, indeed we name it, in terms of its enemies, in terms of the whole of the classical European social struggle. When fragmentation detaches it from this context, and makes it master of a whole region, all sorts of magic inevitably take place. First of all it becomes a universal, sinking beneath the surface of thought to the level of an assumption. Then, almost instantly, it is reborn, transformed into a new nationalism arising out of the necessities of fragmentation itself. Feudalism comes back at us as the French-Canadian Spirit, liberalism as the American Way of Life, radicalism as the Australian Legend. But even this is not all. The European ideology, buried and refurbished, is extended to African and Indian relationships which in Europe it did not have, so that it inspires a series of racial formulations apparently outside its compass. Suárez lies hidden beneath the Latin-American encomienda, Calvin beneath the slavery of Dutch South Africa. By the time we are through, the European ethic, so familiar to us on the streets of Paris and London, has been buried almost completely.

[1] Numbered notes are on pages 319 to 330.

But surely this does not mean that it has disappeared. On the contrary, the very things which hide the European ideology are proof of the enormous new power it has acquired in the fragment world, the very power which produces its problem under the impact of world events today. Where else could an ideology become a moral absolute, a national essence, a veritable way of racial life?

2 The Making of the Fragment Tradition

Beneath these metamorphoses, these psychic inflations and disguises, a purely mechanistic process is at work. That process begins with the escape of the fragment from its original European enemy, the flight of the Puritan, as it were, from the hungry clutch of Laud. But it goes far beyond that. For the fragment is protected against a whole series of later enemies as a result of its original movement, enemies which in the renewing process of European history arise out of those it has escaped. Marx fades because of the fading of Laud. There is a stifling of the future as well as an escape from the past, and it is at the heart of the process of fragmentation that the one is determined by the other. Nor is even this all. Once the fragment has escaped the European challenges past and future, once it has achieved its curiously timeless place in Western history, an unfolding within it takes place which would have been inconceivable in the constricted atmosphere of Europe. To continue with the American example, Jacksonian democracy burgeons, the New Deal flowers, because both the right and the left are missing. The fixity of the fragment liberates in the end a rich interior development.

If we look more closely at the European struggle, it will not be hard to discover why the escape from past leads inevitably to an escape from future enemies. There is a process of contagion at work in Europe, enormously subtle and ramifying, in which ideologies give birth to one another over time. This process actually begins with the feudal world which, in a queer Hegelian sense, helps to generate the very attack against it. That world not only gives its own "class consciousness" to every Enlightenment ideology, bourgeois or socialist, but it holds out as well the memory of a corporate community which, in the midst of revolution, men seek to recapture. Marx no less than Rousseau yearned for that community, which is why there could be such a thing as "feudal socialism," a kind of reactionary Marxism which sought to absorb the industrial question into the medieval framework. But even within the Enlightenment world itself there is a complex contagion. Whiggery inspires with its first grand liberal formulations the Jacobin who later assails it. The Jacobin inspires with his more radical version of the Enlightenment the socialist whom he ultimately fears. So that at every point, from medievalism to modernity, and within modernity itself, the European contagion is at work. Europe renews itself out of its own materials.

Under these circumstances it is not hard to see why the extrication of the fragment from Europe at any point should have fateful consequences for its future conservatism. When it leaves Europe, it cuts short the process of the European contagion at the point of its leaving. When it leaves its first antagonist, it leaves all of the future antagonists that the first inspires. I have cited the case of socialism fading in America because feudalism has been left behind. We can now see, not only in the United States but in other bourgeois fragments like Dutch South Africa and English Canada, the enormous complexity of this negative connection: Marx dies because there is no sense of class, no spirit of revolution, no yearning for the corporate past. But the same principle, in a different way, holds true of the feudal and radical fragments as well. The French Canadian, having escaped the Enlightenment, escapes also Jacobinism and Marxism, since these later radicalisms are fed by the Enlightenment spirit. He is an American, as it were, but, starting earlier, he has had a wider "future" that has faded. One might suppose, perhaps, since radicalism is the "last" ideology, that the Australian out of the world of Cobbett might have no prospective damage to impose because of his escape from the past. But that is not true. In his case a radical migration in the eighteenth and the nineteenth centuries blocks the doctrinaire socialism of the twentieth, for without the continuing pressure of the English feudal and bourgeois challenges the spirit of Harold Laski loses its source. Australian radicalism, even after the Labour Party, even after the blood and thunder of the early Commonwealth period, remains morally fixed at the point of its origin. So that the process here works within ideologies as well as among them, smothering later versions of a single theme as well as the later themes themselves. There is, in fact, no shrinking of the European past at any point which does not shrink the European future as well.

Given this protection through time of its boundaries, it is not surprising that the fragment should nourish an affirmative unfolding not to be found in Europe. Every fragment, in the dynamic context of the Old World, contains a potential whose development is constricted by the multiplying challenges it confronts. Europe gives us a series of strangled social visions. Thus the feudal order has the solution of Tory socialism, of Young England and the French Legitimists, for the problem of modern industry. But where liberalism has already hit, and the masses have become infected with it, how can this idea ever be completely appealing? But this does not mean that liberalism is in perfect shape. Its utopia is a utopia of individualists where Jacobin democracy would come spontaneously to power. But precisely because feudalism still has a grip on the land, and socialism is emerging to claim the factory, that utopia is perpetually frustrated. The Jacobin must stave off the Tory and the Marxist, which means that his Whig opponent crushes him again and again through the manipulation of various interests. Needless to say, the socialist does not emerge unscathed in this situation. He has a glorious vision too, as we know. But not only is that vision challenged by aristocratic and bourgeois forces, the proletariat itself, the very hope of the future, continually "sells out" to those forces. The Marxian lamentation on this score is a matter of legend, and in its very bitterness summarizes the frustration of every social idea that the Old World has. Europe develops many teleologies but because it intertwines

8

them with one another, because it locks them together in a seething whole, it gives none of them the freedom to evolve.

The fragments provide that freedom. By extricating the European ideologies from the European battle, by cutting short the process of renewal which keeps that battle going, they permit precisely that unfolding of potentialities which the Old World denies. The story here is marvelous, like a succession of Cinderella dreams. Bossuet, Locke, and Cobbett, miserable men abroad, all wake up in worlds finer than any they have known. When the revolution hits France, French Canada clings to the spirit of divine right, and if Latin America is touched by the Enlightenment, the underlying tide of feudal traditionalism moves forward there as well. When the masses organize in the bourgeois fragments, whether English Canada, the United States, or Dutch South Africa, the tortured European Jacobin becomes a mighty man. Instead of being hemmed in by the forces of the land and the factory, he has absorbed them, has become himself both peasant and proletarian, so that he is able to isolate the Whig and knock the props from under him. The fulfillment of radicalism in Australia speaks for itself. After the depression and the great strikes of the nineties the Labour Party mastered the Australian scene with an ease unheard of in the annals of European socialism. In every case the conservatism of the fragment unlooses the drama, the embryonic *telos,* that Europe has contained and stifled. The world has shrunk, but precisely for that reason, it has blossomed as well.

Now there is nothing mysterious about this mechanism of fragmentation. A part detaches itself from the whole, the whole fails to renew itself, and the part develops without inhibition. The process is as simple, as intelligible as any historical process we normally take for granted. And yet it is in the nature of fragmentation, perhaps its greatest irony, that it prevents both the European who stays and the European who leaves from understanding the pattern involved. The European who stays is bound to think of national histories in terms of the revolutionary process which it is the genius of the fragment to escape. He can understand an England in which the bourgeoisie carries the aristocracy along with it, a

9

France where the two fight it out, or even a Germany where the *Junker* dominance persists. But how is he to understand a North America where the bourgeoisie, having escaped both past and future, unfolds according to interior laws? On the other hand, the men of the fragment are in no better position: they are the European in reverse. They take their world for granted as he takes his, and if he cannot understand the European mechanics of an isolated bourgeoisie, they, being isolated, cannot understand that any European mechanics are involved. Peering outward from the interior of the fragment, they can even attribute their history to the open land of the frontier.* Of course each side could find out the secret of the other if it wanted to. Europe could study itself bit by bit, and the fragment could study Europe as a whole. But given life as both live it, why should either attempt to do so?

And yet we must not assume that this burying from sight of the fragmentation process is due entirely to this inherent matter of separated perspectives. Does not the fragment do everything it can to hide its European origin, its ideological character, its "fragmentary" existence? Does it not claim to be an absolute principle, the great spirit of a nation, the clue to racial truth? Actually there is a splendid collaboration between the unconscious perspectives generated by the separations of fragmentation and the psychic needs of the fragment itself. Which brings us back, after a view of the mechanistic process of fragmentation, to the moral inflations and disguises which it generates.

* This subjectivity is in fact the source of the Turner thesis and the ultimate reason why it cannot successfully be extended to other societies. The rise of American democracy is a product of the European logic which governs the unfolding of a liberal fragment, but Turner, like the average American, "cannot see" Europe. He is, however, able to see the open land on which the European drama is enacted. Since the American democratic outcome is not to be found in the larger setting of Europe, and since the visible land is new, it is easy enough to fall into the notion that the outcome is due to the land. But this makes it necessary to insist on the same result wherever there is land, and the social variety of the fragment cultures instantly challenges the idea of such uniformity. The Turner thesis is blocked in application. Indeed it is threatened with exposure. For as soon as the variety of the fragments is confronted, the significance of their differing European origins comes to view, and the frontier begins to be discredited as the explanatory factor even in American terms.

10

Louis Hartz

3 New Nations Out of Old

Being part of a whole is psychologically tolerable, but being merely a part, isolated from a whole, is not. It is obvious that there is a major problem of self-definition inherent in the process of fragmentation. Universalism itself comes fairly easily. The fragmented British Puritan can make Calvin universal in New England simply by virtue of his migration. It is nationalism that is more difficult. What "nation" does the universal Puritan belong to? He is no longer completely "English." Being English means sharing a community in which there are not only Calvinists but Anglicans, indeed all of the future organicists whom Anglicanism will proliferate and New England will also escape. It means being connected precisely to that totality, past and future, which the fragment has fled. Nor are Englishmen unaware of this fact when they look at the migrant Puritan: they see him as a mere "colonial." What then is to be done? How is wholeness to be recaptured? There is only one way out, determined practically by a bootstrap necessity. The Puritan must convert Puritanism itself, the one thing he has, into a new nationalism which denies the humiliation of the old. He must convert it into "Americanism," a new national spirit under the sun, grander than anything the world has ever seen. Or, if he happens to be a French-Canadian Catholic rather than a New England Puritan, he must subject that ethic to the same process. Or if he is an Australian radical, he must do the same for the spirit of the Chartists. It does not make much difference which segment of the European revolution we are dealing with: they can all become substitute nationalisms. If one becomes "Americanism," another becomes the spirit of the French-Canadian race, and another the national legend of "mateship."

It may seem that there is something meretricious about this, a sleight of hand, forgivable perhaps because of the moral necessity out of which it arises. In fact this is far from being the case, and we will not be able to understand the force of the fragment nationalism if we do not grasp its utter his-

11

torical honesty. The need for the new nationalism obviously increases as the fragment loses more and more of the European homeland, as future enemies begin to wither because old enemies have been left behind. But as this happens, new generations emerge within the fragment to whom it is, in sober truth, a "nation." The conversion of ideology into nationalism is not accomplished by the first settlers, whether they are Spanish treasure seekers, transported convicts, or embattled Pilgrims. These men still identify with the European homeland. But their children are not in the same position. Their children do not remember the "old country." They have lived inside the fragment all their lives, their battles have been the battles of its unfolding, and to them it is a true land. Indeed there are moments when, the process of detachment from Europe having finally matured, the new generations burst forth with a "discovery" of their national essence, amazed that its novelty has never been recognized before. These can be moments of great literary expression, as when Whitman discovered American democracy or Furphy Australian mateship.[2] In terms of "honesty" it makes no difference that what is discovered is really something very old and European, in this case bits of Puritan and Victorian England. It does not even make a difference that the peculiarity of the fragment language, now cherished as something remarkable, reflects this antiquity, as when American English or Canadian French or Brazilian Portuguese turn out in surprising degree to be stamped archaically with the spirit of the migration. The new generations of the fragment have lived inside this culture, not outside of it, and to them it is national. And who, on their own terms, is to challenge the view they advance? Europe invented the fragment, but it did not live inside it, never tasted its interior concreteness, the intensity of its closed life. The French language of Quebec resembles the Norman of the seventeenth century, but in Paris modern French is spoken.[3]

To be sure, this forgetfulness of context, this "discovery" of self, can be discouraged by lingering connections with Europe. But what is interesting is how it proceeds even in the face of all of them. We find it in Australia and English Canada

12

despite the imperial tie, despite the absence of an "American Revolution" or a conquest from the outside. Indeed we find it even among the creoles of Latin America, who require precisely their European origin in order to rationalize their class position. When feudal cultures are manufactured out of Europeans and Africans and Indians, the aristocrat of course has good reason to remember the "old country." And indeed the other classes have good reason to develop an indigenous nationalism which does not so much forget Europe as reject it. But quite apart from the discrimination that the peninsula exerted against the creole, which was obviously peculiarly painful in this context, the Iberians born in Latin America found it impossible to hold on to the European whole. Even when they went back to Spain and Portugal, indeed precisely when they did, they remained alienated members of a departed fragment. Did not Bolívar himself discover the American world in Madrid and Salamanca? [4]

The new nationalism, produced by the process of fragmentation, fortifies that process in turn. The relationship is reciprocal. Nor is this reflected alone in an intensified escape from the European past, in the assault on Old World "decadence," which invariably occurs at the nationalist moment. It is reflected also in an intensified escape from the future. Thus if the historical instinct of the fragment is to shut out the Enlightenment, there is the French-Canadian clergy to invoke the sacred memory of New France for the purpose. If the instinct is to eliminate Marx, there is Senator McCarthy to invoke "Americanism" for the purpose. Of course precisely because the genius of the fragment is to depart from the resources out of which these demons arise, there is always an imbalance between the intensity of the nationalist outcry and the reality of the threat which it meets. The *Institut* liberals of the eighteen-sixties in Quebec, whose work every "true patriot" was urged by the church to shun, were hardly a threat to the French-Canadian establishment.[5] The Communists whom the United States has assailed in recent years have hardly threatened to overthrow the Federal Government. But given the sources and the uses of the new nationalism, this strain of hyperbole is to be expected. The

13

nationalism does not arise because of the enemies: in fact it arises because the enemies do not, and cannot, exist.

In the case of immigration the new nationalism may be said to perform more realistic services. To be sure, the issue is the same: the protection of the fragment boundaries, the collaboration with history. But since the immigrant is a man from Europe, with, willy-nilly, the memory of the larger world, he is more of a threat to the fragment than the man who arises inside it, who has lost his connection with the Old World. For this reason, of course, some of the fragments have discouraged immigration, and after the explosive Huguenot impact on South Africa in the seventeenth century, it was prevented by the home government completely. There is no doubt that societies like the Afrikaner, or the French-Canadian, which have tended to renew themselves from within have presented us with the purest cases of fragment traditionalism. But the power of that traditionalism is better illustrated in its proven capacity, despite all fear, to meet the immigrant challenge. And here the new nationalism plays a part. By consciously articulating the fragment ethic, it provides an instrument for absorbing the immigrant into it. This takes place regardless of the substance of the ethic, and works in the case of Australia and Brazil as it does in the case of the United States. But the United States, not only the greatest of all the immigrant fragments, but with a genius for transparent terminology, has coined a word for the process. Together with Americanism there is "Americanization."

And yet the greatest service of fragment nationalism to the mechanism out of which it arises is to be found in still another place. It is to be found not in the protection of the fragment boundaries but in the help which it gives to the interior drama that unfolds as a result of that protection. In the simplest sense this is purely strategic, the provision of a set of symbols for the conquering hero to use. Thus the leaders of the Australian Labour Party seized with a vengeance on all of the mateship nationalism that the flowering of the nineties produced: the radical *telos* was pushed forward. But the issue goes actually deeper than this. Precisely because the internal unfolding of the fragment is suppressed by the European competition it has no European name. To be sure, there are labels of a minor sort which Europe supplies for the actors inside the fragment. But precisely because they are minor they are not heroic, and given the middle- and lower-class nature of many of the fragments, they are often touched with contempt. Could America live by calling Andrew Jackson "petty bourgeois"? This is not a matter of the villains of the fragment, the Whigs, as it were, who are in any case blackened. It is a matter of the heroes, the men at the heart of the legend, whom the children must admire. The greatest contribution of the new nationalism is that it solves this problem. It rescues Andrew Jackson from the ignominy of his European life, and instead of labeling him "petty bourgeois," gives him a name to match his glory. It calls him a "great American."

And so the nationalism that buries the sight of the fragment arises out of the process of fragmentation and implements it: implements its escape from the past, its closing down of the future, its interior unfolding. The moral change emerges out of the mechanistic process and facilitates it. In Europe the social ideologist is not called upon to supply the national identity or to preside over the national historic evolution. Countries like England and France have an identity which transcends any ideologist and a mechanism of development in which each plays only a part. But in the fragment this is not the case. The European whole is gone, the mechanism has shrunk. There the ideologist is called upon for a special duty: he must define a new national situation, hide "ideology" itself. But is this a misfortune? Is this a disadvantage? Hardly. It is true that the ideologist must give up his identity as a "conservative" or a "liberal" or a "radical." But he receives in return what in Europe he longs for most passionately, what he would die a thousand deaths to have: the national emotion. To gain that emotion is in fact the greatest of all of the Cinderella experiences of the fragment ideologist. For who can fail to see, even without reading Rousseau, that an idea with that emotion behind it cannot be beaten? * A

---

* The effect of the nationalist conversion can be measured vividly in two-fragment situations such as those which prevail in Canada and South Africa.

man may quarrel with a concept, but dare he shout down the national anthem? Dare he defy the spirit of a race?

4 The Racial Question

If nationalism buries the European identity of the fragment, so too do its racial involvements, its encounters with Indian tribes and African slaves. This is not owing to the creation of still another name for the fragment ethic, another "Americanism," as it were, for the racial issue is quickly absorbed into the ordinary nationalist language. It is owing to the fact that the European revolution out of which the fragment arises does not know racial distinctions, so that the racial formulations of the fragment are outside of its obvious and recognizable vocabulary. "Feudalism," in other words, is not a matter of color, a tribute, perhaps, to the cosmopolitanism of the European class ethic. But this does not mean that the racial constructions of the fragment are not dictated by the European ethic and the whole mechanism for retaining the fixity of that ethic which fragmentation provides. They are. If we go beneath the surface of the racial attitudes, we will soon encounter the familiar figures of Suárez and Locke and Cobbett, each struggling in his own terms to deal with an unfamiliar world.

Apart from this development, the fragments would face one another as ideologies do in the European setting. But that is far from being the case. Feudalism and liberalism confront one another as "nations" in Canada, not as these ideologies do in either the British or the French settings of Europe. To be sure, there are lingering memories of the purely European identifications here, which are not to be discounted. But one easily sees, beyond this, the transformation of competing social ethics into nationalisms: it is to be corporate and Catholic to be French in Canada, to be Protestant and liberal to be English. And of course the clash between the two further intensifies the nationalist transformation, giving it an "alien" force of fixed proximity to feed upon, something more effective even than the domestic subversive or the foreign immigrant. The same is true in the South African case where, though the nationalisms are brought closer together by a common Protestantism, racial involvements exacerbate them beyond any type of tension Canada has known. In both cases the added passion that nationalism gives is proved by the fact that only a kind of hands-off federalism can bring the fragment ethics together at all. Not even in ideologically "fragmented" France has it been necessary to develop the relation between liberal and feudal traditions that the distinction between Upper and Lower Canada represents.

The problem is complicated further by the fact that, since the European ideologies do not know race, battles break out within them over their application to race. These obscure the fact that actually both sides are seeking to apply the ideologies. Within the feudal fragments which seek to absorb the Negro or the Indian into the hierarchical structure the question is whether the non-Westerner should be lower in status or higher. Within the liberal and the radical fragments the issue is actually more decisive. Since the inclusion of the non-Westerner into the human group at all requires full equality, during the era of slavery he is totally excluded by theories of either property or race, which make "liberal slavery," if we can use the term, harsher in practice than feudal. But by the same logic, once humanity is conceded, the liberal ethic is more compulsively generous, since it demands completely equal treatment. Not only is emancipation therefore a more revolutionary matter in the Enlightenment fragments* but the struggles within them over race are more passionately doctrinaire, adding a special force to the flame of fragment nationalism that burns equally on either side, the "Americanism" of Calhoun and Garrison alike. Even in South Africa, where the Dutch found their American North, as it were, in the English, the explosion which took place after the first encounter between the fragments re-

---

* A word should perhaps be said about my use of the term "Enlightenment" in this study. In referring to the "Enlightenment fragments" I mean those which embody various shades of either liberal or radical culture. At the same time it must be pointed out that the process of fragmentation, by removing the fragments from the European social struggle, makes impossible the ideological intensity of an eighteenth-century mood arising out of that struggle. Indeed, the very term "Enlightenment" as we ordinarily use it implies such a struggle, a finding of light after darkness. In the case of the fragments the darkness fades with migration and the light is soon taken for granted. Moreover, this principle applies even to the feudal cultures, for without a social challenge Maistre quiets down just as does Rousseau. This is the French-Canadian case. In Latin America the situation varies, but the variation betrays the fundamental peculiarity of the fragment experience there. With the fabric of community scarred and an alienated creole class created, the Enlightenment is introduced in a French and iconoclastic form; but because the underlying tide of traditionalism is heavy and accepted, that introduction does not cut deep. Save for a few variations of this sort, the term "Enlightenment" in the fragment context serves the purpose of describing progressive social content rather than the formal nature of intellectual experience.

flected the racial polarity of the Protestant ethic in this matter.

But these struggles, exacerbated by their very internecine character, cannot be confused with battles among the European ethics themselves. The principle of fragment extrication governs here as well, once removed, as it were, through the racial formula. Latin-American treatment of slave and Indian was harsh, but it was far freer from a sense of property and race, far more involved in distinctions of status, than was the treatment of the non-Westerner by the British and the Dutch. Again fragment identifications are revealing, for whether we are dealing with the aristocratic nationalism of the Spanish creole or the democratic nationalism of the indigenous peoples, all groups are presumed included in the fragment whole. It is this very principle of inclusion which divides the warring nationalisms of the Enlightenment fragments, and when the latter shift to a Sir Walter Scott feudal plane, as the American Southerners did before the Civil War, the falseness of their position is transparent.

The future, too, is insured. Of course the Enlightenment enters into the amelioration of the lower groups in the feudal culture of South America, as in the emancipation of the slaves. The class struggles induced by race are one of the reasons, in contrast to French Canada, for the intrusion of the Enlightenment into the feudal atmosphere of the fragment in the first instance. But the doctrinaire passion of a Garrison could not by definition be introduced if only because an earlier tradition of apartheid did not exist to react against. The bourgeois fragments, in turn, are saved from the disturbances of the socialist formulae on race. To be sure, insofar as racial exclusion goes, radicalism can do just as well as liberalism, which is a clue to the common nature of the Enlightenment fragments on this score. Chancellor Harper himself could find nothing to object to in the racial outlook of the British South African Labour Party, although Marx, in that European world outside the racial issue, might. But there is also the inclusion side of the Enlightenment, and here the bourgeois ethos might be threatened by a Garrison of collectivist leanings. That threat has been duly exorcised.

18

There is, of course, nothing to prevent the South African Labour tradition from producing such a Garrison, as happened in the case of Mr. S. P. Bunting and the Communists after the First World War.[6] But in America, where that tradition has been excluded, socialism of any kind has played little part in the struggle for Negro rights. Even the battle of the Negro himself has been concerned, as in the case of the immigrant, with full inclusion in the American world.

Thus the racial issue is swept up in the process of fragment traditionalism, and like any other issue, religion or land tenure or politics, responds to its general principles. The past is excluded, the future shrinks, and the logic of the fragment unfolds, in this case ambivalently. This has the effect, of course, of strengthening the fragment ethic by extending still further its empire over the national life. But since its impact is to exclude all possibilities other than those the fragment contains, it also has the effect of giving to the citizens of the fragment the notion that there can be no conceivable ways of dealing with the non-Western impact, the challenge of alien Indian and African cultures, save the ways they instinctively elicit from the ideological code they have made universal. Absolutism appears again. The American cannot think of the Negro apart from the separatism of Calhoun or the egalitarianism of Garrison, and the Brazilian cannot in all reality understand either of these categories. And this in turn gives the fragment ethic a new role: exclusive defender of the Western faith. Needless to say, this role is charged with a special passion, and in terms of insuring the fixity of the fragment it is a splendid addition to the roles of absolute reality and national spirit.

The psychological metamorphoses of the fragment do indeed provide an increasing number of services for the citizen in it. They reassure the citizen that the world is really one, that it consists of French Catholics or Australian radicals or American bourgeois. They give the citizen a glowing sense of nationhood, a national anthem to sing and to communicate to his children. They provide the citizen with a shield against the Saracen, the only imaginable moral way of dealing with the man outside the West. Is it surprising, after adding these

19

services up, that the citizen is attached to the fragment? Is it surprising that he fails to see it as a "fragment" at all?

5 The Return to Revolution

This is the reason for the peculiar trauma of the fragment as it is suddenly forced back, through the world events of our time, into the context of revolution. It does not return as an ideology. It returns as a world, as a nation, as a way of racial life. Its "conservatism" is bound to be more powerful than the classical Wellingtonianism of the European revolution. Wellington, coming out of the same world as his opponents, at least knew them. But the fragment does not know its opponents, or at any rate it has forgotten them long ago. For it they are bound to be a challenge to reality itself: Martians successfully landed on earth. And yet the impact of the new world situation is inexorable, forcing the European revolution back upon the fragment, working indeed through the very mechanisms which created the fragment universe itself. I have said that that universe was finally developed not by the first European settlers, but by their children, who had never seen Europe, had lived wholly inside the fragment. But are there not new "children" now? Is not a new generation arising in the fragment to whom life "outside" it is instinctive? And is not this group in danger of "forgetting" all of the psychic magic, all of the wonderful metamorphoses accomplished by its predecessors?

We can see now, with a kind of sudden Hegelian retrospect, that inherent in the whole legendary process of "escape" from Europe there were mechanisms canceling out its results. On the simplest plane, these were technological. The Spaniards came to Latin America in the slow vessels of the sixteenth century, the British arrived at the African cape in the frigates of the Napoleonic era, and today we fly from Quito to Johannesburg with the speed of a jet. Was there not all along a "fatal contradiction" technologically here, a shrinking of the universe through the mechanisms of flight bound to end flight itself? But this was not all. As the globe contracted, the

Western revolution that the fragments escaped was spreading throughout it with increasing rapidity, so that ultimately it was bound to overtake them, if only from a distant place suddenly made near. If Holland was left behind, there was still Russia, China, the awakening African states. The historic mechanism by which the fragment, having escaped one enemy, escaped another could not prevent the new challenges. For this was not a matter of the internal resources for challenging itself that the fragment had. It was a matter of external impact, and what French Canada may have lacked in the way of Enlightenment resources, or even Australia in the way of communist resources, the new world clearly possessed.

To be sure, there cannot be a literal return by the foreign route to the original conditions of the European revolution. You cannot precisely duplicate the struggle between the Mountain and the Gironde by means of diplomacy, even of war. Not that the fragment does not have internal problems despite its fixity, especially in cases where race or class distortions have taken place within it. But these become quickly absorbed into the world impact, entangled with it, so that even here the result is different from the classical revolutionary encounter. Even if the French Revolution had involved the South African racial question, the peculiar mixture of domestic and foreign elements in the South African dilemma today would have been unknown to it. But this world twist to revolution does not mean that the problems the fragments encounter as a result of it are less acute. On the contrary, they can be made more difficult. Together with sheer violence, or the threat of it, there emerge a whole series of new and agonizing connections through "leadership," through "aid," through alliance. A knock-down, drag-out fight with Filmer or Marx on the European stage might well be preferable to the tortured relationship that the American bourgeois has to the Bolshevik revolution today.

In this context, "reaction" changes its shape. It ceases to be a matter of a specific social viewpoint, opposition to the Reform Act, as it were, but a resistance to the displacement of the fragment universe. And this, again, involves impulses which are obviously not to be found in the Wellingtonian

21

pattern. One of these is the passion to flee again, to duplicate in the face of all reality the original voyage, which comes out in "isolationism." Another, also unknown naturally to European conservatism, is the intensified exploitation of the old nationalist gift, so that in desperate moments, as under McCarthy or Verwoerd, the fragment rocks with the cry of "treason." Finally there is a kind of hysteria which arises not merely because of the Martian challenge, but because all of the instinctive methods for dealing with it, out of the fragment past, do not work. Isolationist South Africa withdraws from the Commonwealth, but the world is still there. Loyal America deports the Communist, but the Bolshevik revolution is still there. The fragment reactionary exhausts himself in a thousand Treason Trials, clerical excommunications, and congressional investigations. But after all of his effort, the Martian remains. Indeed, as in a horror tale, he keeps coming closer all the time.

This is not all, of course. If the fragment Wellington cannot prevent the world from engulfing him, he cannot prevent the new generations in the fragment itself from responding to the experience that they have. The cry of "treason," coming out of the interior of the fragment, even if implemented with all of its nationalist dynamite, cannot forever prevent men from seeing what they see outside it. The man who has left the Platonic cave is never the same. In the time of the jet, of two World Wars, of the advancing European revolution, the fragment reactionary is destined to be shattered not only by the Martian he cannot allay but also by the new generations who are deserting his milieu as he deserted Europe. For all of his cries, they will deny that the world consists of the Peruvian highlands. They will reject the proposition that "Americanism" is the instinctive emotion of all humanity. They will challenge the idea that the Afrikaner has devised the only way of racial life. Indeed they will go a step farther. They will recapture the memory of Europe itself, and in the very teeth of the fragment hysteric, they will expose the relativity of his ethic. They will announce, outright, that the fragment is a "fragment."

As the fragment world passes, destroyed by the same

"honest" response to experience which created it, even a critic of its values cannot fail to have a nostalgic pang. Life inside the fragment did have its satisfactions. With the past gone, the "future" closed off, amid timeless Catholic and Jacksonian unfoldings, who can deny the even tenor of things? And yet it is a fact, obvious in the whole shrinking process of fragmentation, that that evenness, that security, was purchased at the price of a larger vision. It is no accident that none of the fragment cultures, not even Latin America with its myriad "Enlightenments," produced a major tradition of social philosophy. Where life is fixed at the point of origin, how can philosophy flourish? Where perspectives shrink to a single value, and that value becomes the universe, how can value itself be considered? The exposure of the fragment universe by the world impact of the present time, reversing the history of the fragment, is bound to be traumatic. But it brings with it a moral liberation, an enlargement of consciousness, which for its own sake would well be worth the struggle. It brings, for the first time in the fragment settings, the hope of philosophy. The new generations that are shattering the confines of the fragment today, from Cape Town to Lima, from Montreal to Sydney, will in the larger world find a richer life than the life they have lost.

Chapter Two

Fragmentation Patterns:
Feudal, Liberal, and Radical

1 Extrication,
Atrophy, and Unfolding

There is an obvious chain of cause and effect in the stages
out of which the fragment tradition arises: the extrication
from Europe, the atrophy of the future, and the unfolding of
the fragment potential. Once the voyage is under way and
the European shore has begun to fade, processes are set in
motion which only the forcible return of the revolutionary
context can alter. Indeed, in some ways the meaning of that
return, for the generation which experiences it, is precisely
that it introduces an element of "freedom" into a pattern
historically determined.

Given the voyage, how could the outcome be different? To
be sure, various parts of Europe could be left behind. If the
voyager happens to desert urban Paris we can imagine him
deserting mercantile Amsterdam instead, or industrial Manchester. There are plenty of possibilities here, in fact a series
of theoretical desertions which the actual experience of fragmentation did not accomplish. But given what is deserted, is
there any way of preventing the effect of desertion? Can the
future, for example, be retained in its European largeness?

24

This is not a question of the citizens of the fragment "rejecting" later ideologies. Rejection implies precisely the kind of freedom they do not have. Because the very seeds of the later ideas are contained in the parts of the Old World that have been left behind, the experience of choice cannot be said to exist, even though, as I have said, the fragment nationalisms are forever crusading gloriously against the "alien" principles. Does the Catholic French Canadian "decide" against atheism? Does the bourgeois American "decide" against socialism? Such questions are, curiously, beside the point.

Nor is it easy to see, given the original voyage, how one could prevent the potential of the fragment from flowering. Where men are not stifled by competition, they not only do what they please, but they do not know that they might be expected to behave otherwise. Again "choice" is not the word to use. Nor ought the determinism here to be confused by the mechanism of fulfillment in the feudal fragments which is often based, as with Catholicism or even Latin-American dictatorship, on popular submissiveness. What is involved takes place as well in the bourgeois and radical cultures where men "vote" and do so aggressively and enthusiastically. The point is that the heroes they choose, the national symbols they support, arise in relationship to Europe out of a larger process of which they are unaware. The American bourgeois elects Jackson and the bonfires blaze. But does he "decide" not to follow John Quincy Adams because Adams is not leading a crusade against the unreformed Parliament or Charles X? The Australian proletarian elects the Labour Party and the spirit of Lawson is fulfilled. But does he "decide" not to be confused by the traditionalist lures of a nonexistent Tory Party? It would be absurd to assume in the case of any fragment, whatever its interior drift might be, that any such calculations would be made. The process of fulfillment, like the process of exclusion, is determined by a shrinking of context which has ceased to be a matter of conscious decision.

What I am discussing here, of course, are not merely elements of cause and effect, but facets of the bottomless subjectivity which swallows up the fragment as even its memory of Europe fades. The latter is an instrument of the former,

25

indeed its most powerful instrument. For it is because men are contained by the fragment that they cannot betray it, cannot give way to the alien thoughts of the future, cannot resist fostering the *telos* of the "present." It is only when that containment is shattered by external experience, and objectivity begins to appear, that determinism is converted into choice. That of course is what is happening today, and it is the clue to the significance of the new generations that are arising in the fragments now. Those generations, because of their new and wider experience, are beginning to "decide" about the very things that fragmentation made inevitable. They are beginning to "decide" about feudal traditionalism in Latin America, and even if they accept apartheid in South Africa, they are making a "decision" there as well. Indeed, in the context of a growing objectivity, choice is as inescapable as was its absence before. The new generations of the fragment are liberated by the very determinisms amid which they live.

2 Feudal Traditions

The feudal fragmentation, starting earliest, has the longest "future" to exorcise, the longest reach, as it were, of all of the detachments from Europe. There is no real Whiggery, and thus no Jacobinism. And since there are neither of these manifestations of the Enlightenment ethos, socialism cannot arise, at least with the "normal" evolution that we find in Western Europe. And yet, despite this bleak train of fixity, there is a remarkable creativity about the unfolding of the feudal ethos which it makes possible. To be sure, this would not be so if the feudal fragments had had a perfect record, the total exclusion of all urbanism, all industry. But even they, whether in Quebec or Brazil, are ultimately hit. And what the Catholic church, the corporate tradition, the authoritarian spirit, all do to absorb and contain the materials of "modern history" is something that even the most ingenious Disraelis and Montalemberts of Europe would have to admire.

26

It might be asked, however, even if feudalism "fragments," that is, leaves Europe and goes to another place, will it not in the end produce an Enlightenment out of its own resources? After all, prior to the first Whig thrust in Europe, there were only the Middle Ages. The answer, apart from all psychology of movement, is that the full *ancien régime* did not move outward, a full "Spain," a full "France." The migration in both the Canadian and South American cases was primarily military, clerical, and rural. Feudalism itself, so to speak, shrank. Nor does the fact that many of the French-Canadian seigneuries and Latin-American encomiendas fell into the hands of adventurers and bourgeois alter the matter. Not only were these men themselves recruited to the aristocratic ethos, as in the case of the bourgeois of Europe itself, but whatever dilution of aristocracy they involved led not to liberalism, but to the increased power of the church. The result was that the feudalism of the fragments was not only divorced from the seeds of the urban European Enlightenment, but was made more doctrinaire by a kind of clerical aristocracy. This point can be seen even when we contrast Latin America with Spain or Portugal. But when we contrast French Canada with France, the classical home of Voltaire's rationalism and D'Holbach's atheism, it stands out with crushing force.

There are, of course, great differences between French Canada and Latin America, quite apart from the relationship of their mother countries to the drift of the European liberal movement. We cannot easily say of the twenty republics of the South, even in Spanish or Portuguese terms, what John Commons once said of French Canada: that it was "a bit of medieval France, picked out and preserved for the curious student of social evolution." [1] The breakdown of organic medievalism in Latin America is a great differentiating matter.* And yet in and through that breakdown the logic of the

---

* Terminologically, of course, one can quarrel indefinitely here. Can one call Latin America "feudal" given its revolutionary tradition and the fact that even in the Iberian peninsula itself, the development of classical feudalism was inhibited? But I have already suggested that no fragment comes out of Europe a pure ideological archetype, and even if it did, it would inevitably be modified by the imperial relationship and racial encounters. Dutch South

27

feudal fragmentation can be seen to persist, often producing strange results, heartbreaking betrayals, as it were, of the Enlightenment. Indeed, one of the factors which produced that breakdown, the manning of the feudal ranks by alien African and Indian races, from another angle actually intensified the feudal spirit by contributing new traditionalisms to it. French Canada and Latin America have not had any outstanding cultural or diplomatic involvements. But it is not accidental that the fiercely nationalist Emile Bruchesi, writing in Montreal's *L'Action française* during the nineteen-twenties, saw

---

Africa is "bourgeois," but the primitive nature of the Boer economy and the native involvement clearly modify the classical norm of liberal culture. British South Africa is touched in origin with the radicalism of the early Industrial Revolution, and is actually capable of yielding some type of labor tradition, but it is deeply conservative in other respects. One could go on in this vein. The value of the European ideological categories is not that they fit completely, but that they give us a point of analytic departure. They permit us to seize the phenomenon of fragmentation by employing comparatively the experience of the European whole which is governed by those categories. Once this is accomplished, we are not prevented in any sense from appreciating deviations in the fragment from the European archetypes. On the contrary, we are provided with a context which makes those deviations meaningful. The turmoil in Latin-American history stemming from the collapse of imperial legitimacy, an alienated creole class, and the introduction of new races into Iberian feudal culture becomes intelligible in terms of a twisted fragment situation. The failure of that turmoil to result in a general modernization of Latin-American society also becomes intelligible in these terms. The theory of fragmentation, beginning with the European archetype itself, permits us to define a situation unknown to either the "traditionalist" or "revolutionary" experiences of Europe—a tug of war between the fixity of a fragment and the energies arising out of its breakdown. This in fact, rather than any "1789," is the Latin-American situation.

Nor ought the utility of the Western norm to be obscured by the fact that the deviations from it, not only in Latin America but elsewhere, are partially derived from the impact of African and aboriginal cultures, non-Western in character. One can view every situation in which the West meets the non-West as a situation involving two fragments, equally significant analytically, comparable to the interaction of the European fragments themselves in Canada or South Africa. But if we adopt the Western norm for certain analytic purposes, the distortion of that norm by the non-Western fragment will measure perfectly, from its own angle, the degree of compromise which it itself has been forced to make. We do not in any way limit the examination of American history from the standpoint of the Iroquois or the Cherokee by viewing it from the standpoint of the vicissitudes encountered by a European liberal fragment in the process of fragmentation. The categories of the Western revolution are like any historical categories man can devise: they neither "perfectly fit" nor exhaust historical experience, but they help to illuminate a relevant portion of it.

28

them as "natural allies." [2] Bruchesi, assailing the exploitative capitalism of English Canada and the United States, urged French Canada to turn instead to the Catholic, rural, and aristocratic traditions of its sister culture in the South.

Certainly the Whiggery with which both of the bourgeois North American fragments begin, the Whiggery of the "capitalist revolution," is missing at the outset in Montreal and Lima alike. The mercantile element that did exist in French Canada, even prior to the flight of many of its members at the time of the Conquest, did not as a force disentangle itself from such groups of clerical and seigneurial power as the Château Clique. In its heyday, if one can use that term, it was not a Girondin force. Nor can one say that the Latin-American creoles represented such a force, devoted as they may have been to the French Enlightenment, defiant as they may have been of the Inquisition. They were concerned centrally with their exclusion from imperial power, and after their aims were accomplished they quickly united with the church hierarchy and the new military corps to resist a leftward trend. In Chile, where this process proceeded apace, Francisco Bilbao wrote a classic essay amid the liberal enthusiasms of the forties in which he put his finger precisely on the point. After examining the basis of "Chilean feudalism" in politics and society, in religion and on the land, he lamented the failure of a libertarian middle class to arise, "like the bourgeoisie in Europe." [3]

The Jacobin thrust assails the Girondin but it would not exist without it: in the European revolution we do not appreciate adequately the degree to which big wealth, through its own Enlightenment force, awakens in the mass of the people the resistance against it. But in the feudal fragment, where that force is missing or stunted, how is the awakening to proceed? French Canada shows us the problem here. To be sure, the issue is clouded by the presence of a popular nationalist emotion which arises at the instant of the Conquest. Even though that emotion is associated with the persistence of the old Catholic hierarchical culture, it demands "liberty" and therefore gives the appearance of a popular democratic drive. But it is not hard to disentangle the two elements here. There is a democratic movement in French Canada, but when we abstract the nationalist elements from it, it shrinks in force. Louis Joseph Papineau, the leader of the movement during the eighteen-thirties, assailed the oppression of the habitant by the English, but did so with much less force in connection with the seigneur: he was himself a landowner and prided himself on his social status. But the main point, whatever the complex question of Papineau's own position may be, is that on the score of simple democracy the *Patriote* group was not clearly in touch with the illiterate habitant. Andrew Stewart at the time of their famous Ninety-Two Resolutions said that they represented only a professional elite,[4] and there is reason to believe that the habitant did not understand even the slogans they inspired him to emblazon on placards.[5] If this alienation existed in the case of the *Patriotes* of the thirties, it prevailed even more in the case of the Rougists of the forties, French Canada's "1848." Certainly one can hardly imagine a popular movement, a Jacksonian drive, for example, being crushed by the clergy as the Rougists were crushed.

Wider explosions took place in Latin America after Independence, but they do not disprove the presence of an underlying passivity, an underlying traditionalist tide. As we know, they ended in the anarchy that produced the age of the great *caudillos,* and this result underscored more vividly than anything in French Canada the incapacity of the people to assume Enlightenment responsibilities. In part we are dealing here with the sheer collapse of legitimacy due to the withdrawal of the historic Spanish absolutist power, but this itself would not have been a factor had the Latin-American populace been able to shift successfully to a democratic ethic. F. García Calderón, the Peruvian critic, once compared the *caudillos* with the Bonapartist phase in French history.[6] But the parallel ought not to be pressed too far. If the creole revolutionaries were not Girondins, and the Jacobins scarcely got under way, the *caudillos* could not really be Napoleons. Difficult as it may have been for France to shift from feudal to modern norms, it did so more successfully than Latin America, and Napoleon himself of course embodied the modern spirit decisively, not least in the land settlement which he underwrote. Without denying the constructive achievements of some of the *caudillos,* we have to say that they did not represent the same force. In very large part they were the projections of a preliberal tradition which included not merely Spanish rule, but an even earlier habit of Indian absolutism as well.[7]

The Whig is gone, the liberal democrat incapable of arising: what is to be said about the Marxist? Feudalism of course goes into the socialist brew, as the liberal fragments show us in a negative way, and in the case of the feudal fragment which smothers the Enlightenment from the beginning there is a powerful type of appeal which the Marxist can make when the comparative impact ultimately hits. He can promise a single leap across the whole of the modern experience that has been suppressed, a combined development into the last stage of industrialism and democracy. But until this kind of appeal can take hold, he is badly disadvantaged by the Enlightenment atrophy, for he needs a rationalist and egalitarian spirit on which to build. He needs the Jacobin as the Jacobin needs the Whig. Thus it is not surprising that the classical history of Marxism even in Latin America is not impressive. Comte is a larger figure, which gives the whole traditionalist situation away. For does not Comte offer the medieval world of authority at the moment he offers the modern world of progress? To be sure, especially after the First World War, various types of socialism penetrate the Latin-American labor movement. But they do not transform the culture, and above all they do not touch the great hacienda tradition on the land, one of the great sources of the later Marxian threat. In French Canada, of course, the situation is far "purer." There, where even a superficial revolutionary tradition does not exist, Marx is flailed by the classical hysterias of fragment nationalism. The "Padlock Law" of the Duplessis regime, unanimously adopted by both houses of the Quebec legislature and drastic in the powers it gave to the attorney general, is symbolic of the matter.[8] French nationalist orators claim in a single breath, without any sense of paradox, that the French have saved Canada from "American invasion and from communism." [9]

Could there be a finer place for the flowering of the feudal ingenuity? There is "room" in the New World, but after a fashion subtler than is usually realized. If Cardinal Taschereau can condemn the Knights of Labor in Canada, there is room for the national Catholic syndicates.[10] Of course, given the socialist impact, the situation is different in Latin America: Toledano is no agent of the church. But the strength of Catholic unionism in Latin America as well shows us that we are still dealing with Bruchesi's "natural allies," and so does the Perón-Vargas tradition of authoritarian labor organization. That tradition, to be sure, is hostile to the Catholic syndicates, invariably tends to destroy them.[11] But it emerges out of the traditionalist order that Catholicism itself exemplifies, a situation in which the masses have not been effectively activated by liberal influence. Indeed, in the Vargas instance we almost have a streak of legitimate Toryism, for the tradition behind him is that of the paternalism of the Brazilian monarchy and the "big house" of slavery days. Vargas as the "father of the poor" would not be acceptable to "feudal socialists" like Carlyle or Berryer, but from the Latin-American shore he is stretching out a hand in that direction.

Actually, in European terms we are close to fascism here, and it is not surprising that both the disciples of Perón and those of Duplessis found a good deal to interest them in Generalissimo Franco. European fascism, flowering in those societies in Europe itself which had a hard time getting beyond the feudal point, is a natural source of inspiration for the feudal fragment in the modern time. In the case of Latin America there is continuity here, but in the case of French Canada we find again the vivid light which the European national contrast throws on the medieval fragmentation. While the Popular Front was burgeoning in Paris, the clergy of Quebec did not find the resources even of the French right, of the Maurras tradition, sufficiently nourishing. They traveled to the places where 1789 had never successfully struck and viewed admiringly the outcome there. They found their greatest hero actually not in Spain but in Portugal, where the philosophical Salazar had best pursued the corporatist message of the Papal Encyclicals. There, on the Western coast of the Iberian peninsula, away not only from the North American bourgeois fragments, but also from the France which centuries ago had betrayed them, they found the proper method for dealing with the modern world.[12]

When, as Sarmiento put it, the Middle Ages are carried outward by settlers, when step by step the Enlightenment withers or is nullified, when traditionalism itself seizes "modern history," we have the classical pattern of the feudal fragmentation. We also have a pattern which is peculiarly explosive as all of the fragments return to revolution. For is there not a specially heavy debt to the future here? As the determinisms of the fragment gradually become matters of "choice," are not the choices here dramatic? These are the obvious questions to which we are led both in Latin America and French Canada. But before we turn to them let us examine the process of the flight from Europe, the closing down of the fragment, and the unfolding of its purposes, as this process appears in the bourgeois and proletarian cultures. Nor will this be useless in evaluating the current dilemma even of the feudal fragments. For certainly one of the most remarkable things about fragmentation is that, despite all cultural diversity, it yields in the end the same formal problems.

3 The Behavior of
the Liberal Fragments

What happens in the bourgeois instances is that the Enlightenment which the feudal migrations left behind in Europe, and which in Europe is caught between right and left, flowers apart from all antagonists. It departs from Filmer as in the earlier cases Filmer departed from it, and since socialism is compounded of a mixture of Filmer and its own liberalism, it escapes the Marxian threat as well. And this in turn, by the rationale of external protection and internal flowering, releases a domestic development impossible in the European scene. Ironically this development does not put the Whig part of the bourgeois community in the saddle, for if Whiggery fails successfully to appear in the feudal fragments, its work is already done in the liberal fragments through the universal spread of the bourgeois faith. It is robbed of the mechanisms that Europe provides for its support, and is overwhelmed by a Jacobin tide that Europe manages to contain. The teleology of the liberal fragments is not only liberal but democratic.

To be sure, this process works itself out differently in the different fragments, and it would be a blind traveler indeed who did not sense the difference between Ottawa and Kansas City, Kansas City and Cape Town. The bourgeois spirit of the Dutch Reformed church is more relaxed than that of New England Puritanism or the Anglicanism of English Canada. The democratic spirit in English Canada is etched with a Tory streak coming out of the American Revolution and in the American South and South Africa by the elitism of racial biases. There is no need to deny such distinctions. As in the case of the feudal fragments, we are concerned with both general processes and the individuality of the settings in which they evolve. I think it is reasonable to say, however, that in the case of the bourgeois fragments the unifying themes are even more marked than in the case of Latin America and French Canada. There may be an "aristocratic" touch to the American South, but it is a long step away from the old English feudal order that Bentham and Price assailed. There may be a Tory touch in English Canada, but the fragment, despite the Cooperative Commonwealth Federation of recent times, has not yielded a major socialist movement. There may be a mitigated capitalist ardor in South Africa, but the Boer community is a democratic community of individualists. We are dealing with a surprisingly parallel set of developments.

The European bridge between feudalism and socialism, which the bourgeois fragmentations explode for their own protection, is made up of strangely contrasting elements. On

34

the one hand socialism seeks to recapture the memory of the organic medieval community, and it is the fact that the memory of this community has been left behind and buried beneath new liberal absolutisms and nationalisms that militates in the first instance against the emergence of a series of Marxes in the fragment commonwealths. Neither the Boer nor the American nor the English Canadian is instinctively inspired to think in collective terms, in terms other than those of Veblenian "self-help." But it is also the spirit of revolt against the hierarchical nature of the feudal community which these inveterate individualists lack. Precisely because their individualism was detached from the medieval root, and did not struggle against it, it was untouched by the flame of revolution which, out of European liberalism, entered together with the collective mood into the manufacture of socialism. They were Benthams, as it were, without the class or the millennial passion. Nor can one disprove this by pointing to such outbursts as the American Revolution or the agitation of Dutch burghers against the East India Company. These manifestations were national and not class matters. Unlike the French Revolution, or even the "French period" in Holland itself, something South Africa only remotely experienced, they could not sow the seed of the European social revolution.

Thus protected from the left because the right is gone, the bourgeois fragment flowers as it cannot in Europe. But the very process of this protection shows us why Whiggery, the elite component of the fragment, is bound to fall. To begin with, if there is no revolution because the feudal order has been escaped, if there is no flaming Enlightenment because the medieval antagonists are gone, then one of its crucial functions is already served. What does not successfully get under way in the feudal fragments is accomplished from the outset in the liberal. But this is not the loss for Whiggery of a sentimental role, a mere touch of radical grandeur. It is the true beginning of its strategic collapse. For one of the ways it manages to keep the people behind it in Europe is enlisting them precisely in its antifeudal campaign, in its struggles against an unreformed parliament or Bourbons out

35

of hand or German princes. When that struggle is gone, why should the people accept an elitist Whiggery? Francis Place might knuckle under to the British Whigs during the eighteen-thirties because they are taking a step in the right direction, but why should George Brown, of Canada West, or Andrew Jackson, of Tennessee, knuckle under to the Whigs of Kingston or Washington? What steps are the latter taking? Indeed, to the extent that there are feudal remnants in the bourgeois fragments, for example, primogeniture in the United States or the landed reserves of the Anglican church in Canada, the Whig is usually involved in their support. As a matter of fact, in the Canadian instance, the Family Compacts willingly associate with the Château Clique of seigneurial and clerical power in order to present a common front against the democratic tide. Where, under such circumstances, can one find the popular appeal of reform? Where, indeed, can one even locate the "progressive" side of the Whig personality?

To be sure, in Europe Whiggery has mechanisms other than revolution for keeping the people behind it. It allies against the people with the very aristocracies it fights, as when Brougham and Guizot turn around and become defenders of the traditional order; and it terrifies the people, or at any rate the peasantry and the petty bourgeois, by pointing to the dangers of proletarian upheaval on the left, as was the case in the France of 1848. These strategies, though somewhat devilish in light of the grand egalitarian role that Whiggery assumes in its revolutionary action, are not ineffective. But is it not of the very essence of the new position of Whiggery in the bourgeois fragments, of the same position which submerges its "progressive" side, that these strategies are unavailable? If a House of Lords cannot be found to reform, can one be found to lean upon? In the South African interior even the dream of that House is meaningless, but when we get to North America, there are the classic frustrations of Alexander Hamilton. Moreover, if radicalism dies as a result of the flight from feudalism, is not the cry of "leveler" thereby robbed of its effectiveness? The only place where this cry really worked to sustain the power of Whiggery was in English

Canada, where the Family Compacts capitalized on the memory of the American revolutionary mobs which had driven many of the Tories to New Brunswick and elsewhere. But even there, though wrapped in a more aristocratic atmosphere, Whiggery ultimately fell. Put simply, the Whig sustains himself by manipulating the European periphery of right and left in which the bourgeois fragment is encased: eliminate the periphery and he falls.

The democrat who emerges to defeat him displays in his very personality all of the strategic losses that Whiggery experiences. He is to be found in the European struggle, too, as the Jacobin, but there he is mainly an urban man of the "shop," alienated from the passivity of the peasant by his liberalism and terrified of the proletarian because of his faith in private property. The fading of the European periphery gives to this figure an enormous access of strength, indeed converts his enemies into his friends. For the peasant now becomes an individualist farmer, the proletarian a bourgeois unionist. The European "petty bourgeois" grows great through the Canadian Clear Grit Party and the American Federation of Labor. Of course this very spread of individualism means that the Whig, if he converts to equality, can find a link with the people he cannot find in Europe. In a dynamically capitalist world he can even enchant them, as Horatio Alger did in the United States, with a promise of some of the Whig gold. But so long as he permits his elitism to show, he is doomed. The national democrat will rise in his might and bring him down to the proper level.

In every case the chemistry which produces this democrat is a marvelous thing in the way in which it subsumes all of the social forces that the bourgeois fragment has left behind in feudal Europe. Essentially the matter is ideological, the infection of alien elements with the spirit of the small bourgeois. Even in the case of the South African Boer, who resembles the classical peasant because of his remoteness from market and credit concerns, the achievement is remarkable. For it is not feudal submissiveness which goes with the primitive economic outlook of the Afrikaner of the interior. The *Voortrekker* evinces a legendary independence. More-

over, the very simplicity of the economic setting in the Afrikaner case means that a true Whiggery, the kind of thing
which comes in North America as in Europe out of big
commerce and industry, does not appear. The rich cattle
owner is differentiated from the poor woodcutter, but not
in a social way. This means that there is a kind of spontaneous democracy in the community, the "Jacksonian logic,"
as it were, fulfilling itself with scarcely a battle. And that is
precisely what we find reflected in the political constitutions
of the Dutch Republics beyond the Orange River. The Com-
mittee of J. P. Hoffman which drew up the constitution of
the Orange Free State created instantly a vigorous republican
constitution. Indeed, here was a case, even among people who
"only know one book—the Bible," [13] where the law of Moses
was replaced by a summary of the American Constitution.
Both the President and the members of the Volksraad were
elected by practically universal suffrage.[14]

When we come to North America democratic victories are
not quite so easy, but the magic of European bourgeois universalism is more obvious. Here all shadow of the European
peasant, even economic, is gone. The British tenant of the
Disraelian type has become an aggressive entrepreneur, echo-
ing the Jacobin spirit of the "shop" in the vast context of the
North American land. The cry against "monopoly" in the
United States, from the time of Jefferson to the time of Leon
Henderson, is well-enough known. But the same cry, if only
a touch more muted, was heard in Canada. There was the
same attack on financial institutions, with William Lyon
MacKenzie lashing out at the "Bank Gentry." [15] There was
the same fear of railroads and transportation firms, showing
itself especially in an assault on the Grand Trunk Railway.
There was even the same attack on trusts during the later
era, though this was kept in abeyance for some time by the
limited resources of small capital. Indeed, there is a sense in
which the transformation of peasant into farmer is most
vividly highlighted in the Canadian context, for together
with the new agrarian individualists of Upper Canada we
have the habitants of Lower, whose passivity infuriates the
democratic liberal reformers. Does it not illuminate the lib-

eral magic to see George Brown, leader of the Clear Grits during the fifties, ultimately inheriting the anti-French passions of Lord Durham himself? [16]

If the peasant goes, so does the proletarian, with the result that the Whig is adrift in a world of too many friends. To be sure, the individualist magic with respect to labor takes a longer time to show itself, for while all of the fragment cultures begin with agriculture, the rise of an urban proletariat can be much delayed. In the Dutch South African case the Boer did not become proletarianized until the twentieth century when, as a matter of fact, the British fragment provided him with a radicalism out of its own tradition. Even in the case of the United States and Canada it is not until the late nineteenth century that the struggles of industrialized labor appear. But after this has been said, the genius of the bourgeois transformation is evident. It is not Marx, but Gompers and the American Federation of Labor, instruments of "wage consciousness" rather than class consciousness, which emerge triumphant in North America. Nor does "international unionism" here mean merely geographic proximity, for French Canada, no farther away than English, yields in its Catholic unionism a historic barrier to the Federation.[17] Moreover, if we have to wait until the later era to see the full fruit of the bourgeois proletarian magic, even the rural and relatively primitive industrial situation of the earlier time reveals, in the very starkness of its exclusion of socialism, the ultimate mechanism involved. Is there clear evidence at all of Fourier and Proudhon, even Owen, in the English-Canadian agitations of the thirties? Reformers like Bidwell and MacKenzie may have been influenced by Roebuck, Hume, and Attwood, but that is as far as their "alien" influence went.[18] In New York Thomas Skidmore became touched with a wider view, but he was rapidly disciplined by his bourgeois brethren. There was simply no operative Red Republic in either Canada or the United States, and needless to say in the Afrikaner states, during the democratic age. And that is one of the crucial reasons why "1848" led not to the frustrations of Lamartine and the Second Republic, or even to the miseries of the Chartists, but to solid democratic achievement.

The swift attainment of popular government is of course the mark of the new democratic giant who arises within the liberal fragments. That process may be accelerated in the Dutch republics by the simplicity of the egalitarian ethos, or it may be delayed in English Canada by a Tory touch, imperial arrangements, or the presence of the French feudal fragment. But as a process, it is uniform. Moreover, it is not to be judged alone by political matters, the achievement of manhood suffrage or elective office. The new Jacobin leaves his mark on the whole of the culture, and because he represents its inner drift, he is the hero whom the fragment nationalists discover, celebrated alike by Olive Schreiner and Walt Whitman. What is involved is a core of emotion, a quality of individualism which, despite immense cultural diversity, gives to Boer and American and Canadian alike something in common as against feudal and radical Europe. The European traveler immediately sees it, often vaguely ascribes it to the New World. But it is in fact the product of a contracted version of the Old World, which is why the European traveler, whether he is a Tory or a Whig or a radical, usually responds so quickly to it. It is a product of the escape from his own feudalism which, in turn, meant an escape from the organic and revolutionary sources of socialism. It is a product of his own bourgeois experience permitted, because of this extrication, to unfold as it could not unfold in Europe. On the world scene today this "sport" of European culture, bred in isolation from Europe itself, has become a familiar matter.

4   Radicalism

If the process of fragmentation worked according to its archetypical forms, a radical fragmentation would involve a relatively simple problem. Coming at the end of the European ideological spectrum, it would have none of the "future" to exorcise, and containing a relatively homogeneous proletarian class reality, its internal efflorescence would be characterized by no major struggles. Australia, however, involves many departures from this norm. For one thing, it does not contain, as it were, the "final" radicalism of modern times, so that there is still an element of the future that has to be cut off; and for another, its class content embraces many extraneous Whig and capitalist elements even on the land.[19] And yet the rationale of the European fragment is apparent in and through these characteristics. Whether or not we are dealing with a "simpler" form of the process, we are clearly dealing with the same process.

Though it produced a Labour Party which lasted down to the crises of the very recent past, dedicated to the principles of socialism, there is no doubt that on any scale the British South African fragment is far less radical than the Australian. Save for a moment during the twenties when it helped to put the Hertzog government into power, the South African Labour Party was a comparatively limited force. Nor is this entirely because the Labour tradition, originating in terms of the simple demands of mining labor in a British ideological context, ultimately became entangled in a major way under the leadership of Colonel Cresswell [20] with the effort to exclude native labor competition. We know that White Australia has played its part in Australian Labour history, even though it is true that the contradiction imposed on socialist principle by the struggle against native labor on the spot is more vivid and direct than any arising from an exclusive immigration policy. The difference is not even due to the fact that the reliance upon native labor prior to industrialization by the entire white community served, as Bryce saw,[21] to discourage a working-class consciousness. The very root of the Australian fragment before socialism arose in either place was socially more radical than that of the British South African, which actually contained a number of officers of the Napoleonic wars to whom Jacobinism was anathema. Stamped as the British settlers were with many of the progressive ideas of the early English nineteenth century, reflected in their political struggles with the mother country,[22] they lacked the proletarian spirit which came out of the early convict establishment and the subsequent waves of radical migration, both British and Continental, which characterized Australian development.

And yet even in Australia, as we know, the doctrinaire Marxisms of the twentieth century have failed to develop. One need not point here to the weakness of communism which, even in England, failed to take significant root. One can point to the absence of the theoretical discipline of the English Labour Party, of the Webbs, Laski, and Cripps. In large measure this has been owing to what Australian radicalism did not have to fight, feudalism and a powerful bourgeoisie: again the "future" shrinks because the past has been left behind. For it is the continuing pressure of these older forces which renews the doctrinaire passion of European radicalism, renews its utopias. The easy triumph of the Labour spirit in Australia, like the easy triumph of liberalism in the bourgeois fragments, robs it of the Jacobin, the doctrinaire, edge. Indeed, in both cases that ease leads to a distrust of the theoretical mind not merely because self-evident truth requires no expositor, but because the intellectual, or the "tall stoop," as he is sometimes known in Australia, represents an elite outside the triumphant mass. There is a fear of brilliant leadership in the Australian Labour Party, reflected in the persistence of caucus control, which in itself does much to rule out the doctrinaire left.[23]

The unfolding of the Australian fragment, because of the elitist interests it contained, included the defeat of an early Whiggery as well as the triumph of a later socialism. And it was, of course, the fact that the feudal establishment was missing on the spot which, in the first instance, as in the bourgeois fragments, insured the collapse of the Whigs. To be sure, there was a division within the early Australian elite between the Exclusives and the Emancipists, the one representing the old colonial magnates, the other representing newer wealth and the demand for a liberal ex-convict policy. As the battle between these two elites evolved, the latter took on for an instant a "progressive" side which, as with European Whiggery, mobilized the people behind it. But only for an instant. Once the battle of the Emancipist Whigs was won, and they turned to the idea of aristocracy, they were laughed out of court, not only indeed in Australia, but in Gladstone's London as well. The Australian Colonies Government Act repudiated William Wentworth's dream of an aristocratic establishment for the South Pacific. And, of course, when the Emancipists denounced the people as a threat, they could scarcely be more successful than were the Whigs of the liberal fragments. Because of the actual radicalism there the cry of "mob" has frightened the petty bourgeois a bit more in Australia than in the United States. But even in the age of the Communist menace, in part because of the sobriety of the Australian collectivist, its utility has been limited.[24]

And yet the very fact that it is a radical democracy which does the work of overthrowing the Whigs, a democracy dedicated much less to the capitalist dream than to mateship, shows us at once why after their defeat the Whigs of Australia were destined to a direr fate than those of America or any of the bourgeois fragments. In all of them they could somehow relate through their capitalist individualism to the passions of the mass, and in the United States they were able to do so in a vivid way through the Horatio Alger promise of the Republican Party. But where the democrat is collectivist in orientation this method does not work. What came out of the bourgeois fragments of North America as the problem of social reform arose at the opening of the twentieth century was, logically enough, an analogue of European Liberal Reform, the kind of individualist radicalism that we find in the Progressive movement or the National Progressive Party of Canada. But what big business had to face in Australia was the emergence of a Labour Party which seized the nationalism of the fragment and which, even in defeat, determined the context of Australian politics. Other parties, the Country Party and the Liberal Party, became, as Professor Hancock put it, the "parties of resistance" to its impact.[25] They take as their point of departure, ideologically no less than strategically, the basic Labour ethos.

If again we accept the notion that socialism is the "last" ideology, the European revolution thus comes to an end in the South Pacific. Australian socialism may not be the most

43

radical of socialisms, but in the context of a series of fragments which cannot produce socialism at all, some of which indeed are made hysterical by the thought of it, it is an impressive "advance." And yet if Australian history brings us to the end of the ideological revolution, it also brings us closer to the reversal of the whole fragmentation pattern. Nor is this correlation unreasonable. The proletarian spirit of the Industrial Revolution could not have moved outward from England, nor the spirit of 1848 from the Continent, until in historic time these appeared. The lateness and the shortness of Australian history is at once a reflection of its fragment content and the coming of the time when all fragmentation would be impossible. It is as if Cobbett and O'Brien and the Chartists, so to speak, just got in under the wire. But let us turn now, not merely in the case of Australia, but of all the fragments, to the dilemma they currently encounter. In terms of the pattern of fragmentation that we have now seen repeated so often, the movement from Europe, the shrinking of the future, and the development of the fragment ethos, just what has happened?

5   The Twentieth Century

I suggest this: the "future" has returned. There is a legend about the past catching up with individuals, but in the case of the fragments, the future has caught up with them. This does not mean that the modern fragments have not, as a result of world affairs, become involved again with the whole "underdeveloped" world. But even this involvement, this return, as it were, of Filmer and Philip II, has been defined in terms of the agitation of the traditionalist cultures by aspirations for modernity which have quickly become entangled with the most radical phases of the European revolution, socialism and Bolshevism. Everywhere the fragments now encounter the radicalisms they escaped when they left the moving stream of European history. And it is this meeting, this delayed

rendezvous with Babeuf, which has yielded the internal turmoil into which the fragments have been plunged.

Delay itself heightens the dramatic impact of the revolutionary encounter, and this is above all clear in the case of
the feudal fragments, where the atrophy of the future shut
out so much of modern history. The fact that these fragments
confront not early capitalism, but advanced industrialization,
not early Whiggery, but the Bolshevik revolution, heightens
their problem enormously. Nor is this reflected merely in the
conservative who, challenged by a vision starker than Maistre
encountered, is driven to a passionate clinging to the fragment myth. It is reflected even more vividly, and certainly
in a more complex way, in the innovator who yearns, precisely because of the more distant point he sees on the horizon,
to overleap all of the earlier stages of development he might
have experienced had he never left the scene of the European
revolution. The one thing which characterizes him, whether
in Quebec or Argentina, is impatience. It is as if, after the
long wait of fragmentation, waiting has become unendurable.
And it is here that the lure of extremism appears. This can
be nationalist extremism, the spirit of the Quebec Liberation
Front and its "suicide commandos." Or, as we have seen, it
can be the extremism of Marx, the very ideology that the
Enlightenment atrophy in the feudal fragments originally
militated against. In this context of impatience Marxism,
which in Western Europe inherits industrialism and democracy from the liberal movement, promises both, as well as its
own organic virtue, to men who before have refused the taste
of liberalism. Of course it is not the same Marxism, and
Castro is a good deal different from Sidney and Beatrice
Webb. But that is the heart of the matter.

The impact of delay in the Enlightenment fragments, the
great racial dilemmas of South Africa and the United States
apart, is less marked. For these fragments, if in a traditional-
ized and nationalized form, embody modernity itself. To be
sure, they also face on the world plane their socialist future,
the Marxes they escaped. But that encounter does not throw
them into a turmoil with respect to social policy. They have

45

battles over policy, but those battles are almost entirely contained within the traditional framework. And they are solved within that framework reasonably well, even when, as with various types of Liberal Reform, the state is employed to repair or stabilize the economy. From the Marxian point of view this gives them the queer appearance of successfully functioning antiquities, old Ford cars, as it were, that somehow keep running. But in fact that point of view is fallacious, and the experience of the fragments is designed precisely to expose the fact. Socialism does not arise inherently out of the requirements of advancing modern industry. Indeed, given the way in which socialism re-creates the feudal community, it can be argued that the liberal fragments contain an ethos more thoroughly "modern" than its own. The North American, feeding the bourgeois dynamo, cannot dream even of a futuristic kind of feudal peace.

This does not mean, one must hasten to say, that the Enlightenment fragments are without their problems as they face the return to revolution. What it means is that, again the racial question apart, their problems begin peculiarly as problems of international adaptation and struggle. If they can handle modernity in their own way, and indeed must, the rest of the world is not in the same position. Their experience cannot be duplicated: it is a part of history, irrevocably lost. For this reason the United States and the other modern fragments—Australia as well, given the pragmatic mood of its radicalism—are destined to deal with a world they cannot out of their own experience understand and for which they cannot out of their own experience prescribe. That world, including Latin America and French Canada, must achieve modernity through methods other than the *Mayflower* voyage. Extremisms of right and left offer such methods, and for that reason the struggle against them by the Enlightenment fragments calls for a leap of the imagination outside of their own experience. But that leap is as difficult as any that could be made in the realm of domestic social policy. It is resisted by Wilsonian theories of liberal imposition, by demonological theories of Bolshevism, by sheer isolationism. It is resisted, in short, by every regressive impulse of the fragment.

And yet have we not seen that this conflict, the conflict between obscurantism and enlightenment, is in the end the one that all of our cultures encounter? The feudal fragments may be agitated by issues of internal social policy, but in the last analysis these too raise the issue of the capacity of the fragment to break with its past. The oligarchies of Latin America may be concerned with one thing, the ultrapatriots of the United States with another, but they display in common the impulse of the fragment to flee in the face of new experience. They call those who challenge that impulse revolutionary and, in terms of the fragment myth, they are right. But one thing is clear. In terms of the threat of social revolution, it is they who are the allies of subversion. For it is they who paralyze the response of the fragment to circumstance, and doing so, build up the resources for the extremist appeal. Nor does it matter whether the issue is internal or external, changes in land tenure or policies of diplomacy. The Peruvian land-owner who cannot dream of compromise at home gives as much aid to revolution as the American businessman who cannot dream of deserting the criteria of Horatio Alger in foreign aid. But this is standard revolutionary procedure, and here indeed we are back at the classical process of the European revolution. Was not Wellington the legendary ally of the threat of violent change?

This struggle between regression and advance, emerging as the old fragment determinisms become matters of "choice," is not prefigured in the classical internal alignments of the fragment. It is not anticipated in the flowering of Catholic syndicates, the defeat of the Whigs by the petty bourgeois, or the battles of the Labour Party in Australia. It may become entangled with these issues, as when a rationalist tide among the French-Canadian clergy inspires them to accept the CCF or an obscurantist tide of the McCarthyite type in the United States hurts the Progressive movement. But the new battle cuts across the old alignments. And the reason is obvious. Those alignments reflect the interior drives of fragmentation itself, while the new struggle is generated by an exterior impact. The new struggle reflects not the era of escape, but the era of return. This is why the old alignments cannot give us a clue to its outcome. It is also why it will be decided finally by the new generations emerging in the fragment to whom the old alignments become increasingly empty.

Chapter Three

The European Fragment,
Africa, and the Indian Tribes

1   Race and Ideology

It was inevitable that the fragments of Europe should absorb
racial relationships into the whole intricate process of escape,
exclusion, and development by which their traditionalism
was forged. An experience so great as that involving the African and the Indian could hardly be left hanging outside the
general drift of the culture, its ethic and its nationalism. Indeed, that experience in every case was so closely intertwined
with all of the other experiences of the fragment, from economic production to religious worship, that one could expect
the most heroic effort to be made to extract from the European ideologies the message they contained for the racial relationship. That message was found in every instance, whatever
the problems were. Nor did its implementation cease because
the alien peoples tinged the fragment culture with their own
traditions. Catholicism was charged with the spirit of African
cults in Brazil, and with Indian religions in Mexico, but it
was nonetheless an effective weapon for imposing the European feudal ethos on men who had never known it. The instinct of the fragment to pursue its historic path is vividly
seen in the racial area.

This is not to deny that an ingenuity was needed here which was not required when the European principles were directly and immediately applied. If the Latin-American encomienda is as much the product of the feudal spirit as the concept of aristocracy itself,[1] it nonetheless requires a larger act of the imagination to invent it. If the slavery of the American South or Dutch South Africa flows from the bourgeois outlook, or at least one phase of it, the idea of that slavery is not to be found in any of the European bourgeois writers or theologians. To be sure, there is one method for implementing the Western ideologies, especially in connection with the unco-operative aborigine, which is simpler: extermination. Actually this method, the method of the "Indian War," is a kind of escape for the fragment and represents a duplication by violence, as it were, of the original voyage. But it is by no means without its problems. For one thing, the elimination of the recalcitrant aborigine is never complete, so that on the fringes of many of the fragments, in South America as well as North, there are alienated native populations which raise peculiarly agonizing problems. Moreover, where the native is exterminated, the African slave is usually imported, for the hunger for labor persists. And with the slave a more permanent, and hence more complicated relationship has to be worked out.

It will always be an interesting facet of the European fragmentation that the racial relationship was in one crucial sense easier for the feudal cultures than for the liberal or the radical. The feudal cultures had a concept of status which could be revamped for the purpose, in terms of either slavery or the encomienda. The Enlightenment cultures did not. In their case a human being was entitled to full equality, so that if he was to be enslaved in any way, his very humanity had to be denied. Of course, once that humanity was conceded, a person was bound to receive full equality, and this meant that the conscience at least of the liberal and the radical fragments was far more demanding than that of the feudal. The doctrinaire demands of a Garrison in the United States, a Dr. John Philip in South Africa, were the reverse manifestations of the exclusion principle. But it was this very oscillation between moral extremes, this very "revolutionary" character that the Enlightenment imposed on the issue of race, which characterized the difficulty of the matter. We are dealing with nothing less than Civil Wars and Great Treks, radical overturns in outlook. And the only way these could be escaped was, as in Canada and Australia, to have the good fortune of limited contact with African slavery or native subordination.*

Here the great distinction is between the feudal spirit and that of the Enlightenment in general. The gap within Enlightenment culture between liberalism and radicalism diminishes in significance, since both are involved in the moral polarity imposed by the egalitarian idea. To be sure, since radicalism comes late, during the age of emancipation, we are robbed of the chance to see it as an instrument of slavery. It is itself the instrument of emancipation in South Africa through the British impact, and Australia does not import slaves, although convict labor is a kind of substitute for them. But of course slavery is not the only instrument for expressing the spirit of egalitarian apartheid, and indeed as a later proletarianism emerges, the radical ethos has special ways of its own of doing so. The British South African Labour Party hurled the slogans of Marx himself against the native when he began to compete with the white worker, although it is true, of course, that the Communist element arising out of it has tried to appeal to the native. It was the crusade for White Australia which in that fragment actually "knit the first Federal Labour Party together." [2] We do not have to be cynics to see that the proletarian, like the bourgeois, can discover the exclusionist side of the Enlightenment coin.

I do not mean to affirm that the compulsions of social logic, whether coming from feudal or Enlightenment ideology,

* The distinction between feudal and Enlightenment ethics is also reflected, of course, in the response to alienated aboriginal groups. Given the absorptive quality of the feudal fragments, the "Indian question" becomes a matter of completing a process of inclusion already begun on a status basis, and hence becomes, as in Mexico, a "social question." In the Enlightenment cases there is an oscillation between separating the aborigine off and making him a full "citizen," as in the United States. I have developed this distinction in Chapter Four, under "Indian Wars and the Slavery Question," pp. 95-99.

51

from the spirit of Spanish Catholicism or British Protestantism, exhausted the racial issue in the fragments. Indeed, here is a case where the mandates of ideology are peculiarly intertwined with the larger range of factors out of which every fragment nation is made. For one thing, nothing ideological can explain the fact that the Incas of South America were more susceptible to subordination than the Iroquois of the North. Everywhere the type of aboriginal contact is independent of the fragment. Moreover, the peculiar shape of the national traditions themselves is deeply relevant. Spain and Portugal had a legalized tradition of slavery within their own borders, something which had fallen into disuse in England long before the British colonists moved outward, and this clearly helped to impart an element of status to the racial relationship in Latin America.[3] In addition, the countries of the Iberian peninsula had had historic contact with Africa while Northern Europe did not. There was, as Freyre has argued,[4] an ancient element of racial cosmopolitanism here which facilitated the absorption of the non-European into the feudal structure.

But after all of this has been said, the role of the class ethic stands out. We cannot, of course, here measure the detachment of the ethic from its competitors in European terms, since Europe does not confront us with a series of racial applications to match its ideological diversity. The feudalization of race in Brazil cannot be contrasted with anything the European bourgeoisie developed, since that class did not have African slaves. The internal turmoil of the Enlightenment over exclusion and equality cannot be contrasted with anything the aristocracies of Europe experienced, since they did not import the African either. This is the whole reason why the racial question is curious in the context of European ideology: ideology generates the answer to it, but does not before migration really know of its existence. But that need not alter our pattern of analysis. We can accomplish our comparative result by contrasting the fragments with each other, noticing the emancipation of each from the dilemmas which the other habitually possesses. Thus the contrast between the feudal ethos and the liberal springs as vividly to view if we compare the slave practices specifically employed in Brazil and the United States as if we were studying the contrast between each ethos and something it had left behind in the Old World or subsequently avoided in the New. On this plane, once removed, as it were, from the European reality, the principles which govern the behavior of the fragment are as vivid as elsewhere. There is the same detachment from challenge, protection of ethos, and unfolding of potential. Above all there is the same psychic magic, the same nationalization of ideology, so that the racial formula becomes one of the most firmly rooted parts of the fragment myth. Can the Brazilian see himself as a "Brazilian" without it? Can the Afrikaner see himself as an "Afrikaner"? This of course is why the racial question in all of the fragments in which it appears has been charged with enormous emotional force amid the challenges of the modern time.

2 The Feudalization of the Race Relationship

If what I have said is correct, the extrication of the feudal fragments from the liberal and radical impact in the racial sphere was an extrication, not from a moral challenge, since that impact led in two directions, but from a painful type of ambivalence. It was an emancipation from the spirit of both the Great Trek and the London Missionary Society, of John C. Calhoun and William Lloyd Garrison. This does not mean that the feudal fragment did not have its troubles because of race: I have already indicated how racial struggle helped to scar the organic fabric in Latin America in contrast to French Canada. But this struggle was, as it were, "inside" the fragment. The mestizo, mulatto, and other racial groups who revolted in Latin America after Independence were not in the position of the American Negro or African native had they revolted. One could just as easily say that they were in the position of the American Jacksonian or the poorer Afrikaner, participating in the fragment. Indeed, it is only because of their inclusion that we can speak of a feudal culture at all in Latin America: otherwise we would have only an "aristocracy," and in places like Brazil and Mexico, where the European population was small, a very limited one at that. The result is that whatever battles took place, breaking down the Latin-American organic cohesion, they could never be battles as in the bourgeois fragments over the basic question of cultural inclusion. There has always been racial tension in Ecuador, but Juan Montalvo had something different in mind when he assailed the United States for excluding men of color from the "common society." [5] The issue is purely one of perspective. From the angle of the classical Burke race scarred the Latin feudal community, but from the angle of the embattled Lincoln the Latin feudal community absorbed race.

How could the bourgeois spirit of separatism flourish when the whole drift of the Iberian fragments was to constitute their class identity out of the very material of the new races? There was a kind of theoretical reciprocity here. The feudal ethos of the Iberian fragments needed the new racial groups, those groups needed the ethos. If there was to be a "middle class" in a culture dominated by a Spanish aristocracy, this would be the mestizo group. On the other hand, without the sense of class that this involved, the mestizo elements in Latin America would have been disinherited. They would hardly have been in a better position than the products of miscegenation in the Enlightenment fragments. They would have been plunged into the ambiguous position of the South African Griqua or indiscriminately ranked with the Indian and the African groups themselves. It was the "medievalism" of the Spaniards and the Portuguese which helped to avoid this result.

Nor does the Enlightenment spirit of exclusiveness intrude itself as we move lower in the class hierarchy: to the Indian. We are not dealing here, of course, with a matter of simple brutality in human relationships, although that factor is involved. The Spanish encomienda could be a cruel instrument of exploitation. It is notorious that the Laws of the Indies promulgated by the crown in defense of the Indian were not easily enforced. But it is one thing to say this, and it is another

54

to say that the Indian was viewed outside the pale of humanity. His status, low as it was, linked him to the total culture. Nor was this revealed alone in his formal relationship to the Spanish crown or to the encomendero who was charged with the task of protecting and instructing him. It is revealed as well in his Christianization, something which did not trouble the Afrikaner in the relationship to the aborigine and which the North American easily forgot. The church accepted the Indian as a human soul, along with others, in the essentially medieval hierarchical world which it rationalized.

Indeed, we cannot even say that the separatism of the Enlightenment, the spirit, as it were, of Chancellor Harper, functioned in connection with the Negro slave. To be sure, slavery was by definition the harshest of the positions on the status ladder. But it remained, in and through all brutality, a matter of status, amenable to change and mobility. Again one can point to the formal responsibilities of the master,[6] to the absorptive role of the church, or even to other factors, such as the wide range of occupations through the social system for which the Iberian recruited the slave population. But the crucial index here is to be found in the practice of manumission.[7] In a bourgeois community where the Negro is either an item of property or an equal human being, a free Negro under conditions of slavery is an enormous paradox. How can an object of property be "free"? Or if it can be free, it must be human and hence all Negroes must be free. But in a feudal context, where the slave is accepted as human and given a status, this paradox does not exist. Manumission is merely a rise in status. It does not threaten the rationale of slavery itself, and it does not threaten the fragment ethic as a whole since that ethic is grounded in social differentiation. Hence it is not surprising, while manumission was sometimes even prohibited by law in the United States, that it took place easily and on a very large scale in Brazil.[8] The Negro himself could purchase it, and there were a number of traditional circumstances under which it was granted to him.

Under such conditions the work of Wilberforce could not be done. Given status, the lot of the slave could only be "improved." He could not suddenly be transformed from a living tool into a living human being. It is easy enough to see that the elimination of Enlightenment apartheid was, at the same time, an elimination of Enlightenment emancipationism. This applied to the Indian, and even when the cause of the Indian became tied up with democratic movements. With Las Casas behind them, not even the most subversive defenders of the aborigine could discover him as a human being.[9] But of course the most vivid illustration of the escape from absolute emancipationism lies in the slavery area. Nor, again, is this fact any less true when the struggle for emancipation becomes radical. In the seventeenth century the Jesuit Pedro Claver in Cartagena sought the religious amelioration of the African slaves,[10] in the nineteenth the secular Joaquim Nabuco sought their instant liberation in Brazil. But in both cases the point holds.

In Brazil it is of course true that the monarchy was active in the movement for emancipation,[11] and even though this finally alienated its support among the planters, it is also true that the Conservative Party pushed through the famous partial emancipation measure of 1871. But looking at the matter from the angle of the later abolitionist movement, with its societies and its banquets and radical demands, we cannot say that "liberal abolitionism" was at work. Could liberation mean what it meant in the United States in 1861, when the number of freed Negroes and mulattoes already vastly exceeded that of the slaves? Could it mean in São Paulo what it meant in Georgia when those freedmen were already functioning throughout society?

We can say, in other words, that in the feudal context the question of the slave could not be millennial, could not involve a wholesale overturn of human conceptions. It is not accidental that emancipation took place violently in the Enlightenment fragments where slavery had taken serious root, but peacefully in Brazil. The story is often told of the United States minister James Partridge, who, when flowers were thrown in the Brazilian Senate in 1871 at the passage of the Rio Branco bill, gathered some of them up and said, "I am going to send these flowers to my country to show how a law is passed in Brazil which caused the shedding of so much blood in the United States." [12] It is true that in some of the Spanish areas emancipation was accomplished forcibly at the time of the revolutions for independence. But this is not to be compared with the struggles in the United States or South Africa. Many of the royalist landlords and mineowners were the holders of slaves, and their elimination led easily to emancipation. The revolutions themselves, the struggles of Bolívar and San Martín, were not centrally concerned with this question. Nor is it a genuine comparison here to say that the Emancipation Proclamation by Lincoln was itself a form of retaliation. [13] It is true that the Proclamation was an instrument of civil war, but the issue of slavery lay centrally behind the war itself. The fact is, the Latin-American fragments, by absorbing the African like the Indian into their status system, indeed by creating that system out of their ranks, were saved from the radical oscillations of egalitarian morality.

What freedom from the Enlightenment moralisms meant was that the feudal ethos could flower without challenge. And yet even though neither Calhoun nor Garrison was there to disturb the process, one can hardly dismiss this as a simple spontaneity, something happening without design or effort. This was clearly one of the great achievements of all fragmentation, without question greater than any of the applications of the Tory or the Catholic spirit to the economic materials of the modern world. Granted, there are qualifying aspects in the ledger. Racial struggles did mar the hierarchical pattern. Insofar as the Indian was concerned, a portion of the population was never absorbed into the Iberian fragment system: down to the present time, from Mexico to Bolivia, the record of this limit remains. And the Indians who were absorbed, of course, conspired themselves to help the process in many ways. It is legendary that the labor system, the religion, even the traditions of chieftainship in Aztec and Inca culture played significantly into the Iberian pattern. One needs only to look at the fate of the Catholic French Canadians, seeking a similar result with the Iroquois, to appreciate the importance of this reciprocity.

But after all of this has been said, and even after we have

taken into account the original racial cosmopolitanism of the Spanish and the Portuguese, the extension of feudal culture remains a remarkable achievement. What is involved here is a kind of constitutional inventiveness we identify ordinarily with the Enlightenment and not with the "reaction," with Sieyès and not with Mariana. And yet, precisely because this was inventiveness for a feudal purpose, it brought neither the Iberian nor the Indian nor the African into the modern world. A price was paid for this Latin paradox. The hierarchical ethos permitted Latin America to escape the revolutionary oscillations of the Enlightenment fragments in the matter of race, so that today it does not experience the explosions of Johannesburg or Little Rock. But if race is feudalized, there is still the problem of feudalism, with all of its attendant experiences on the land and in the city. That is no minor problem as the European revolution descends again upon its fragment children. So a final question has to be asked. Can Latin America transcend its hierarchical spirit in the same peaceful fashion that that spirit itself permitted it to transcend race? Will the remark of Partridge, made in the Brazilian Senate on the memorable day of emancipation in 1871, apply to the medieval ethos itself?

3   The Enlightenment Polarity

It is often said that the slave cultures of South Africa and the American South were "feudal." But when we look more closely at those societies, as well as others bearing the mark of the Enlightenment norm of equality, it is clear that their battles over race are fought out in terms of the moral extremes which that norm imposes on human relationships, in conscience if not always in fact. Indeed, as we observe the detachment of those battles from the moderating sense inspired by the feudal outlook, what stands out is how deeply the Enlightenment principle in its unfolding is associated with both of the positions they involve. Democracy, as we have seen, is the outcome of that unfolding. But what kind of democracy

58

are we talking about? Are we talking about the Greek democracy of a white community made even more egalitarian in outlook by the fact that a group of Negroes flourish beneath it? Or are we talking about a real democracy in which everyone, including the Negro, has the Jacksonian right to vote and to live the bourgeois life? Ironically the democracy which arises in the Enlightenment fragments because they escape external challenge can collaborate with either phase of the dualism that their sense of equality imposes upon them. There can be the democracy of Calhoun or of Thaddeus Stevens, of the Dutch Republics or the British impact which inspired their independent creation.

It is not likely that in ordinary speech the "feudal" concept of South Africa and the American South will ever disappear, since the bourgeois ethic in these places is in fact impaired by the racial experience. Nor is the matter one of slavery alone. Even after emancipation a quite unbourgeois contempt for physical labor can prevail,[14] and the relationships of semiservitude which arise at that time can actually resemble the feudal bond even more than slavery itself. In South Africa it was after the abolition of slavery, in areas like Natal and the Transvaal, where native families lived on the land of whites and gave them only a portion of their labor, that a system closest to the European manorial order was developed. But at any historic point in the bourgeois fragments it can easily be proved that we are not involved in a genuine feudal ethos. Nor do we even have to point to the spirit of an aggressive capitalism here. To be sure, the "feudal" philosophers of the Reactionary Enlightenment in the American South before the Civil War[15] were given away very badly by their persistent capitalist passions. But in South Africa, where those passions were not nearly so much in evidence, the crucial distinction was even more obvious. This lay in the spirit of apartheid, the moral exclusion of the Negro, which flowered institutionally in the native reserves created in South Africa as colonization expanded. That spirit was also to be found in the American South, in the midst of all of the fine hierarchical paternalism that George Fitzhugh celebrated,

59

even though a difference of circumstance precluded the native reserve. It is this development which the experience of Latin America instantly throws into focus.

In other words, given fragmentation, the Enlightenment ideologies no less than the feudal unfold freely. If Latin America escapes the South African Nationalist Party and the NAACP, the bourgeois fragments escape the mood of the Portuguese colonists. This does not mean for an instant, of course, that they escape their own internal turmoil. It merely means that they can begin it without inhibition. And they do, first of all by fighting the full egalitarian outcome of the Enlightenment faith through definitions of the Negro as property or as an inhuman species of race. Locke is turned upside down, and he is a defender of the chattelized Negro rather than the Negro person. But there are wider sources of inspiration here. The very experience of fragmentation is relevant, for as we have seen in connection with the destruction of the aborigine, the racial detachment mirrors the primitive detachment from Europe, itself a kind of apartheid. If the mechanism of separation can be used in connection with decadent old Europe, why should it not be used in connection with the Negro? Here is "flight" within the very context of exploitation. And even this is not all. There is the Calvinist religion, not only with its Old Testament pictures of slave-owning patriarchs, but also with its sense of the chosen few, the curious democracy of a limited virtue. Put all of these themes together, and do you not come close to the trekking Afrikaner, the Jerusalemgangers of the Transvaal and the Orange Free State who instantly adopted, for the white, that is, practical manhood suffrage? Do you not, shifting to North America, come close to the fundamentalist areas of the American South?

The democratic unfolding of the fragment can fortify this entire drift, nourishing the sense of a Greek democracy, embellishing Calvin with a touch of Pericles. Even where the emergent democracy of the bourgeois and the radical fragments fight Whig elements of wealth on questions of race, we cannot assume that they will favor equality for the non-European. Hinton Helper cried out against the "lords of the lash" [16] even within the American South before the Civil War, but he was not a defender of the Negro. Indeed, in the context of advancing industrialization it is often vividly plain that the proletarian interests are the most passionate defenders of the Greek idea, the "interests" they fight those most ready, if only for economic reasons, to go beyond it. The South African Labour Party fought the mineowners against the employment of native workers. The idea of a White Australia has been a genuinely proletarian plank for the Labour Party of Australia. In every culture touched with the spirit of apartheid, we must beware of assuming that the agitating mass have as their goal the emancipation of the masses below them. The Enlightenment, in its democratic form, can be peculiarly exclusive.

And yet there is always, regardless of how much passion, how much religion is expended, the other side of the Enlightenment and Reformation coin. Aristotle himself, who was not troubled by addictions to Locke or to Calvin, could not successfully dehumanize the slave. And if the slave once becomes a Lockean owner, a member of the priesthood of Calvinist believers, what happens to the whole structure of exclusion? It is in the nature of things, of course, that the philosophy of apartheid in this respect digs its own grave. Nor, anywhere, does it do so more dramatically than in the case of the unfolding of the democratic *telos* of the Enlightenment fragments. For if there is Greek democracy, there is true Lockean democracy. One can shift from Pericles all the way to Abraham Lincoln. To be sure, this shift tends to be a regional matter, found in the North rather than the South, among the British rather than the Afrikaners. But that does not alter the point. If Garrison arises amid the democratic enthusiasms of the North, he still speaks the language of the South. If the London Missionary Society arises out of English Evangelical Protestantism, it still speaks the Reformation language of the Afrikaner. There is a wider gulf in the latter instance, of course, not merely because the Dutch faith remained fixed at an early seventeenth-century point, but also because it had never, like that of the South, been entangled in the "Jacksonian movements" of its opponents. But even here the issue is clear. Actual democracy is merely an extension of Greek democracy. Or, of course, vice versa.

I have called this situation "revolutionary." And there can be no doubt that the emancipation of the slave in South Africa and the United States involved not merely doctrinally but actually an upheaval that the feudal fragments did not experience. The Civil War, the explosion that came with the British impact, both testify to this. At the same time it is also true, as is perhaps the case with all revolutions, that emancipation by no means led to a perfect turning of the Lockean lever. Outright slavery was abolished, but the spirit of separatism continued. From this angle it can even be argued that the American South won the battle of Reconstruction. Certainly we know that after the Boer War the British surrendered much of their humanitarianism on the race issue, agreeing to leave the political status of the native unaltered in the Dutch Republics.[17] The issue thus is converted in fact into a matter of degree. At the same time the moral issue does not change: that issue in the bourgeois fragments cannot be a matter of degree. This is why the problem persists in issues of conscience like the "American Dilemma"[18] and finally in the civil-rights struggles of the present moment.

Those struggles have become enormously exacerbated by the world pressure of the present time. Who can deny that in facing the current revolution the conquest of the spirit of apartheid in the bourgeois fragments is one of the greatest problems of all? This is their "feudalism," their "backwardness," their "underdevelopment." And one cannot help noticing, given the way in which the feudal fragments managed to escape this dilemma through their very class ethos, the principle of compensation involved here. To be sure, the very rootedness of the inclusionist as well as the exclusionist view in the liberal ethic itself suggests that there are resources in this area for the bourgeois fragments which they do not possess in others. The fact that the forward movement of emancipation is dictated by one aspect of the fragment faith itself gives that movement an enormous access of strength. And yet if this is the good fortune of the bourgeois and liberal fragments, their compensation in turn, does not the problem of the limited view of the fragment absolutism remain? Can we not view the battle for civil rights as a compulsive imposition of the fragment faith, a kind of Wilsonian reconstructionism which is the other side of apartheid as the Wilsonian mood is the other side of "isolationism"? And can we not view it, also, as a struggle for the humanity of the Negro in its own right and for its own sake?

4 The New Era

One is tempted to say that the "prehistory" of the fragment has ended, that its history is beginning. For as it returns to the scene of revolution, as it encounters its "future" and begins to exercise "choice" with respect to its past, it enters a world larger than any that it knew even in its forgotten European home. But this issue, though it has come about suddenly, certainly as suddenly as any revolution ever hit any *ancien régime,* is not an issue which will be settled in an instant. It is fated to last over time, and even though the most intense moral battles may be fought as a result of it, over social emancipation or racial policy or sheer intellectual freedom, its resolution cannot easily be hastened. And the reason is clear enough. It will be settled only by the new generations to whom the experience of isolation is itself "alien."

It is interesting to compare, again, these generations which in our time are brought back to the world with the earlier generations in the fragment who, after the original settlement, lost contact with it. The determinisms are precisely antithetical. After the first settlers, fresh from Europe, have died, and their descendants begin to live entirely within the culture abstracted from the Old World, it is inconceivable that a contact with the larger whole, even in terms of the memory of oppression, can be truly maintained. The "insider's" view takes over, with all of its subjectivity, and ultimately its nationalism. What happens to the memory of the European world is that it is usually totemized in a static symbol, the voyage of Pizarro, of van Riebeeck, of the Pilgrims, which children dutifully learn about but which is remote from their own experience. The fragment lives, inevitably, its interior life. The men emerging in the fragment today, however, are losing contact precisely with that interior life. Indeed, is it not remarkable how far away from that life every one of the fragments has drifted in the very recent past? I am not referring alone to the sheer extent of travel outside the fragments, the technological matter. I am referring to the acceptance of an involvement with cultural diversity, the rise of an almost automatic assumption of cosmopolitanism. Whatever position within the fragment a man takes on an issue today, does he not take, somehow, the outer world into account?

In other words, we are fated to "remember" what an earlier generation "forgot." And yet what is involved here, of course, is not a return to the original colonial situation. One of the buried sources of fear in the face of a modification of the fragment nationalisms is undoubtedly the sense of that past situation, the intolerable ambiguity of being part of a whole and isolated from it. But not only is it in the nature of the current situation for isolation to end, but also the "whole" that is returning is wider than the old European nation. And the status of any fragment within it is not dependent on the European class ethic. Indeed, here is a curious advantage that the fragment derives from the expansion of the European revolution, for that revolution has produced a sense of equality which makes the old colonial contempt it received, a mixture of imperial and social snobbishness, impossible. "Anticolonialism" is itself in fact a vital part of the revolution, however distinctive the imperial experiences of the fragment may have been. It is a false fear which sees in the world involvement the return of the British governor, the Imperial viceroy.

And yet if colonialism is gone, we must not underrate the complexity, even the ambiguity, of the new situation. If that situation does not create again the sense of being half in and half out of a European country, England or Holland or Spain, it surely creates a new type of diversity. The fragment ethic now becomes one among many, not only in Europe but in a setting which embraces Asia and Africa as well. The French Canadian exchanges a partial "Frenchness" for a partial place in a culture wider even than that of the Canadian dualism. The Australian exchanges his English ambivalence for a world ambivalence. From this point of view, in fact, the world impact creates a much larger problem than any that the fragment solved through its nationalist discoveries, its manufacture of cultural universalisms.

But is not this the very clue to the enrichment that the new condition brings? It was the security of life in the old fragment that destroyed its philosophy. Of course the fragment always has excuses for its past theoretical poverty: it was crossing the Kansas Territory, fighting the aborigine. But philosophy does not depend on whether a culture is "busy": it flourishes in moments of the most desperate preoccupation. What smothered philosophy in the fragment cultures was the false certainty that those cultures created for themselves. The whole mechanism of their past development can be viewed in terms of the drive for this certainty: the destruction of the past, the shutting off of the future, the interior unfolding, above all the psychic metamorphoses associated with the whole process. The end of that mechanism is creating more and not less insecurity, but it is liberating the perspective of the fragment for the first time since its original voyage from the Old World. It is igniting again a spark of philosophy that died in the course of that voyage. This imaginative renewal, with all of its trauma, is today the mark of the new era that the fragment enters.

Part Two

Five National Histories

Chapter Four

United States History in a New Perspective

by Louis Hartz

1 The Expansion of Comparative Analysis

The comparative analysis of American history involves two strokes: the relationship of the United States back to the larger European context from which it came, thus exposing its history as a form of liberal fragmentation, and the comparison of that experience with other types of fragmentation. The first action uncovers the nature of America in terms of the interacting forces from which it was extracted in the Old World, the second illuminates that result in terms of other societies with a similar fate. The traditional interpretations of American history do neither, because they are projections rather than analyses of the experience of fragmentation, reflecting that forgetfulness of original context, that triumph of subjectivity which everywhere is at the heart of the traditionalism arising from detachment. Ultimately this is the difference between the view I am urging here and the large interpretations of Turner and Beard in the twentieth century or even their predecessors of an earlier era.*

* I have already commented on the way in which the Turner thesis, by seizing on the "native" factor of the frontier, reflected the loss of memory of

Certainly the fixity of the American liberal tradition, which stands out so vividly against the moving pattern of European history, becomes even more persuasive as a fact when viewed in terms of the other Western fragmentations. Even if we had not started our comparative analysis with the American liberal tradition, even if we had begun at the point of French Canada or Australia, we would be bound to arrive at the mechanism of extrication, atrophy, and unfolding by which that tradition was forged. Inevitably, once we saw the withering of the Enlightenment in the Catholic Canadian setting, we would have seized upon the meaning of the socialist atrophy in American culture. The miseries of A. A. Dorion and the Parti Rouge would have led us to the miseries of John Spargo and the American Socialist Party. At the same time the very flowering of socialism in Australia would have led us to the strategy by which democracy arose in the bourgeois context of American history. To see how the Australian Labour Party emerged out of a fixed radical setting would have been the prelude to seeing how Jacksonian democracy emerged out of a fixed liberal setting. Nor could we

---

Europe in American history as a whole. The same type of subjectivity, from a different angle, characterizes the work of Beard and the Progressive historians. If they did not stress the perspective of the covered wagon, as it were, they stressed the perspectives of the internal battle involved in the unfolding of the American fragment, an angle of vision equally subjective. The nature and even the outcome of that battle were determined by a logic that was European, but it was in the very nature of that logic that the participants in the struggle should be so divorced from the European context as to forget it almost completely. The result is that Beard, when he projected the view of those participants, became, like Turner, a datum for the student of fragmentation rather than a contributor to his work.

On the other hand, the European historian is in very much the same position. Presumably if the American historian misses the European rationality of the fragment, the European historian ought not to do so. But he rarely includes the fragment cultures within "European history," even though their history illuminates crucially every important development within modern Europe itself. In this study I have stressed European history as a clue to the fragment, but it is obvious that the order of this relationship can at every point be reversed. And yet, clearly enough, both American and European historiography are victims of the separated perspectives that the analysis of fragmentation itself explains. It is the conquest of that separation through the objective experience of our time which will in the end expose the historical continuities that have been obscured. That experience must ultimately force a surrender of the false distinction between "European history" and "American history."

have avoided, watching the moral efflorescences of French Canada and Australia, perceiving the nature of our own. We would have come to the meaning of "Americanism," to the historiographical hiding of the fragmentation process, even to the peculiar psychic turmoil that Bolshevism and world war have yielded in the twentieth century. In short we would have come via Quebec or Sydney to everything in the American experience that, starting from London or Paris, we originally found in America when we encountered the American liberal tradition.

But the expansion of comparative analysis to the European fragments does more than underscore the process of traditionalism in the American case. It highlights, from a series of new angles, the liberal substance of the American tradition as well. The dynamic ideological relationships of Europe cast a vivid light on the more static life of the fragments, but the fragments by virtue of their very traditionalism provide an angle that Europe does not supply. Of course there is the large racial issue that Europe does not encounter, and in this context the fragments take over the comparative task, in the immediate sense, completely. But what I have in mind is the insight that comes from the juxtaposition of sheer continuities. Put the American businessman alongside the Latin-American creole landowner, for example. The latter can be as reactionary as the American, but does he not in his very fixity illuminate the prejudices of the American in a forceful way?

Nor need we work alone with gross contrasts here, the gap between La Paz and Kansas City. The bourgeois fragments themselves, if they illuminate the Protestant individualistic substance of American culture, provide also delicate contrasts which etch lines of detail in the American fragment portrait. English Canada and Dutch South Africa show us clearly enough that America is a middle-class fragment, but they show us equally clearly that it is so in a distinctive way. Its individualism is intense, its capitalism aggressive, its "Americanism" doctrinaire. It is, if one can use such language, the Marxian archetype of the bourgeois fragment. Marx himself knew little of fragmentation: if he had, I believe that his historical theories, including his explanation of socialism, would have been a good deal different. But he seized, perhaps arbitrarily, on an archetypical purity in the bourgeois culture which actually is relevant to the bourgeois fragment that has rejected him more passionately than any of the others. America is the clearest case that we have in fragment terms of a "capitalist democracy."

Always we are dealing with mutually checking analyses, Europe and America, America and the other fragmentations of Europe. The concept of the fragment, the common experience deriving from the extrication from Europe, is the bridge between the two analyses. As the comparative study of American history expands, there can be no doubt that our confidence in generalization increases. We gain, so to speak, a whole series of new witnesses to testify to the quality of the national drama. Latin America joins France, French Canada joins England. But this is not all that happens. Each of the fragment cultures, as the romantic would say, is "unique," a special blend of European national tradition, historical timing, racial encounter, accidental incongruity. A whole series of new slants on the American experience is thus provided by them. To be sure, we will have to jump about a bit in order to exploit this resource, the Latin-American revolutions becoming peculiarly relevant at one point, the Australian military establishment at another. But there is little danger that we will lose our bearings. The behavior of the fragments as abstractions from the European revolution, revealed in terms of both Europe and their own history, remains the dominant fact at every point.

2   Colonialism and Independence

Early American history contains a number of miracles, duly celebrated in the national legend, which the process of fragmentation does much to illuminate. We had a liberal Enlightenment, but it was contained within the limits of sobriety. We had a revolution, but we escaped anarchy and military dictatorship. We developed a Constitution, and it has

72

lasted down to the present time. Moreover, twentieth-century trends in American historiography made these miracles even more miraculous than ever. For those trends discovered a genuine "social revolution" in which class relations changed, a "critical period" in which anarchy and proletarian revolt prevailed, a "reaction" on the part of the elite which sought desperately to clamp the lid upon an exploding community. In the context of Fiske and Beard and Jameson the political achievements of the early American, remarkable to begin with, cease to be of this world: they are the work of a god, a fabulous Rousseauian or Solonesque Legislator who converts disaster into prosperity and creates an inheritance beyond their understanding for the mere human beings who follow him.

In order to explain what actually happened it is necessary to disturb these images rather badly. We must disturb them in connection both with timing and with the social experiences they portray. For the great agitations of the eighteenth century were in fact resolved in the seventeenth, when the *Mayflower* came; and they were resolved not through self-controlled revolt or fabulous constitutional invention, but through migration, through leaving the "old world" behind. It is obvious, from the standpoint of both Europe and the fragments, that what steered the Americans through the vicissitudes of the Revolution and the Constitutional Convention was a liberal cohesiveness which had been established from the outset in colonial life. To be sure, in the context of the fragments we do not gain the vantage point for seeing this fact that the French or the Puritan or even the Russian revolutions provide, since fragmentation by its very nature precludes social revolution. But there are compensations. The contrasting light of the other fragments brings out vividly the original nature of the American liberal establishment, and the Latin-American revolutions, upheavals within the context of feudal fragmentation itself, provide a point of departure to which we must give special attention.

It is not hard to see that the theory of colonial resistance to England was an application rather than a repudiation of the doctrines of the American colonial past. There is a secularism

73

in revolutionary thought which the seventeenth century does not display, and Jefferson on this score is symbolic of a shift. But that secularism, that reliance upon an autonomous natural law, contains the whole individualist essence of the earlier period, even discounting the fact that in New England it was ministers like Jonathan Mayhew who led in significant part the thinking of the revolutionary movement.[1] All that one needs to do here is to compare the political implications of the Catholicism of the feudal fragments with the American development to see the issue involved. It was a doctrine of divine right which came out of the Catholicism of both French Canada and Latin America, and when in the Latin case the imperial power was assailed, the past had in fact to be contradicted: there was an "Enlightenment," a collapse of continuity. To be sure, there were Anglican espousers of divine right like Jonathan Boucher among the Americans, just as there were religious revolutionaries like Mexico's Hidalgo among the Spanish. But the general drift in the American case is obvious, as in the Latin. The Americans when they turned to Locke were extending, rather than contradicting, their intellectual heritage, which precisely is why they turned to Locke rather than to Rousseau after the fashion of the Spanish creole. Rousseau and the French thinkers symbolize precisely the break with tradition which, because of a liberal inheritance, the Americans were able to avoid.

Nor is the issue one of doctrine alone. If the American "Enlightenment" was temperate, it was also because the actual culture of the colonial establishment made unnecessary a major social transformation and indeed supported empirically the liberal formulations of resistance doctrine. We are coming to accept the fact that colonial society even prior to 1776 was remarkably fluid, for all of its stratifications ranging from the elite around the royal governor to the back-country farmer, from the rich merchant to the artisan. A flood of light from the fragments confirms this. The simple principle of freehold tenure stands out vividly against the background of both French-Canadian and Latin-American land practice, and insofar as religious diversity or class equality goes, one could hardly desire starker antitheses than those to

74

be found in the power of the French-Canadian clergy or the minute distinctions of behavior and privilege which separated the ranks of society in Portuguese or Spanish America. Nor, if one goes all the way to Australia, does the light cease to shine on the social liberalism of colonial America. The prison establishment there, associated with estates worked by convict labor, throws the culture of the independent American farmer or trader into a special kind of relief. To be sure, there was some convict transportation in the American case and the establishment at New South Wales in 1788 was created in part to replace North America for this purpose.[2] But the convict element in America was overwhelmed by free settlement: it generated neither a military elite nor a proletarian tradition. From every angle the Declaration was socially "real" to a remarkable extent in America before it was signed. And this was why its signers, for all of their high resolve, for all of the pledging of their lives and their fortunes, remained remarkably cool in the process of signing it.

Of course, the continuities here were not merely social: inevitably they were political as well, and this was of the greatest importance for the specific outcome of the revolutionary activity. In a Protestant, individualist culture the institutions of self-government immediately take root, and by the time of the Revolution a tradition of popular assemblies had been evolved which made Locke quite a common matter of fact. This did not exist in the Latin-American case, but the reason was not merely that the creole was excluded by a rigorous imperial policy from any participation but that in the *cabildo.* That exclusion did, to be sure, produce an alienated class which turned toward French thought. But the creole was an aristocrat, and even if he had been taken into the Spanish system as the Canadian seigneur was taken into the French, there would still have been the passivity of the mass of the people as there was in Canada. The American experience, elitist as it may have been before the Revolution, presupposed a spread of liberal sentiment as well as a specific type of imperial policy. No doubt an early period of "salutary neglect," the significance of which was felt throughout the community as a whole, helped the American tradition of participation to get established. But the popular force which challenged the later reversal of that policy flowed from something much deeper than an accidental habit. It flowed from the political institutionalization of a liberal spirit which had shaped every phase of colonial society as well. And this was why the doctrinal articulation of that spirit was a matter of intoning tradition, not shattering it. Of course, when the Latin-American revolutionaries read the Declaration of Independence they did not see this fact any more than did most of the French radicals. Even as late as 1887, General Mitre, Argentina's famous president and scholar, was interpreting the Declaration as involving "a theory of government independent of all precedent." [3]

What the actual situation, apart from French or Latin-American misinterpretations, meant, of course, was that the frames of government adopted in 1776 at the call of the Continental Congress were grounded in solid experience.[4] There were reforms, some of them vivid, as in the case of the Pennsylvania constitution, which adopted not only practical manhood suffrage, but a single-house legislature as well. But at no point did the current of change produce anything like the break with tradition that republicanism produced in Latin America. Indeed, the issue cuts deeper even than this, for what was involved in the American continuity was not merely political forms. It was the sense of responsibility wrought by the habit of political participation. Everyone knows Tocqueville's famous analysis of the inexperience of the French revolutionaries, and it practically applies to the Latin-American creoles even though they are not an innovating bourgeoisie. But it does not apply to Sam Adams and Patrick Henry, far apart as these men may be with respect to "conservatism" and "radicalism." The American was not an alienated figure suddenly hurled to power: he had "belonged" before, and his exhilaration was therefore kept in bounds.

But if the political participation of the American had been nourished by the liberal spirit, it minimized inevitably the possibility of anarchic conflict. The American, in other words, precisely because he had experience, was saved from even

confronting the frightful dislocations which men of inexperience inevitably encounter when they take over the affairs of
state: to him that hath shall be given. In some sense the Latin-
American record reveals this even more clearly than the
European revolutions, for though the feudal tradition was
not uprooted in this record, it displays a peculiar kind
of violence arising out of the breakdown of organic community. When we look at the sheer slaughter of royalists
in Mexico and Argentina, the driving out of the Tories by
American "mobs" seems almost genteel. When we study the
racial upheavals in Venezuela, which on occasion threatened
all property owners with extinction, the "rebellion" of Daniel
Shays seems exceedingly constitutional. By the end of the
Latin-American wars the class to which Bolívar himself belonged in Venezuela had been decimated by social struggle.[5]
In the great legend of the "critical period" Washington was
deeply alarmed by news of the uprising of Shays. But had
Shays and his friends gotten hold of Washington, they would
merely have petitioned for mortgage relief. In 1821, at the
height of the Latin-American revolutions, a critic in the
North American Review expressed an instinctive reaction:
"How can our mild and merciful peoples, who went through
their revolution without shedding a drop of civil blood, sympathize with a people, that are hanging and shooting each
other in their streets, with every fluctuation of their ill organized and exasperated factions?"[6]

In part the bourgeois continuity of the Americans can be
defined in terms of the issue of legitimacy. Given their liberal
cultural heritage out of the fragment, given their previous
implementation of that heritage in political action, when independence was proclaimed the structure of legitimate authority did not break down: in some ways it was actually
clarified. Just the reverse was true in Latin America, where
the imperial power symbolized legitimate authority. Indeed,
in the American case, as we know, because the Acts of Trade
reversed an earlier policy of imperial neglect, the Americans
were able to denounce Britain itself as revolutionary. To be
sure, the Latin-American creole originally began to revolt
when the Napoleonic invasion had deposed Ferdinand VII,

and his initial claim was a claim of pure legitimacy. But even at that moment he was beginning to undermine the imperial structure, and he was shortly at war with the Spanish monarchy itself. That war, in its removal of the historic fount of legitimate power in Latin America, throws one crucial aspect of the American Revolution into vivid relief. Paine had been translated in Bogotá. But whereas his antimonarchical sentiment struck at true authority there, in the United States it did not do so. On the contrary, it is probably reasonable to say that by 1776 monarchy itself had become largely obsolete, "illegitimate" in America. Paine's utilitarian attack upon kings struck an instant chord in a culture already generally utilitarian.

It is only in the context of this social cohesiveness and this continuing legitimacy that the smooth republican outcome of the American Revolution can be understood. The need for the Latin-American *caudillo* simply did not exist: there was no anarchy out of which he could arise, no vacuum of legitimacy which he could fill. There were officers in Washington's army dissatisfied with the state of things, a Colonel Lewis Nicola or a Major General James Mitchell Varnum, but had these men desired to do so they could never have pursued the path of Bolívar's lieutenants, which led to the military domination of Latin America.[7] To be sure, some Americans feared a military dictatorship, and some also feared a monarchy. In fact, both were ruled out by the historic character of the American fragment. An army was needed to liquidate British rule, but it was not needed for any other purpose. Monarchy was eliminated, but because it too was not needed, there could be no "restoration." Mexico's Iturbide was as inconceivable as Argentina's Rosas.

Actually it is the Brazilian situation which casts the American most clearly in perspective here. Iturbide had a disastrous career, as did the other invented monarchs of Latin America. But Dom Pedro I, himself of the Portuguese royal line, by continuing the monarchical tradition generated stability in Brazil for a long period, which the Spanish states did not have. We can say this: the Americans accomplished the result of Brazilian monarchy without it, and probably could have done so only without it. The American Whigs who yearned with John Dickinson[8] for a monarchy undoubtedly wanted precisely what the Portuguese line did impart to Brazil: an anchor, a ballast. They had the yearning that San Martín expressed in connection with monarchy for Latin America. But the frustration of Dickinson was of an entirely different order from that of San Martín. For whatever might be said about the monarchical problem in the context of Latin-American absolutism, in America the dream of kingship missed the character of the fragment community. It missed the very source of stability and continuity itself in the culture.

What emerged, despite the early Whig lamentations, was a republican Constitution which worked. Inside the American fragment 1787 is bound to look like a "reaction," but the exterior view as always modifies this perception. Even in connection with the greatest of the achievements of the Federal Constitution, the centralization of a larger degree of power in the hands of the national government, this is so. If that achievement seems like a simple reaction against the weakness of the Continental Congress under the Articles of Confederation, it nevertheless could not have taken place were it not for a fabric of fragment unity which had underlain the Articles also and made possible the orderly movement to the Federal Convention. In this sense the original migration, despite colonial diversity, endowed us from the outset with a kind of "national unity." Not only what the European kings had to do in connection with feudalism, but what the Latin American *caudillos* had to do in connection with the local *caciques,* America was able to avoid. The Federal Convention helped to create a nation, but it also inherited a nation.

One sees this vividly enough when we place the American federal question alongside that of countries consisting of two European fragments. Would Madison's reasoning in the *Federalist Papers* have been able so successfully to unite the British and the French in Canada, the British and the Dutch in South Africa? Would the Connecticut Compromise have worked so easily in these cases? The very fact that the federal issue was debated in terms of large and small states in the Federal Convention, in terms of the Virginia and New Jersey plans, is proof in fact that major cultural battles did not exist. To be sure, the slavery question ultimately shattered the work of the Convention, and there were at the time rumblings of it, as in the provision extracted by the South that there should be no federal interference with the African trade for twenty years. But the sectional holocaust on this count was still in the future. Moreover, the fact that it came, no less than the contrasting difficulties of Canada and South Africa, proves the basic point. The success of the federalism which "reacted" against the Articles of Confederation lay in an antecedent unity of fragment culture.

But the deepest sense in which the Constitution worked through an inheritance from the past is not to be found in the federal area. It is to be found in the sheer effectiveness of its republican system of government. The fact that that system worked, unlike so many in South America patterned after it, was traceable to the cohesiveness of the liberal fragment. One is reminded of Miranda's conversation with Sam Adams in 1784. Miranda asked why the American constitution made no place for "virtue" and gave so much room to property, which he regarded as a "poison." [9] The Venezuelan had little grasp of American facts. Virtue was suffused throughout the American world, and it was associated precisely with property, the pervasive presence of the bourgeois spirit. Of course the American constitutionalists themselves, if they did not dislike property, did not think very highly of American virtue. It is a commonplace that the philosophy underlying the Constitution, even that consciously articulated in the *Federalist Papers* contains a bleak view of human nature. Reading the American writers, one would suppose that one were in Miranda's world rather than theirs. This is why they placed heavy reliance on checks and balances, as we know. But did those checks work in the Latin-American context? Did they unify the Spanish fragment? Whatever the Americans thought, their republican virtue was insured by a cultural heritage out of the past, ultimately out of the first of the seventeenth-century migrations. It was this heritage which had given them a tempered Enlightenment, a traditionalistic revolution, ultimately a successful republican constitution.

I believe that this analysis would have been confirmed by the experience of the other bourgeois fragments had they also had national revolutions. But of course since English Canada did not have a sharp break with the imperial tie and in the case of Dutch South Africa the tie was broken through conquest, there is no immediate vantage point for analysis. What stands out in this context, indeed, rather than a parallel, is a contrast. For the fact that the Americans in a national revolt, in a new constitutional document, enunciated the liberal ethic in the course of a revolt for independence facilitated peculiarly the conversion of the ethic into nationalism. Here is one of the sources of that peculiarly driving "Americanism" that the other bourgeois fragments lack: Jefferson in the Declaration articulates the spirit of both the American migration and the American Revolution, the latter sharpening the nationalist significance of the former. The Puritan ethic becomes all the more vividly "independent," all the more vividly a nation in itself, as the American colonies overtly break with the mother country. Since the ethic itself is used to justify the break, the continuity between the ideological and national separations is practically perfect. The American troops lay down their lives for an idea embodied in a country, or, if you want to reverse the order, for a country embodied in an idea. It is the peculiar fate of the American bourgeois fragment not only to have a "revolution" but also through that revolution to accentuate the nationalistic transformation of its original fragment norm.

This means, of course, a colossal blending and confusion of figures in the heroic era of American history. The men of the *Mayflower* sink into the ranks of the men of the Revolution, and the Daughters of the American Revolution celebrate them both simultaneously. But do not the men of the Federal Convention also enter the homogenized group? Are they not celebrated at the same time? The truth is, one of the best proofs we have of the empirical continuities that we have seen at work in the movement from colonization to Constitution is the American fragment legend itself. If those continuities had not existed, could the DAR honor so easily in a single breath Winthrop and Jefferson and Washington?

Time itself is no explanation here. In France the royalist still curses the Jacobin, and in Latin America, our tortured feudal fragment, the mestizo is suspicious of the creole. What this means is that the multiplicity of figures absorbed into the American heroic myth of the early era discounts somewhat their heroism. The revolutionaries were successful because they were not quite such "revolutionaries," the constitutional inventors were successful because they were not quite such "inventors." But this mitigation of heroism can be tolerated, especially since it is unlikely to penetrate very far into the community. It is better to have an intelligible ancestor than one who is merely heroic.

3   The Rise of the National Democracy

If the Revolution and the Constitution are related to the abstraction of American culture from Europe, the victories of Jeffersonian and Jacksonian democracy are related to it no less clearly. The whole familiar drama of early American history could only have taken place within the context of the American fragment. For it was of course the fact that the European aristocracies had been left behind which robbed the American Whig of the chance to dominate America by leading a campaign against them, or turning around and allying with them. It was the fact that those aristocracies had been replaced by a uniformly liberal culture which gathered peasants, "petty bourgeois," and proletarians all into the ranks of democratic liberalism, producing an egalitarian giant ready to take full advantage of the Whig dilemma. In other words, the very spirit of community that tempered the revolutionary "Enlightenment," contained social strife, and insured a republican outcome yielded also the victory of American democracy. Today both the Revolution and the rise of democracy are centers of historical controversy. But the resolution of the issue in both cases, diverse as the specific questions seem to be, is precisely the same.

Unfortunately for comparative purposes, the fragments do

not confront us with the case of a victorious Whiggery against which we can place the twistings and turnings of the early American elitist Whigs. In the feudal fragments Whiggery does not get under way, in the Enlightenment fragments it collapses. At the same time there are certain imaginative transpositions that we can make which will illuminate the American problem with special force. Given the interior perspectives of the American fragment, the early Whig is a "conservative," and if he is of the Fisher Ames type, he is a diehard "reactionary." But is it not sobering to conceive of the Whig, if only for an instant, in the setting of the Château Clique or the military and social aristocracies of Latin America? Does not his color change with remarkable rapidity, and do we not begin to see, even if the record itself does not provide us with the precise situation, the incipient beginnings of the classical European strategy? Put Alexander Hamilton in Quebec. Does he not become a revolutionary? It is inconceivable that Hamilton could have lived for long under the dominion of Bishop Ignace Bourget without challenging the whole structure of clerical power. Surely he would have tried to shatter the old rural economy, for if the dynamic agrarianism of Jefferson was anathema to him, the static life of the French-Canadian land would have made him even more restless. In the end, inevitably, he would have confronted the French with a National Bank. As a matter of fact, we do not need to exercise our imagination wholly here. The disturbing impact that the English-Canadian merchants had upon the French provides an adequate clue, for Hamilton came himself, in a most specific way, out of the English capitalist tradition. Of course, our illustration places Hamilton inside the French-Canadian community, rather than, as in the English-Canadian case, outside it, for it is only in these terms that we can begin to see the revolutionary aspect of Hamilton, which the American fragment prevented from flourishing. And it is only in these terms also that we can see him begin to make a popular appeal against the *ancien régime*.

In Latin America the situation would probably have been even more explosive. Like all good Whigs, Hamilton viewed military elites with suspicion.[10] The *caudillo* dictatorships of

83

Páez and Rosas would have distressed him. But, once again, the state of the Latin-American economy would have made him instantly an apostle of the capitalist revolution. He would have tried to transform the world of the hacienda into the world of Birmingham and Manchester. To be sure, the degree of popular support he would have received here is open to question, since the masses in Latin America were governed by distinctly preindustrial norms. But that is not our problem now. It is in the nature of the feudal fragments that they have their fixity: what we are trying to see is how the American is transformed in an alien setting.

Hamilton becomes a revolutionary: but he also becomes at last a successful conservative, satisfying his frustrated yearning for elitist supports. To be sure, as Hamilton makes the classical Whig about-face in the feudal fragments, as he shifts from Brougham before 1832 to Brougham after 1832, he encounters a few inconveniences. The seigneurial elite in French Canada is not quite the British aristocracy, and the collapse of legitimate authority in Latin America is distressing. But there are compensations. The access of clerical traditionalism in French Canada, distasteful as it might be from some points of view, does control the great popular beast marvelously. Even in Latin America, there is always Brazil, at least until the Republic is established, where one can find the solace of those good monarchical and aristocratic continuities missing in New York and Philadelphia. The situation is not perfect, but it is adequate. Surely it is better than a situation in which one encounters the mob without any protection at all. In the feudal fragments, at any rate, the Whig can always find some ally.

The drama of Hamilton as revolutionary and conservative is interesting, but of course it is not enacted in the United States: here Hamilton falls before the mob. But this situation can be dramatized in terms of the very feudal fragments through which Hamilton is imaginatively transformed. For in those fragments, not in imagination, but in fact, there are a series of weak and relatively feckless democratic movements which throw the great Jeffersonian and Jacksonian upsurges into a vivid light indeed. Of course, the fecklessness of those movements derives in large part precisely from the fact that a few antecedent Hamiltons were missing to set the Enlightenment off, but that is not our main concern now. What is relevant at this point is how the American democratic movement, arising out of a liberal society which has replaced the *ancien régime* with a mass of individualist peasants and individualist proletarians, differs from one which tries to get started where the population is in a precapitalist and preliberal frame of mind. In a general way, of course, it is not hard to document the comparative difference of mentality here. One glance at the habitant and the peon is enough to put the economically speculative and politically activist outlook of the American democrat into fairly clear focus. Tocqueville did not have a better point of departure for the analysis of these qualities in France itself. But as a matter of political mechanics, the American democratic movement is highlighted in a peculiar way when we put it alongside democratic actions which try to represent, to work with, the masses of people in the feudal fragments.

Compare Andrew Jackson with French Canada's Louis Joseph Papineau. One instantly, of course, sees a difference: Jackson is brought to the White House in a blaze of glory, Papineau spends a considerable time in exile with a price on his head. But the social mechanisms involved are more significant than this specific outcome. Jackson's democracy, and that of his followers, is the simple democracy of the American common man, but after one has abstracted anti-British nationalism from it, one is never quite sure that the Papineau movement is in fact such a movement quite apart from Papineau's own seigneurial position. Jackson, to be sure, was a slaveholder, but this cannot in the same sense be counted "against" him: the matter here is not one of general justice, but of the processes that arise in a fragment. The American fragment displayed a logical democratic unfolding within its own context, despite the slave. It is surely doubtful whether, robbed of its nationalism, the French-Canadian democratic movement of the thirties would have approximated the Jacksonian comparison even to the extent that it does. Even its pro-Americanism, its admiration for American republican institutions, and its yearning at various points for annexation to the United States was wrapped up in this fact. In the American case, of course, the imperial issue had ceased to be a factor in domestic politics in 1776: the democratic upheaval was a clearly domestic and clearly authentic force.

But this is not all. American democracy received the active support of the American people, and this is one of the clearest evidences of their liberal character. I have already referred to the political responsibility of the American in the course of the Revolution. But this is a complex matter, involving not merely a temperate outlook, but also a high capacity for participative activity.[11] That capacity is as much a function of the Calvinist spirit as the capitalist ethos of the average American, and politically it is crucial. One need not affirm that American democracy welled up, after the fashion of Rousseau, spontaneously from the people. This is a legend which is belied by the obvious work of Jacksonian party organizers. But one can say that there was a remarkable reciprocity between the organizers and the people. The people "understood" the organizers very well indeed, and, moreover, kept on understanding them.[12] It is this understanding which is in doubt in the French-Canadian case. French-Canadian nationalism, to be sure, was easily communicable to the habitant. But again, that is not the point. There was also nationalism in the American democratic case, but it consisted precisely of the democratic consciousness of the people at large. It was an emotion compounded of their "understanding."

The distinctiveness of the democratic tide which overwhelmed the Whig in the American liberal world comes out no less vividly if we place it in the context of the later Rougist development in French Canada: compare Jackson with Antoine-Aimé Dorion. In light of the fate of the Rougists, crushed by the church and transformed into a symbol of collective shame, the Jacksonian movement appears universal and irresistible. The Supreme Court itself could not terrify Jackson, even though it was nourished by the same liberal consensus which generated his own electoral strength. We need hardly imagine what would have happened if the clergy of any American church, Catholic or Protestant, had tried to assail the Tennessee warrior. Of course it would never have occurred to Jackson that he would be seriously challenged by the church, which reminds us of something crucial but often forgotten: that the American democratic movement did not have to become involved in significant anticlerical crusades. That advantage is driven home to us not only by the French-Canadian experience, but also, of course, even more vividly by the Latin-American.

And yet defeat, even defeat by the church, is not the most significant vantage point for assessing American democracy that we can find in the record of the Parti Rouge. Even more revealing is that it is, more obviously than the Papineau drive, the work of an intellectual elite, gathered around various newspapers and journals. Jacksonian democracy had its publicists, even its "intellectuals," like Clinton Roosevelt[13] and Orestes Brownson, but these played a minor part in its full victory. This meant, to be sure, that it did not respond to winds of doctrine such as the ideas of the French Revolution of 1848 which inspired the Rougists, and it also meant that the movement reflected a characteristic American lack of ideal intensity. But there was this compensation, even in intellectual terms. If Jacksonian democracy produced no major set of illuminati, this was precisely because of the "enlightenment" of the average voter who participated actively in it. The Parti Rouge purchased its doctrinaire mood at the price of a popular alienation from the people far more marked than that of the earlier democratic drive. In the American case the participative "rationality" of the average voter precludes, as it were, the theoretical rationality of the intelligentsia. This is a state of affairs which can be criticized from various points of view, for that participative rationality, bred of the liberal tradition, is not always the fount of critical enlightenment. But this situation is at the heart of the American democratic success.

The same situation is seen, in slightly different light, from the angle of Latin America. There "1848" may be a somewhat

87

less elitist affair, for example, in Chile, where the reception of French doctrine coincides with an outbreak against the conservative Portales dictatorship and the emergence of a new liberalism within the congress bent on controlling the clergy and extending the suffrage. But the anarchy into which this throws the state, leading to the emergence of a new dictatorship, reminds us merely that participative responsibility in the Jacksonian sense involves sobriety as well as "rationality" —the temperate Enlightenment of the Revolutionary era again. And this leads us back to the peculiar collaboration between leader and led in the American democratic movement, for the progressives in Chile were perpetually frustrated because they could not count on a liberal society to back them up. Jackson would have been as uncomfortable in the company of Lastarria as in the company of Dorion, and would have been no more able to appreciate the doctrinaire idealisms of the former as of the latter: he was speaking the language of the common man as they were not. Indeed, the clubs of students and youth formed in Chile to worship Lamartine would have meant nothing to him. If anyone had told Jackson, or Van Buren, that he ought to think of organizing the university students, he would have responded with blank amazement. If the universities of Latin America, and France itself, could turn out progressive brigades of political importance, in the United States one of the few historians of student life is able to report that "the students, instead of being a disturbing and revolutionary element . . . were inclined to be more conservative politically than the average citizen." [14] Again, where the culture is a culture of institutionalized, habitual, and visceral liberalism, the "intellectual elite" is not needed by the liberal movement.

Thus both Jackson and Hamilton are transfigured in the settings of the feudal fragment, but in different ways: Hamilton becomes an effective Whig in the European sense, with various parts to play, and Jackson shrinks to a tenuous and alienated position. In both cases the process intrinsic in the American liberal fragment becomes obvious. But it is not merely the feudal fragments which have a story to tell. When we turn to the

Enlightenment cultures, the same process is illuminated in other ways. Here there are parallels with the American situation, but in the context of these a whole series of distinctions arise which pinpoint the most specific aspects of the American democratic movement. In a curious way the Australian experience suggests this: that American democracy was peculiarly unsusceptible to effective defamation. In a limited sense this comes out when we consider the whole Emancipist question which dogged the rise of popular government in Australia. Jefferson and Jackson did not have to defend the American common man against the charge of a convict past: on this count, again, he was in a social sense on a par with his opponent. From the Whig point of view this was also a loss. Had Hamilton or Fisher Ames been in Australia, they would have been able to belabor at least a portion of the "mob" with the convict charge, and even if this would not have prevented their ultimate demise by precisely the American logic of isolation, they would nonetheless have had some better lease on life. They might have mingled, at least for a while, with the Exclusives of Camden Park:[15] as it was they faced the full democratic tide almost instantly.

But the freedom from successful defamation enjoyed by the American democrat involved, of course, far more than this. If he could not be assailed in terms of a convict past, neither could he be assailed successfully or divided against himself as a leveler: he was, all around, a remarkably "good bourgeois." Had the American Whigs been provided with the radicalism of the "diggers" and the Ballarat Reform League in Australia, they might have done rather better than they did in their defamation of the popular beast. None of this proletarianism was authentically socialist in the later sense, but its spirit was still markedly removed from the entrepreneurial individualism which characterized even the early American labor movement. Ely Moore, Seth Luther, and their colleagues, for all of their bombast, were thoroughly reliable in the middle-class sense. Not one even of their economic objectives challenged the integrity of property, and politically their action was characterized by a minimum of violence. We can already see here, of course, as we can see even during the social upheavals of the American Revolution, that underlying mechanism of the American world by which the socialist vision was to be blotted out. The early American labor movement foreshadows a future of larger industrialism, but it foreshadows also the atrophy of the "future" which the American fragmentation involved on the count of radicalism.

The bourgeois fragments place the matter in a somewhat different light. For one thing, the *Voortrekker* republics show us something we can easily miss: how indispensable to our concept of Jacksonian democracy is the Whig enemy against which it fought. From the classical European angle, all attention is directed at the ease with which Whiggery was subdued in America, and that is as it should be. But when we encounter a bourgeois situation simpler and even more homogeneous than the American, in which Whig elitism does not arise and manhood suffrage is adopted without a struggle, we are reminded that the gnashing of the Hamiltonian teeth is a vital part of the national past. If we extend Hamilton's imaginary travels in this analysis and remove him to the Transvaal or the Orange Free State, we create a situation in which his American misery is compounded. In the Volksraad of the Free State the attainment of his objectives would not only have been difficult, but out of the question. If Jefferson was a problem in the matter of industrial promotionalism, would not the independent Boer pastoralist have been a greater one? If an aristocratic establishment was impossible in the United States, would it not have been perfectly outlandish beyond the Orange River? Hamilton would have had no one to talk to. At the same time, Jefferson would have had no one to assail, and the classical force would have gone out of the American democratic movement. Of course it would have been replaced by the "democracy" of the struggle against the British, as was true in the case of French Canada. But this is not a domestic egalitarian matter, however productive it may be of nationalism. And the essence of the Jacksonian legend is a victorious popular revolt in the do-

90

mestic sense. Ironically, what the *Trekker* experience reveals is that that legend depends on a society which is homogeneous, but not too homogeneous.

A contrasting light, however, comes out of English Canada: the legend cannot sustain an elitist barrier stronger than the one it had. There is no doubt that had Jefferson or Jackson moved in a world as dedicated to the imperial tie as the one encountered by William Lyon MacKenzie, they would have been discredited to some extent, as he was, by the suspicion of an unwanted republicanism. Here we see, from still another angle, the significance for the American democratic evolution of the fact that the imperial bond was eliminated permanently in 1776. Moreover, the democratic purity of the American fragment stands out in relation to the Tory touch, inherited in part from American loyalism, which restrained egalitarian feeling in Canada. I have mentioned the good fortune of the American democrat and his unsusceptibility to effective defamation. There is no question that this comes out in contrast to the English-Canadian radicals, not merely in the imperial sense, but in the "mob" sense as well. As always, even in the context of the bourgeois fragments pursuing a similar path, the quality of the United States stands out.

The context of Europe and the other fragments makes it possible to understand the triumph of American democracy, and yet of course the inward forces which made that triumph possible precluded a preoccupation with the other countries. I have placed Hamilton in Latin America, Jackson in Australia. But had they actually had the perspectives generated by such experiences, they would clearly have disturbed the pattern of American history as we know it. The easy triumph of democracy in the American context depended in part precisely on the subjectivity of life within the fragment. Had Jackson been preoccupied with the constructive progressivism that American Whiggery might have shown in French Canada or Latin America, could he have denounced it as he did? And, indeed, had the Whigs told the American people that in fact, north or south of the border, they might have been quite "liberal," would anyone have cared? But the issue involves even more than indifference. The very conversion of the fragment ethic into a national absolute played a significant part in the United States, as elsewhere, in determining the outcome of alignments. Thus the emotions of an incipient "Americanism" came to the support of the democrat. In a sense, the very fact that the Whig might have had functions elsewhere which he did not have in the United States, or that the democrat was intrinsically in a better position in the American fragment, reflected itself in the strategic capacity of the democrat to belabor his opponent in nationalist terms. Jefferson had already read the Federalists out of the national community; Jackson carried on his work in connection with their successors.

Of course this very matter is illuminated by a comparative view of the fragment nationalisms themselves. Thus even on an imaginative plane one of the things which would make the American Whig uncomfortable in French Canada is the conversion of Catholic corporatism into a nationalist tradition, and one of the things which would discourage the American democrat in English Canada is precisely the degree to which mitigating imperial and class factors reduced the excitements of democratic nationalism. The American experience is confirmed even amid different results. But in terms of the process of fragmentation it is not the relationship of the United States to other fragments which is involved in its growing nationalism and subjectivity. To be sure, the prevailing indifference to other colonial cultures, revealed in historical writing itself, is a mark of the inward view. But the implicit object of the nationalist transformation in all cases is to master the problem of the old partial relationship to Europe. Hence what is interesting, as Jefferson and Jackson hurl nationalist slogans against their opponents, is the way in which in the process they are helping along the "wholeness" of the American fragment. We think of an "upheaval" on the part of the democrat, of a splitting of the nation. But in a deep and secret way the efflorescence of egalitarian nationalism is giving a part of old England, or old Europe, the sense of being a nation. Jackson in this sense may not quite be the messenger of national unity but he is the messenger, as it were, of national "completeness."

This has little to do, obviously, with the impending sectional struggle which even in the heyday of the Jacksonian era was apparent. If Jackson was a "nationalist" as against the Nullifiers in South Carolina, they too were participating in the conversion of the liberal norm into a national spirit. They were merely offering a different interpretation of the meaning of that norm, and indeed they claimed the national spirit too. To be sure, the matter is not without relevance ultimately. In the end, as abolitionism intensified, and the South was finally driven out of the Jefferson and Jacksonian camp, the very achievement of cultural wholeness through the inflation of the liberal norm into nationalism would be assailed. The Southerners, in their classic desertion of Jefferson and the Declaration of Independence, were not only challenging the North but also undoing a process by which they and the Northerners both had achieved an identity as against England. The fact is proved by their immediate effort to invent a new form of cultural identity through the development of the "feudal nationalism" of the Scott-Disraeli type.

But during the Middle Period of American history itself all Americans were participating in that unfolding of the teleology of the American fragment which both the victory of democracy and its association with nationalism involved. They were "forgetting" Europe together, becoming "Americans" together. The victory of the egalitarian *telos* had the effect not only of intensifying nationalism but also of intensifying, within its terms, the sense of community. The great effort of the Whigs in 1840 to democratize themselves can be interpreted as an effort, so to speak, to "rejoin" the American club. And yet though the sense of community was thus enhanced, one of the most interesting things about it is that it existed in the context of other people who did not share it and were not subject to its mechanisms. There were two groups that remarkably did not belong to the "American" club: the Indian and the Negro.

4 Indian Wars
and the Slavery Question

As the comparative view of United States history gradually develops, it is safe to predict that the history of the American Indian will rise markedly in importance. The neglect of the subject which has been traditional stems entirely from the interior perspectives of the American fragment which have prevailed in historical study. Since it was the fate of the American fragment to destroy and exclude the Indian, life inside it has had a dwindling contact with him. How could he then be perceived? How could he be appreciated as a problem comparable to that of the rise of the "common man" or the emergence of the trusts? But, of course, once we get outside the national fragment the very fact that the Indian was thus eliminated, could thus be neglected by the European logic of the culture, becomes a matter of very great importance. Our own past historical emphases, as usual, become themselves the data for our new historical work. Moreover, the fate of the Indian turns out to exemplify, in a peculiarly vivid way, that oscillation between exclusion and inclusion which comparative analysis proves is the characteristic way that the American liberal fragment, in common with other Enlightenment cultures, handles the problem of the non-Westerner.

I do not mean to suggest of course that the isolation of the Indian from the national experience has been traceable entirely to the prevalence of our liberal ethic. The character of the North American tribes, in contrast to the more advanced Indian civilizations to the south, obviously had much to do with the matter. Locke is not to be blamed for the nomadic character of the Iroquois. Whatever British Canada may show, where comparable problems existed, the evidence of Dutch South Africa is clear proof that a bourgeois ethic is not incompatible with a considerable exploitative absorption of the aborigine: the Sioux and the Cheyenne, had they been like the Zulu and the Basuto on the Kafir frontier, might well have been converted by the United States pioneer into farm

94

laborers or domestic servants.[16] Moreover, the destruction of unco-operative Indian tribes even in Latin America, as for example in Brazil, testifies to the fact that elimination can proceed in the context of the feudal spirit as well. At the same time the functioning of the liberal ethic, with its peculiar ambivalences, is obvious. The "Indian War" in Brazil was not the racial war of American pioneer legend but one against the heathen, the unconverted, and the war was prosecuted in considerable part by half-breed *bandeiras* who were themselves the product of amalgamation.[17] Brazil, though it destroyed Indians, did not have the peculiar problems of American Indian policy.

Certainly it is obvious at the outset how crucial the isolation of the Indian was to the maintenance of the logic of the American fragment that we take so easily for granted. Had the Indian population, or a mestizo variant, constituted a class within the American fragment, at the very least racial tensions would have distorted the usual alignments. Jackson, instead of rationalizing the extinction of the Indian from the White House, might well not have been there: or he might not have been a "democrat." One of the aspects of American history in European terms is the liberation of the democracy through the liquidation of a threat from the left, but if a disadvantaged racial group had been even sporadically active below the American farmer or worker would not the situation have been altered? In any case it is obvious that the violence involved in the external elimination of the Indian permitted a heightened degree of peace within the American community. Moreover, given the numbers of Indians involved and the character of their culture, this was not the utopian postponement of a subsequent explosion, as in the case of the Negro. Jacksonian democracy also proceeded "purely" alongside the American slave population, but within a short time the entire Democratic Party would disintegrate because of the issues raised by that population. In the case of the Indian, granted the persistence of problems, a genuine threat to the life of the fragment was not in the offing. "Civilization," to use a word bandied about in discussions of the Indian, was slated to triumph.

Moreover, this resolution of the Indian issue made it possible for the nationalism of the American fragment to evolve, like its politics, in almost completely European terms. In the Latin-American case the absorption of the Indian meant that the drift toward a sheer "feudal nationalism" would not only be contradicted by democratic but also by simple racial strivings. The Araucanian Indian becomes a nationalist symbol in Chile, the Spaniard an object of hate in Mexico. In the American case the nationalist legend is indeed touched with the Indian experience, but in an entirely different way: Kit Carson gives to the normal American individualist a heroic touch, as if Indian battle enhanced the pluck of the Alger hero. The Indian, in this context, is a clear outsider. Of course the Indian is discovered, as by Cooper, as a kind of romantic substitute for a missing American Middle Ages. But this romanticism is clearly to be distinguished from either the conservative romanticism of European writers or the indigenous romanticism of Latin-American writers. It did not offer a moral alternative for the American, a challenge to the British liberal ethic. It represented a memory, but without, as it were, operative significance for the culture as a whole. Whether we look at the matter from the angle of the Old World or of the New, it is obvious that the general elimination of the Indian enhanced the simplicity of the unfolding of the European fragment in United States history.

Of course that elimination was not complete, which meant that the very process of exclusion produced a peculiar problem in dealing with the Indians that remained. I do not mean to suggest that the "Indian question" in Latin-American countries where incorporation has largely taken place is not a difficult one. Indeed the percentage of Indians outside the state system in Latin America has posed there historically a threat to the very experience of national unity. But the problem there, where a prior tradition of racial absorption on a status basis has existed, remains a "social question." It is a matter of redeeming, so to speak, through education and economic reforms, a "social class." In the United States, as in Australia and Canada, the situation is different. The tradition of social reform within the American fragment, even that associated with public education or the attack on economic power, has not been related to the Indian population. Jackson, unlike Juárez, was not concerned with saving the Indian masses. The result is that when an effort is made to bring the Indian into the culture a much broader chasm has to be crossed. And, of course, since the culture is compulsively liberal, this is accentuated by the distinction between the tribal and the bourgeois orientations.

True enough, even when the Indian is being eliminated, even when the exclusionist side of the American polarity is at work, the problem is not a simple one. The insulation of the American fragment from the aboriginal impact is purchased at the price of conscience, as Negro slavery always was, for the right of the Indian as a human being cannot be wholly obscured. Indeed, the issue is compounded here by the matter of the Indian treaty, which characterized the long history of American Indian policy. The treaty serves a greater purpose for an isolationist fragment than for an absorptive one, for it recognizes separatism. At the same time the violation of treaties is peculiarly hard for the Lockean conscience, drenched as it is in the morality of contract, and the land grabbing of the United States fragment, especially after it began to hunger for gold, raised a notorious problem of conscience for it. The moral pangs that asserted themselves in the eighteen-eighties over the treatment of the Indian had a superbly bourgeois touch. Unlike Las Casas, concerned with the problem of war against the Indian for purposes of Christian conversion, Helen Hunt Jackson is largely concerned with questions of occupancy and contract right. Her famous *Century of Dishonor* is a humanitarian document, not in the mood of the Counter Reformation, but in the mood of Locke and Marshall.[18]

When in the seventies the United States abandoned the practice of dealing with the Indians by treaty it saved itself from this embarrassment in terms of its own ethic. At the same time, since the lever was rapidly turning toward the radical inclusion of the Indian in the American fragment, curiously, as it were, his "Americanization," the problems posed by the other side of the national polarity were impending. The Dawes Severalty Act of 1887, which sought to convert the Indians into small proprietors by dividing reservation lands, was not "land reform" in the Latin-American sense, designed to break up the haciendas. It was an attack on a tribal structure, and it tried by a kind of Wilsonian fiat to impose the Lockean ethos. Indeed, its creation of private property was rationalized by one Indian commissioner as a happy obstacle to "heresies in the social and political world." [19] The collectivist "future" that the American fragment escaped was being insured even against tendencies arising out of the ancient aboriginal tribal collectivism.

Naturally the Indian did not respond very well to this turning of the bourgeois lever. The story is well-enough known. The Indian clung to his communal habits, did not register that automatic human impulse to be "American" which the proponents of the Dawes Act were sure would assert itself in him. Much Indian land fell into the hands of white settlers, through various methods of chicanery. It is interesting, however, that when the allotment policy was reversed and the principle of the tribe accepted again under Franklin Roosevelt, the polemic which tied the issue to the fragment ethic persisted. The Roosevelt policy was denounced by Flora Seymour as "the most extreme gesture yet made by the Administration toward a Communistic experiment." [20] The ethic of the fragment did not give up easily, even in the face of Indian tribal culture.

But what stands out of course, after these twistings and turnings of the national morality with regard to the Indian remnant are viewed, is the basic fact of separatism, which insured, apart from the Negro, a fairly pure European history for the American fragment. The result both of the bourgeois norm and the character of the North American Indian tribes, this consequence has been crucial to the American development we know, the pivot on which many other things have turned. Granted, it has been a "hidden" factor, or at least one totemized in legend rather than continuously operative and obvious before our eyes. It has been like the *Mayflower* voyage, celebrated but forgotten because not in the nature of things relived. And yet must we not relive the Indian experience now, like the original voyage of fragmentation itself, as we find ourselves amid cultures where the aborigine has played roles of a different nature? Must we not see the continuous significance of the dwindling Indian challenge? Life outside the United States fragment is bound to convert the North American Indian, and his fate, into matters of the deepest historical interest.

Comparative history cannot "discover" the Negro, because, not having been pushed to the side, he has always been seen in the interior of the fragment. Indeed, as I have already suggested, the oscillations of the Enlightenment ethic with regard to him have been one of the central conscious preoccupations of our history. On the other hand, this does not mean that we have understood the character of those oscillations, any more than a conscious concern with Jacksonian democracy or the New Deal has meant that we have understood the process that these developments involve. Inside the fragment the struggles over the Negro have seemed like inevitable struggles over "slavery" or "race." Our radical exclusionist and inclusionist ambivalence with respect to the Negro, like our attitude toward the Indian, has seemed like the fated pattern of all relationships between Europe and the other peoples. It is only when we get outside the fragment that we see that the United States has been in the grip of a very specific mechanism.

Some hint of this fact must have struck the group of Southerners who emigrated to Brazil after the close of the Civil War. There this group, spurred on by the advance enthusiasms of Reverend Dunn of the Confederate army, hoped to find a substitute for the Southern slave culture that they had lost. And in 1867 John Codman declared that the repopulation of a portion of Brazil would years hence be remembered as "one of the results of the Civil War. . . ." [21] It was as if a new fragmentation were under way out of the United States itself, this time a reactionary fragmentation rather than a liberal one, designed to save the one major imperfection that marred the American liberal fragment. But, alas, despite the hospitality of the Imperial government, things turned out very disappointingly. The Southerners expected to find in Brazil a replica of the American South, but instead they were astounded to discover that they had emigrated to a land where Negroes and mulattoes navigated throughout the social system, where the "slave" was a colleague everywhere. They had come to escape proximity to the Negro, but instead they had been hurled more directly into contact with him.[22]

Where the Southerners should have gone, of course, was South Africa: their fragment information was a bit askew. Actually the exclusionist impulse flowered historically more easily in the Afrikaner world, which shows us that the South itself in the United States experienced the Enlightenment ambivalence in a peculiar way. In part this was due to the fact that the Afrikaner had lived from the outset with a large African population, which meant that he had never gone through the phase, prior to the expansion of slavery in the United States, when a kind of disparagement of it in liberal terms had taken place. He did not, as it were, have a Jefferson in his past. He was thus not confronted with the problem of a doctrinal repudiation, some drastic method like Fitzhugh's "feudalism" for justifying himself. When the British impact came, he spoke in terms of the fragment faith as his fathers had applied it. Of course the American South, in a purely national sense, had been linked to the North in a way that the Boer had never been linked to the Briton: there was a world of difference between the sectional agonies which accompanied emancipation in the United States and the inter-fragment struggles of South Africa.* A common history, even a common revolution for national independence, bound

* Quite apart from the post-Civil War Southerners in Brazil, the question can seriously be raised as to whether the secessionist movement cannot be viewed as an attempted "fragmentation" in terms of my general analysis in this study. I believe that the movement is illuminated in this context, and that it in turn casts light on the larger problem. There can be no doubt that in both the Southern and South African settings the instinct created by the previous national migration facilitated the emergence of the notion of the "trek," just as an advancing frontier is easy for European migrants to conceive. At the same time the difficulty the American Southerner had in making the break, and rationalizing it, shows that the force arising out of the original migration in his case was something he shared with the North.

100

Louis Hartz

the South to the North, while the Afrikaner defined both his history and his independence in terms of an antagonism to the British. It was, in other words, much harder for the American Southerner to maintain the exclusionist view than the South African, which is perhaps why the American Southerner, for all his resistance, has been able somewhat more easily to accept the turning of the Enlightenment lever in the matter of race.

This meant, in turn, that the North had a peculiar liberty in developing the absolute emancipationist outlook. To be sure, in a purely federal sense it was as much involved in the South as the South in it: the desperate effort to save an antecedent tradition of unity is something shared by Clay and Calhoun alike. From this angle, the British in South Africa were without constraint after the fashion of the Afrikaner: they had not shared with the Dutch the first migrations of the seventeenth century, the establishment of the original trading company, or the early revolts of the free burghers against it. They were able to implement their reform measures with respect to slavery and the native with a detachment that even Lincoln could not experience. At the same time, the culture of the British, though now influenced heavily by the reformism of Wilberforce and the early nineteenth century, was by no means as unanimously egalitarian in principle as that of the American North. We know that the Southerners in the United States, when they were forced to leave the Declaration of Independence, actually turned to Disraeli and Carlyle for a rationalization of their position. Moreover, the British fragment itself, though imbued with many of the reform ideas, was by no means wholly of the Wilberforce orientation, which accounts in part for the persistence of imperial control. The truth is, the American North, despite its federal entanglement with the South, was in a strong ideological position for implementing the inclusionist side of the Lockean outlook.

Of course in the context of Brazil and the rest of Latin America that very side becomes a distinctive matter. I do not mean to suggest that liberalism played no part in emancipation in this area. We know that from the time of Independ-

101

ence onward the influx of European liberal ideas did accelerate the emancipationist movement there. But the strongly innovative element which the United States extracted from liberalism as it moved toward emancipation could not be found in the feudal fragments because of the prior tradition of status. In Brazil where the mulatto is being advanced by certain writers like Quieroga as the national type, the true "American," as it were, even liberalism cannot produce the explosive discovery of his elementary humanity. Where the slave has already been freed on a large scale, the vision of further emancipation may be glorious, but it is not millennial. In social theory generally, as against the European revolutions or even those in Latin America, we forever have to insist on the quiet temper of the American egalitarian faith. But here is a context where the reverse is curiously true. I have already remarked on the fate of the American Southerners who emigrated to Brazil after the Civil War. Had a group of Northern abolitionists emigrated instead, they would have been homeless in a different way. They might have tolerated the wide presence of Negroes and mulattoes throughout society, but a visionary touch would have gone out of their United States crusade. Garrison may have been our one "apocalyptic" thinker.

At the same time it is obvious that this intensity was itself curiously limited in scope. And the reason is precisely that the American South shared the liberal principles of the abolitionist: Garrison represented, so to speak, a millennium within the bourgeois faith. That is why, though the American situation was "revolutionary," it did not produce an efflorescence of fundamental social speculation. It did not produce a Rousseau. The truth is, none of the usual social categories fit the explosions that race produces within the Enlightenment faith, since those categories derive basically from the European evolution of that faith, which did not encounter, at least immediately, the issue of race. The Enlightenment polarity with respect to the non-Westerner, wherever it appears, with whatever passion, is one of the peculiar contributions of the European fragmentation.

In any case it is obvious from the comparative evidence

that the United States experienced that polarity intensely with respect to the African slave. It excluded, and it included. It rejected, and it "Americanized." This is the same mechanism which prevailed with respect to the Indian. But quite apart from the continuing nature of the matter in the Negro case, which has prevented it from being missed even inside the American fragment, it is obvious that the absorption of the Negro into the Lockean ethos on the inclusionist side has been far more impressive than in the case of the American Indian. At an earlier point I spoke of the absorptive power of the feudal spirit, but here is a case of the absorptive power of the liberal. The Negro is today his own Garrison, implementing the peculiar millennium that the interior of the Enlightenment promises. If his action is explosive, this is not merely because of the world-wide egalitarian spirit of the present time which he reflects and shares. It is also because he is working with what has always been the one "revolutionary" factor in the national history.

5 The Path of Capitalist Development

The unfolding of the American fragment, in the context of its protected traditionalism, did not cease with the first Jacksonian thrust, the first collapse of Whiggery. As in every other case of fragment life, the process continued, extending into later developments the logic of earlier ones. And what this meant in the American case, ironically enough, was the return of Whiggery after its defeat, decked out in democratic clothes. It meant the emergence of Horatio Alger. For there was, in the very European logic which defeated Hamilton in America, a special kind of hope. If the Whig could manipulate neither the European right nor the left, if he was adrift in a community as bourgeois as himself, why could he not capture that community by promising every man in it his own bourgeois prize? If Jackson could not be defeated by power, why could he not be enchanted by wealth? This is the law of Whig compensation inherent in American history and the era of Republicanism after the Civil War is the classic age of its manifestation.

The role of the war itself in assisting the transformation of Whiggery takes on a curious significance in light of the general process of fragment unfolding. For while the principle of Whig compensation, though of course not to be found in Europe, was European in its social determinism, the struggle over the African slave was a matter angular to the original substance of the fragment. Yet without Lincoln, without the war, the shift from Hamilton to Carnegie, from Fisher Ames to Horatio Alger, would not have been as vivid as it was. The idealism of Emancipation itself, the emotional thrust of the Radical Republicans, was a crucial incident in the democratization of big wealth on the American scene. True, the Whig shift was foreshadowed in the election of 1840 when there were a remarkable number of conversions to the democratic capitalist idea on the part of men like Webster and Everett. But the new Republicans of the Garfield and McKinley type, who inherited not only the industrial development, but also the democratic force, of the war, indeed specific war amendments to the Constitution that they could use, were a far more advanced breed. Ironically, the revolutionary moral polarity that Africa introduced into American history assisted the unfolding of an Alger legend that Africa, above all, had never seen.

That legend did more than return the Whigs to power as Republicans: it rationalized, by mixing myth with reality, the peculiar American route to industrialization after the Civil War. For one thing, with the earlier gentilities of American history sloughed away, its values were wholly economic. The contrast with the feudal fragments on this score, even though they themselves were beginning to experience some industrialization, is more vivid than ever. Whatever might be thought about Jefferson or John Adams, can we imagine McKinley saying what Msgr. L. A. Paquet, the famous French-Canadian orator, said in 1902: "Our mission is less to manipulate capital than to change ideas . . . ?" [23] Moreover, if French Canada reminds us of the secular nature of Alger utilitarianism, the feudal display which continued in Latin

104

America reminds us of the universality of that utilitarianism in American life. Veblen spoke of "conspicuous waste" on the part of the American elite, but the very charge proved the generally utilitarian background against which he wrote. The truth is, the Alger hero even after he had made the million dollars was barred from wasting his time on aristocratic pursuits. This was the price he paid for popular support: otherwise he would surely experience Hamiltonian disaster. It was Carnegie, clearly a utilitarian sort, who symbolized the dominant myth.

Moreover, the religion of opportunity had an important relationship to the emergence precisely of the kind of industrial leadership that Carnegie represented. America was, to begin with, a fluid society, but the Alger myth intensified the feeling of that fluidity, thus bringing forth an entrepreneurial thrust which no traditionalist society, in either Europe or the fragments, could finally match. In Latin America, even as the "civilian age" of industry appeared to replace that of the classical *caudillo,* Carnegie would have had to battle a tight rural economy, banking monopolies, governmental elites—in short, the whole apparatus of constraints coming out of a class culture.[24] Carnegie, himself from Scotland, celebrated the fluidity of American life in terms of democratic unity,[25] and that indeed, absorbing the Jacksonian ethic, was the way in which the Alger ethos as a whole celebrated the concept of opportunity. But in terms of American economic development, or at any rate in terms of the peculiar method America adopted for that development, the concept had a special significance.

Nor can we omit the economic importance, in this context, of the role of the humble Alger citizen. He submitted to many of the sacrifices that the American path of industrialization involved. For one thing, he did not instantly demand of the industrial machine its major largesse: he was prepared to wait, save, and work hard, until the million dollars came to him as well. The Latin-American experience of a somewhat later time suggests the contrasting situation in which, after a delay in industrialization, the people may be unwilling to demonstrate this kind of patience.[26] Indeed, what stands out, amid the great "democracy" of the Alger theme, is the degree to which the average American who subscribed to it was willing to accept the sheer inequalities of wealth which arose as industrialization proceeded. The Alger millionaire not only had more money than his Hamiltonian predecessor by far, but also the possession of that money was his very meaning in life. In this context the American, without a feudal ethos, is peculiarly docile. But this reminds us of another point: in the age of industry he is not revolting against a prior elitism, so that all inequalities have become intolerable. To be sure, he has subdued Hamilton, but this has been an easy and almost spontaneous experience. He has not emerged, as in Latin America or elsewhere, out of a highly stratified world which makes him impatient with all differentiation. Of course, he is by virtue of this very fact much more entrepreneurially motivated than the average Latin American, which makes it possible for him to identify far more easily than the other with industrial leadership. In some curious sense the Alger theme developed in the very context of the American liberal ethic a kind of "hierarchical community" revolving around industrial effort.

From one angle, to be sure, this community would seem to be based on a keg of dynamite. An immense acquisitive passion, material hope, is a strange force for binding a "lower class" to its superiors. Consider what would have happened if the cosmic popular hunger manifested in the Alger pattern had been expended collectivistically in the attack on property. A mere touch of "mateship" here would have produced an explosion that the A.L.P. would never dare dream of: Marx himself might be horrified. But the American Republican is unaware of his closeness to proletarian disaster, indeed whips up more furiously than ever the passion for wealth in the average man. And his instinct is sound: what he does not know, the democrat does not know either. Collectivism is the great secret that American history hides from its economically energetic citizens. I have discussed the reasons for this in a number of contexts: the missing experiences of class, revolution, organic yearning. And the Alger era confirms their relevance as do the others. True, the American Socialist Party polled its considerable vote in 1912: there was Spargo, there was Debs. But outside the immigrant areas, very little major strength was shown. We cannot even say that we have had the kind of limited socialism that arose in Latin America around the First World War, tribute to the continuity of the Enlightenment tradition arising out of its scarred organic life. Here we are actually in the position of French Canada, or the traditionalist areas of Latin-American culture itself: indifferent, or nationalistically aroused, in the face of the ideological challenge.

What replaced socialism, if "replace" is the word to use in such a situation, was the tradition of Liberal Reform manifested by Populism and Progressivism. No one could confuse this movement with socialism. Of course there are the usual lights and shadows here. Where a serious Marxian movement does not exist, Liberal Reform even of the milder type, and Progressivism was mild, seems "radical." Where Labour does not exist, even the Liberals seem demonic. And the American Progressive tradition has in fact, for this reason, always been disadvantaged by the Marxian bogeyism of the nationalist fragment ethic. But on a comparative plane the truth is obvious. Progressivism was another version of the Alger faith, seeking collective action for the most part to break trusts and release the individual. The enslavement of Brandeis and Wilson to that faith is the best proof of the success of the new Whig strategy. The fact that some American writers, above all Henry George, had influence in the creation of the socialist movements of Australia and England must not be misinterpreted.[27] George applied to these areas because they were countries with large landed estates: his message was far less relevant here. And the message itself was not socialist: that conclusion was a contribution of the cultures he affected. In America the farthest the Populist or the Progressive movements went in the direction of etatism was probably to be found in the work of Herbert Croly and the New Nationalists who, accepting big industry, dreamt of control. But this mood, nourished by esoteric intellectual influences from Germany, did not cut down to the popular mind. When the First World War was over and the Alger blaze of the twenties began, many of the business controls of the Progressive era were quickly consumed.

The fact that the trust was the great symbol of the Progressive era tells us, of course, very much in this matter. In terms of Latin-American society, as I have said, the American picture was very fluid. Indeed, it was fluid as compared with any European country. But the obsession with monopoly in America proceeded nonetheless, and it was not merely because a mobile society appreciates more vividly than others the choking off of opportunity. The trust symbol was in a much subtler sense a psychic necessity for the American, because it made it possible for him to interpret the economic problem in terms that did not require a departure from the fragment ethic. If monopoly was at the root of evil, then one obviously did not have to surrender to any form of socialism. One could smash the Sugar Trust, and then the necessary individualism would be attained. Even those who reconciled themselves finally to bigness did not explore very fully the alternative to the fragment scheme that they advanced: they were, as reformers always have been in American history when the individualist frontier is reached, vague enough. The fact is that the trust issue was, like economic corporatism in the feudal cultures, a formula made necessary by the fragment compulsion to absorb economic reality into its own historic pattern. Brandeis was playing a familiar fragment part.

In Europe, of course, or even in Australia, this approach would have been pilloried by the socialist as antediluvian. At best it would have been satirized as a hopeless middle ground between Manchesterian capitalism and a true reformist order. But there was no danger that this attack on Liberal Reform would take place in the United States, precisely because the very traditionalism which made it morally compulsory ruled out the Marxist possibility. I have already commented on the fact that the weakness of socialism in the United States actually laid Liberal Reform itself open to the charge of "socialism" in terms of fragment demonology. In terms of the normal situation there was an exchange of miseries here. Wilson could not be assailed as a shilly-shallying "liberal," but he could be assailed as a wild-eyed "radical." La Follette could not be assailed as a builder of halfway houses, but he could be assailed as a destructive iconoclast. The situation was queer, but it was inherent in the position of Liberal Reform in the United States fragment.

The Alger hero, the young man who knocks at the door of opportunity and at whose door opportunity knocks in turn, is a vivid point of departure for setting off the American fragment in the age of its great industrial development from feudal and radical cultures. But he is equally useful in this respect from the standpoint of the bourgeois fragments themselves. Somehow he manages to reflect in his eager and hopeful behavior, his drive and his anguish, the differentiated cultural root, ideologically and religiously, which we have seen at work before in the behavior of America as a bourgeois fragment. He symbolizes our peculiar fragmented version of "capitalist democracy." Canada had a significant industrial development at the turn of the century, but it did not quite develop the Alger hero. Nor is this traceable to the French-Canadian fragment, for Laurier, who presided over much of the development, was a national figure influenced by British liberalism. British Canada itself did not produce Alger. Nor of course did the Boer community, for all of its invincible individualism. Here there is no doubt that, in addition to a more limited capitalist growth, the race question has had a depressing effect. Where manual labor itself is not a tradition, the shoeshine hero of the Alger stories cannot easily flourish. Even in the American South this fact has to be noted; although the gradual return of the South to the fragment fold after the Civil War was marked precisely by its response to the general economic winds of the nation.

The peculiar American amalgam of individualist, democratic, and capitalist intensities out of which Alger emerges involves a blending of the two great traditions of the national history: Hamilton and Jefferson. It is as if the whole of ideological America had flowed into the Alger tale. This is an element of homogenization which in itself is interesting. Of course all fragment cultures are by definition distinctively homogeneous, but there can be matters of degree here, ranging from the conflicts of Latin America through the social struggles of early Australia to the relative historic peace and quiet of French Canada. America, on this scale, becomes quite far advanced in the French-Canadian direction, as it were, as Alger emerges. This may be why Alger not only becomes so distinctive a symbol of the American reality, but also why he so quickly takes over the term "Americanism." It is to be "American" to be involved in the success-failure syndrome, even indeed to suffer its pains and frustrations. At the same time, however, this sheer nationalism of the formula means that no single group can finally possess it. As a strategy for the accomplishment of Whig success, it depended on the effective functioning of the American economy. If the economy broke down, men were bound to inquire into the means of repairing the mechanism, in other words, they were bound to turn to the version of the Alger system offered by the American "left." And that is precisely what happened when the crash came in 1929.

6 The New Deal Formula

The great lever turned again and the Whig entered another Hamiltonian period of disaster. The development was inevitable. For a conservatism which rested wholly on the capitalist promise, an economic crash was interchangeable with political catastrophe. On the other hand, in a land where Marxism had been smothered at birth, there was no possible replacement for a Republican president other than one out of the tradition of Liberal Reform, *i.e.*, one that was Democratic. Of course a number of the dispossessed Republicans denounced the New Deal as fascist and communist. But this attack reflected in its very use of the nationalist emotion the hyperbole arising out of the interior perspectives of the American fragment. As during the Progressive era, the absence of a true socialism made Liberal Reform look "radical" indeed.

It is interesting how the American Whig exchanged one asset for another in this regard. I have already suggested that the main reason for his collapse was that he had no claim to power other than the Alger promise. If he had had some Tory tradition behind him, however attenuated, he might have elicited an allegiance in the face of economic collapse. But since he had himself in the classical Alger days done everything possible to collaborate with American history in reducing his leadership claim to the economic promise, he had no basis for a popular appeal. Hoover fell instantly, a messiah "exposed." On the other hand, the culture which had lured him into this kind of outcome had endowed him with something else, a new kind, perhaps, of Whig compensation: a claim to the national faith.[28] He could still use Alger, but bludgeon Roosevelt with "Americanism." And since in the nature of things, genuinely "un-American" ideologies did not exist to establish Roosevelt's fragment patriotism by contrast, how could one ever be sure that Roosevelt was not himself "un-American"?

Roosevelt's solution to this problem was not to speak philosophically, which would have involved raising the whole question of the nationalist ethic. He spoke of problems, he was a pragmatist.[29] In some ways this very necessity liberated him from theoretical fixations which reformist movements had elsewhere, both in Europe and the fragment world, and the New Deal in fact has a remarkable inventiveness about it. But it is important to realize that the Roosevelt pragmatism was dictated by the most fundamental strategic necessity. If the New Deal assembled all of its specific measures into a pattern of "collectivism," even of the collectivism openly conceded by European liberal reformers, the question of "Americanism" would be bound to arise: Hoover would have been able to strike a real blow. As it was, Alger could remain intact, and a succession of ideologically dehydrated "problems" could be solved. In the end, of course, this very process made things much easier for Hoover's Republican successors. When they accepted the New Deal, or a part of it, they did not have to repudiate their own American individualism. One can call this pragmatism, or one can call it obscurantism, but it was the basic formula by which the American fragment handled the inescapable exigencies of state action in the economic sphere. It was the guise which Liberal Reform had to assume in a culture wholly liberal.

Of course Europe and the fragment world would easily redeem Roosevelt from the authoritarian charge leveled against him, in terms of either right or left. In this context his "Americanism" would clearly have stood out, even if he had been bold enough to be philosophical. No one could confuse the New Deal with the "creole fascism" of Latin America or the "clerical fascism," as some of the British-Canadian newspapers called it, of the French-Canadian right. Even if we turn to "reformist" dictatorships in Latin America, those of Perón and Vargas, Roosevelt emerges as an obvious liberal. He did not need to smash free unions to gain the support of labor, and even the NRA, his great effort at the "corporate state," was mild compared to the Latin authoritarianisms. But the issue is not one of economic organization merely. Roosevelt was a freely elected president: he was as far away from Perón as Andrew Jackson was from Rosas.

The real charges of the "Americanists" centered around the New Deal not as a fascist but as a socialist enterprise. This was the natural instinct of fragment nationalism. In a land where J. T. Lang, the Premier of New South Wales, is not present to demand the nationalization of banking, a figure like Roosevelt who wants only the control of banking is himself a "nationalizer." To be sure, there were radicals on the fringe of the New Deal who desired precisely such a measure, but not only was Roosevelt not compelled to reply to them, which would have brought his liberalism to the surface, but he was not saved from the Hooverite strategy by their presence. He was, in other words, in an entirely different position from the Lyons government in Australia which defeated Lang. Nonetheless the reality of Roosevelt was not altered by this, as reality is never altered by the subjective view of life inside the American fragment. Roosevelt was not a socialist. He was a Liberal Reformer converted into a compulsive pragmatist.

It is interesting how the Roosevelt New Deal inspired the Bennett New Deal across the border in Canada. But, as always, the peculiar intensity of the American situation comes out in contrast: compulsive pragmatism was not quite so necessary in a land where the CCF could arise, although that movement was far from supplanting the major parties. It could not be so necessary in South Africa because of the historic presence of the Labour Party. The Roosevelt dilemma, and the Roosevelt achievement, is an integral outcome of American history in the most specific sense. And not merely Europe but every one of the fragment cultures it produced proves this as well. There is a sense, to be sure, in which Roosevelt "broke with the past," and it would be a mistake to underrate the sense of high excitement which prevailed during the early New Deal days. Certainly the New Deal, as Liberal Reform, went beyond Progressivism, which was far from matching in terms of the assumption of state responsibility the goals of the English Liberals or the French Radicals at the turn of the century in Europe. But it remains in the deepest sense, like the movements before it, an unfolding of the national liberal fragment.

7   Modern Themes

It is a symptom of the obsolescence of earlier social and historical categories that the American today cannot easily unify, cannot easily organize the various issues amid which he moves. He stumbles, as it were, from battleground to battleground. There is the civil-rights agitation, and there is the economy. There is the fate of the New Deal tradition, and there are the conflicts among various types of Republicanism. There is McCarthyism, and there is internationalism. Somehow the American is sure that all of these issues add up to a dramatic moment in the national history, but he cannot define precisely the quality that moment possesses. He is forever at an Armageddon, the significance of which he cannot place. I believe that the concept of the American liberal fragment will help us peculiarly here, will expose a series of neglected relationships running through the issues of the recent past.

When we thrust that experience against the background of the feudal fragments, we see, to begin with, an instant correlation between the turmoil over civil rights and the character of American economic life. That turmoil, unknown in Mexico or Venezuela, reflects a renewed explosion of the polarity of the liberal absolute with respect to race. It is of course in the nature of that polarity, because it embodies doctrinal extremes, that it cannot tolerate an accommodation of degree. There is no doubt that the Garrisonian facet of full inclusion is gradually working itself out in the American community, but until that goal is reached any halt, any surrender to the exclusionist facet, is bound to be temporary. The Negro demands today full and immediate equality, and given the inclusionist logic, that demand can encounter no challenge. For there is, in the liberal ethic, no provision for a "waiting period" for humanity in terms of its privileges, no provision for "adjustment." The nation is making adjustments, as it has throughout the epoch since the Civil War, but every one of them, however necessary, is doctrinally ambiguous. On the question of liberty the Enlightenment is absolute.

We do not ordinarily associate the embattled position of the Reverend Martin Luther King with the broad nature of the American economy, and yet if the feudal fragments show us the bourgeois root of our racial dilemmas they show us, at the same time, the presence of the same root behind our technical outlook. I have already commented on the curious principle of compensation whereby the feudal ethos, being more absorptive in the realm of race, purchases immunity from the storms of Little Rock at the price of a traditionalist social order. If American individualism produces the racial polarity we have experienced, it is the same force which gives us today the habit of economic modernity. That modernity is indeed habitual, the price of all fragmentation, which means that it is actually a very special experience as modernity goes. But it functions, and it does not face major problems of land tenure or the initial production of a utilitarian frame of mind. One writer has referred to the American economic system as involving a "permanent revolution." Actually its

114

permanence derives from its nonrevolutionary origin, as does the timeless and absolute character of American life in general. But there can be no doubt that, since the heyday of the Alger world, its productive energies have been remarkable.

Those energies reasserted themselves after the New Deal. But American Liberal Reform, again precisely because of the results of the fragment ethic, was able easily to adapt itself to that resurgence of the Alger initiative. For it was that ethic which had imposed upon it during the Roosevelt days the requirement of doctrinal silence, of "pragmatism." Not having been able to rationalize the New Deal as "socialism," the New Dealer ironically was able to welcome the resurgence of the bourgeois economic drive. The Truman presidency was a combination of old and new without any sort of doctrinal self-consciousness. Of course the question can be raised whether the Progressive tradition can have adequate independent identity without the Roosevelt drive in classic form, whether its personality is not lost by the acceptance of a streak of the Hoover world. But that is another matter.

The modern fate of Republicanism is intimately involved with this pattern, above all, the struggle between "conservative" and "liberal" Republicanism. The first of these, the instinctive thrust of Hoover, is to discredit the New Deal trend in terms of the liberal absolute itself. Given the empirical triumph of that trend, its very incorporation into the bourgeois "establishment" through the pragmatic technique, this view finds itself increasingly alienated from the history of national policy. But its appeal persists, especially in times of a larger autonomous functioning of the fragment world, because it does express the pure formulation of the fragment conscience: individualism. We are not dealing here with the ethos of the Hartford Convention. That spirit was the spirit of a Fisher Ames Whiggery which put itself athwart the inexorable unfolding of the American fragment. Neo-Hooverism, however, expresses the symbols of that unfolding as they found classic definition after the Civil War, the fusion both of the Hamiltonian and Jeffersonian themes into "Americanism." Roosevelt himself did not dare to repudiate those symbols.

115

It is interesting, in these terms, that "liberal Republicanism" has the same relationship to the conservative that the New Deal tradition itself had. In one sense this may not be surprising, since the mark of the "liberal Republican" is precisely that he accepts a portion of the New Deal program. But in another, arising out of the apparent divisions of the party struggle, it is startling to realize that the pragmatic technique, which saved Roosevelt as against Hoover, is also the technique that saved Dewey from Taft. Indeed, we can say that Roosevelt prepared the ground, not only for the victory of the New Deal but also for its possible acceptance by "liberal Republicanism." Had he given way to the Hooverite demand, had he conceded his "un-Americanism" and rationalized the actions of the New Deal in terms of a departure from the individualist norm, even the departure that the English Liberals or the French Radicals openly confessed, he would not only have insured his own defeat in the American fragment but he would also have made it impossible for the Republican Party to come to terms with his accomplishments. Could Dewey, could Eisenhower have accepted a form of "collectivism"? As it was, since the only thing at stake was a series of morally neutral problems solved in a morally neutral way, the Whig himself could accept the New Deal.

The American fragment absolute, like any ultimate fixation of the mind, comes out then in many ways: civil rights, economic life, the intricacies of political alignment. It is a jewel with many facets. If it were not for this fact, the response of the American mind to the world impact could not have been of the nature we know it to be. Only something fundamental to the whole character of the American experience could have produced that response. I have referred to the peculiar domestic hysterias that ideological challenge since the Bolshevik revolution has produced. These are actually a form of "isolationism," for they seek within the context of the descent of the alien world to repel contagion from it. It is not accidental that after the First World War the isolationist drift of Harding coincided with the flowering of the first of the historic American Red scares. Indeed, as simple isolationism has been forced to decline, the internal moral purge has been the refuge that the isolationist spirit has taken. McCarthyism, like the antiradical spirit of the twenties of which Zechariah Chafee wrote so classically, seeks to isolate America externally from that "future" which internally the process of fragmentation eliminated. Its quality is not that it opposes an idea but that it speaks for the national tradition, the sense of reality, that fragmentation has yielded.[30]

It is not hard to see how this trend becomes entangled with the issue of Liberal Reform and its evolution. Under any circumstances the doctrinaire Whig tactic of discrediting the empirical collectivism of the New Deal in the name of "socialism" was bound to take place. This was inherent in the American polemical situation, as inherent, for example, as Jefferson's effort to discredit the earlier elitist Whigs as "monarchists" and indeed of a piece with it. But in the setting of a Bolshevik revolution and its challenge, this technique was bound to gain added strength. In an odd sense America's Liberal Reform has had to deal with the polemical blows of both the nation and the world. And yet the irony of its position actually lies elsewhere. For the Progressive tradition, by its own contribution to the force of the fragment absolute, has helped to supply the very irrationalist ammunition which has been used against it. In terms of sheer isolationism itself, the sense of a righteous America in a depraved world, the Progressive tradition since the time of Jefferson has made a most notable contribution. In the twentieth century not only Nye but Roosevelt himself, prior to the outbreak of the Second World War, would have to be ranked as major symbols of this trend. But this is not the main point. What is centrally involved is the entire obscurantist attitude of the New Deal tradition itself which, in its pragmatism, has not dared to disturb the national absolute. This has made it possible for the American fragment to accept change, even for the Republican Party to accept it, but it has kept intact the national irrationalism which in conjunction with world affairs has invariably been hurled at the tradition of Liberal Reform itself. The New Dealer without knowing it has worshipped at the shrine of those who have maligned him.

Of course we know that the periodic domestic purge of the American fragment, the continuation of isolationism, is not the only response of the fragment absolute to its re-entry into the larger world. From the time of Wilson, indeed even before then, if we take into account a stream of thought which accompanied our early imperial episodes at the turn of the century, the country has actually sought to project its ethos abroad. Here, perhaps, more than anywhere else, is a case where the unifying rationality of the fragment absolute dissolves a false distinction. For we have tended to pose this trend of "internationalism" in contrast to that of isolationism, when as a matter of fact it is merely the polar opposite of it, no less than exclusion and inclusion are polar opposites in the realm of race. From one point of view, what difference does it make whether we seek to flee the unrighteous world or whether we seek to refashion it in the form of our righteousness? Does not the fragment absolute remain intact? Do we not, in the end, whichever course we pursue, Wilson's or Harding's, seek to isolate ourselves from the experience of true diversity?

Nothing betrays more vividly the interior psychic life of the American fragment than the Wilsonian demand that other cultures instantly behave along American lines. The American cannot grasp the relativity of the form in which his historical substance has been cast. The modernity and democracy arising out of fragmentation could be "exported" if the age of migration were still here and the individual to whom the American package was sent was willing to undertake the *Mayflower* voyage. But the very meaning of the world impact is that that age is over: if America cannot escape a second time, other cultures cannot escape a first. Nor does this principle fail to apply to the other fragment societies themselves, the feudal fragments, for example, with which America has international contact. Latin America and French Canada, whose traditionalisms are themselves underwritten by the powerful conservatism of fragmentation, are hardly in a better position to receive the "message" of Ameri-

118

can history than the Asian mainland. The fact is that modernity today where it does not exist must be manufactured "on the spot," even in the fragment cultures, in relationship to an earlier mode of life from which no physical voyage is possible. It is a deceptive superficiality that modernity and democracy look alike wherever they are found. Beneath the factory, beneath the polling booth, the gap between migration and revolution stretches out wide and deep.

The American failure to understand revolution, however, derives not merely from the formal experience of fragmentation. It derives from the point at which the American detachment from the European development took place, the bourgeois point, which by the complicated mechanism of fragment evolution cut off the socialist "future." Hence it is an inability to understand the appeal of socialism itself which is involved. McCarthyite virtue at home is accompanied by bafflement with respect to the origin of sin abroad. But it is precisely the promise of modernity which socialism offers, in the context of the traditionalist order, which is the root of its appeal. This is not merely a matter of "catching up," or indeed because the Marxian promise is one of transcending capitalism, of overtaking the bourgeois world. It is a promise, also, of continuing the corporate ethos in the very process of the modern development. Life within the American fragment, which does not know that ethos, as either a burden or a lure, as either something to forget or something unforgettable, cannot seize the meaning of this promise.

Need we be surprised that the Wilsonian is bitter? From the interior of his liberal splinter he offers the world unlimited amounts of "self-evident" truth. But the world, instead of accepting it, often turns toward the obvious falsehoods of Marxism. What is a rational man to do when the very mechanism of natural law breaks down? There is more than a touch of irony in the fact that circumstances of national power should have made of America the leader of the resistance to the Bolshevik revolution. It is as if history actually had an interest in the vivid doctrinal contrast. For a fragmented liberalism is of course the most powerful manifestation of the bourgeois tradition that can be found. But

119

more than this, even among the liberal fragments, as we have seen, America stands out as the purest form of the "capitalist democracy." The persistent distinction between America and the other bourgeois fragments reflects itself in the end in a different range of doctrinal intensities on the world plane. If history had chosen English Canada for the American role, the international scene would probably have witnessed less McCarthyite hysteria, less Wilsonian messianism. Even if it had chosen Dutch South Africa, it would probably have witnessed less of these, though the antiradical fear in racial matters in the Afrikaner world far exceeds in hysterical intensity even the McCarthyite mood. But history did not make these choices. It gave the leadership of the struggle against Communism not only to a fragmented Adam Smith but also to the purest case of this phenomenon available. The modern "war of ideas" has clearly been affected by that choice.

And yet I have been speaking of what might be called the "classical period" of the American return to revolution. That period is fading, because the objective difficulties yielded by the initial American response have evoked, inevitably, a challenge to the response itself. This has even articulated itself doctrinally, so that we have gradually come to possess a tradition of thought transcending the compulsions of the American absolute that we have never had before. The twentieth century, as against the Red-scare trend, has created a conscious philosophy of "civil liberties" which prior to that trend did not exist. The nationalist response to the Russian revolution witnessed also, by a queer dialectic, a rich revolt, as with Mencken, against the confining fetishes of the American fragment. The collapse of McCarthyism in our time was the prelude to an attack on "conformity" which the fragment tradition had never seen before. The individualist substance of the American absolute, under the pressure of its own hysterias, is broadening out into a larger, richer personalism. A dialectic is at work which promises to make a deeply significant contribution to the theory of freedom.

Nor is the sense of legitimate diversity which the new view reflects confined to the domestic sphere. It is matched by a deflation of the Wilsonian compulsions on the world plane, so that gradually, as a whole, the American fragment "universe" is being replaced by the real universe amid which America actually lives. The American today is a vastly more sophisticated world traveler than he was in 1914 or even in 1941. This does not mean that the new realism, either domestically or abroad, has yet become our dominant outlook. As in the case of every other fragment, America is in a transitional state between the old and the new, fighting the same battles over and over again, gaining with time and the emergence of new generations an increment of cosmopolitan wisdom. One of the illusions of the twentieth century has been that, after a given triumph of enlightenment, the interior perspectives of the American fragment had finally been transcended, that hysteria and projection had disappeared forever. But those perspectives have invariably had a resurgence, providing another round of battle. America has not extricated itself from its fragment shell. It is fighting for that extrication.

As that battle proceeds, can the historical concept of the "fragment" itself be avoided? In this study I have placed the American, as I have placed the South African and the French Canadian, in Europe. And then I have placed him in all of the fragment settings: Jefferson has been in Chile, in Australia. In terms of the subjective historiography of the fragment, these may seem like fantastic voyages. But the American is taking precisely these trips today, and he is grappling with the problems of communication these trips create. As he seeks to solve these problems, he cannot fail to consult historical tradition, cannot fail, imaginatively, to bring Jefferson with him. But I would not urge the concept of the fragment as a response to cultural need alone. That is a source of energy, as it was for every previous historical analysis inside the fragment, including the Progressive categories of the recent past. But is not the wider view intellectually defensible in its own right? Is not comparison the true historical "experiment"? In American historical work, due in part to Germanic influences, we have spoken much of "objectivity." But this concern has actually masked the deeper plunging of historical study into the fragment interior. The theory of the fragment, at the very moment that it illuminates our national dilemmas, promises in a new sense the fulfillment of that "objectivity." And yet this is merely to repeat, from another angle, what I have argued before in connection with all of the fragments, from the North Atlantic to the South Pacific: that the shattering of the fragment confines is the beginning of "philosophy." It is the Hegelian virtue of our necessity that the difficulty of the present time drives us toward a new enlightenment.

Chapter Five

The Heritage of Latin America

by Richard M. Morse

1 The People

For the past twenty-seven thousand years the sprawling, geographically variegated continent-and-a-half now occupied by the twenty nations of Latin America has been a melting pot for tribes and nations of the world. The prehistoric migrations from Asia, which lasted for millennia and brought to the Western Hemisphere the peoples known to history as Indians, were followed after 1492 by tens of millions of migrants from Southern Europe, from Africa and, in lesser but significant numbers, from all other parts of the world.

The term melting pot, however, is most often associated with the society of the United States. Here it characteristically refers to the later phases of immigration from Europe, when newcomers from north, central, south, and east Europe were added in large numbers to the original nucleus from the British Isles. It also tends to suggest more strongly the diversity of the immigrants' national origin than a diversity of class and occupational background. Applied to Latin America, "melting pot" has similar connotations only for the southern countries, notably Argentina and southern Brazil. For here the Indian and Negro fractions of the population are small, and since the late nineteenth century there has occurred heavy non-Iberian immigration. Persons of Italian and

German descent number in the millions. There are important contingents of Slavs and Near Easterners, while contemporary Brazil has nearly half a million inhabitants of Japanese descent.

Even this southern "sub-melting pot," however, exhibits typically Latin-American patterns of acculturation. A Brazilian sociologist contrasts race and ethnic relations in the São Paulo region with those prevailing in the United States. In Brazil color prejudice occurs in a relatively mild (if complex) form, and the public ideology is "assimilationist and miscegenationist." In such a society the immigrant is accepted "to the degree that he offers the probability of ceasing to be foreign." According to the study, which modifies certain stereotypes, Brazilians tolerate less patiently than do Americans the perpetuation of cultural enclaves, and they are more resentful of the public and private use of foreign languages. This attitude hastens the assimilation of immigrants. In Brazil the identification of a descendant of immigrants with his original ethnic group rarely lasts beyond the second generation, while in the United States it may last much longer.[1]

In contemporary Latin America this assimilative "ideology" may be linked to the newly kindled nationalism of a people of "mixed-race" provenience. More significant, perhaps, are its affinities with certain enduring premises of a Catholic society to be examined later in this essay. For what is demanded of the immigrant to Latin America is not so much outward conformity as the inner acceptance of a hierarchical, diversified, and functionally compartmented social order which permits of much eccentricity and affective release.

The drama that is central to the forging of Latin-American society, or societies, is not a narrowly construed history of interethnic or inter-"racial" accommodation. When we survey the whole land area of Latin America—the South American continent, Middle America, and the Caribbean archipelago— we perceive it as the theater for a massive confrontation of three peoples, each at the start playing a broadly different functional role: the Europeans (predominantly the Spanish and Portuguese), the African Negroes, and the aboriginal Indians. The first came as conquerors and settlers. The second came in slavery. The third occupied an ambivalent status as servants and burden bearers for the settler and as his special ward to be Christianized and "civilized."

Gradually the initial categories of "race" and function ceased to coincide. Some Negro slaves became free. Some Indians were uprooted and Europeanized. Occasional whites became peons. Miscegenation produced a host of mixed types. As the schema of this Catholic, hierarchical society continued to proliferate, social and economic function—in an almost Aristotelian sense—took priority over biological origin in determining social status. This is reflected in the term *castas,* which was applied to persons of mixed race and lower social standing.

Of the three main peoples, the Indians and the Africans each contributed greatly more ethnic and cultural diversity to Latin-American society than did the Europeans. The Indians of the Americas spoke hundreds of tongues and were ranged on a cultural scale from technological simplicity and bare subsistence production to the great Maya, Inca, and Aztec civilizations that the missionary Las Casas compared favorably (if somewhat misleadingly) to those of Greece and Rome. The enslaved Negroes came from a congeries of African tribes and kingdoms that were perhaps as culturally diverse as the Indian societies.

Apart from the latter-day immigration to southern South America, the European migration to Latin America has been mostly Iberian. With limited exceptions non-Iberians were denied admittance to the Spanish Indies and colonial Brazil. Incursions of other European nations in the Western Hemisphere were warded off, as happened in the case of the French and Dutch in Brazil, or else they caused the removal of territory from Iberian sovereignty, as in the case of the Guianas, British Honduras, Saint Domingue, Jamaica, the lesser Antilles—and the vast tracts of British and French North America. In the nineteenth century the migration of United States settlers to northern Mexico led to similar territorial amputation.

The Iberian migration to the New World has been of exceptional duration. And although the early waves of conquerors and colonizers were selective, the subsequent flow came to represent a relatively full class, occupational, and regional spectrum of Spanish and Portuguese society. In our own century forty per cent of the nearly one million immigrants to Brazil since the Second World War have been from the mother country, while one of the most important cultural influences upon modern Mexico has been the arrival of large numbers of exiled Spanish intellectuals.

Spanish and Portuguese colonization was fed by a highly orthodox migration, rather than one by which the mother country spun off unmanageable dissident sects. In 1501 Governor Ovando, of Hispaniola, was instructed to admit to the colony no Jews, Moors, or even reconciled heretics and recent converts from Islam. Later, sons and grandsons of such persons were excluded, as well as gypsies and, of course, Protestants. The exclusion was not wholly effective, particularly in the case of converted Jews, or New Christians, who possessed commercial aptitude. There were always clandestine means of reaching America, which Portuguese Jews especially found ways to utilize. During the colonial period, however, there existed no openly practicing heterodox communities of European or Mediterranean origin. To preserve the purity of the faith the Inquisition was established in Peru (1570), New Spain (1571), and New Granada (1610); but the prevalent religious solidarity caused its attention to be directed, with notable exceptions, largely to censorship and petty discipline.[2] The Indians were not even subject to its jurisdiction.

Although from a political point of view the church in Spanish America was practically a national one, its members shared in a spiritual community that was age-old and universal, the "true" Church. The realm of faith, therefore, worked against the factors making for the separatism of America from the mother country and from the medieval Christian heritage. Religious exclusivism was imposed on the Indies by the crown, and by the agents of state and church, to unify the empire. It did not, as in the Puritan colonies, emanate from the settlers as a point of self-definition vis-à-vis the old continent. Crystallizations of religious practice and doctrine that are characteristically Spanish American must therefore be viewed as occurring within a Catholic realm of faith deemed timeless and boundless. Among these mutations one might list: (1) The tension between fundamentalist or millennialist missionary programs and the bureaucratic conservatism of the ecclesiastical hierarchy and the urban clergy. (2) The emergence of syncretic Indo-Catholic and Afro-Catholic forms of worship. (3) The pragmatic, utilitarian, and pedagogical emphasis given to scholastic thought when it was transplanted to the colonial universities.

With regard to social origins the settlement of Spanish America has been called "a work of eminently popular character." Spanish aristocrats of the highest stratum maintained "an attitude of reserve and inhibition" toward the conquest. They took part in it neither as *caudillos* nor as entrepreneurs. They opposed the recruitment of rural workers from their estates for overseas colonization. "It was the *segundones hijosdalgo* [younger sons of the lesser nobility] who in large part fed the expeditions of new discovery and settlement that left for the Indies." [3] These were marginal persons, claimants of social prestige to whom the primogeniture system denied economic security and for whom only bureaucratic, military, or ecclesiastical careers were socially acceptable. The spectrum of emigration during the sixteenth century has been identified as follows:

Friars and priests were numerous, especially after the third decade of the century; members of the upper nobility, almost none; *segundones* of noble houses, *caballeros,* and *hijosdalgo,* doubtless many, and . . . they gave the general tone to the emigration, beyond what their numerical proportion would suggest. The warrior group, more or less veterans in the service of arms, predominates at the start and falls off after the big conquests. Lawyers and intellectuals were relatively few, but here also their prestige and influence are disproportionate to their number. There are many merchants and even more farmers and artisans of many crafts, whose emigration the Crown encouraged with perhaps more tenacity than result. Under the equivocal label "servants and retinue" given to some emigrants there traveled

127

many who are today impossible to identify and were of very diverse social condition. Adventurers and persons of the lowest social status emigrated in great number but without setting the general tone of the nascent society overseas.

Foreigners were few in the emigration, which was legally prohibited to them save for partial and temporary authorizations, above all during 1526-1538. But at the margin of the law they were quite numerous, especially Portuguese, and some Italians, French, Germans, English, etc. . . . But in any case they are soon assimilated by the Spanish population.[4]

Royal decrees of 1492 and 1497 authorized recruitment of criminals for overseas expeditions, but these were rescinded in 1505. The criminal element among the settlers was probably not significant, although as late as 1680 the Laws of the Indies approved the participation of delinquent persons in colonizing expeditions providing they were not under accusation by a private party.

The royal instructions of 1513 to Pedrarias Dávila, Governor of Tierra Firme, ordered that he minimize quarrels among his settlers by including no lawyers among them, and that instead he take "farmers so that there they may attempt to plant the soil." Charles V, who had supported Las Casas' ill-fated scheme for colonizing Tierra Firme in 1520, ordered in 1523 that "as many farmers and working people as possible" be sent to New Spain. In 1565 Philip II authorized passage to Hispaniola for a hundred and fifty Portuguese farmers, at least a third to be married and accompanied by their families.

By and large, however, a society of small farmers failed to take shape. Spain could not export many, and in America the lure of the mines, the possibilities for large-scale, pre-emptive acquisition of land, and the opportunities for exploiting Indian and African labor militated against such a design. Yet two points are well to remember. First, an interstitial class of small, independent, often mestizo landowners did arise, descended from conquerors who had not "struck it rich"— such as the rancheros of northern Mexico. It has been pointed out that in the seventeenth century the vigorous growth of small holdings in Cuba contrasted sharply with the rapid centralization of sugar plantations in British-held Barbados.[5] Second, the ideal of a society of modest but prosperous communities of landholders has always been present in Latin America. It has roots in the Iberian municipal tradition of the Middle Ages and to some degree in pre-Columbian Indian tradition. It was kept alive in the colonial period by latecoming immigrants, who made the towns their battleground for rights to farm in peace. It reappeared, cast in Lockean rhetoric, in the often misconceived or misapplied agrarian laws of the nineteenth century. And the image of a prosperous, independent peasantry still hovers in land-reform proposals of our own time.

The ratio of men to women is another important aspect of the early Spanish migration. Columbus took no women on his first voyage, and probably none on the second. Of the twenty-five hundred persons who accompanied Ovando in 1502, about seventy-five were women with their husbands. Laws were soon passed prohibiting the emigration of single women or of married ones without their husbands. Then in 1511 the House of Trade was ordered to let single women sail as deemed necessary, and a year later Morisco women were authorized to take passage as "white slaves" so as to reduce intermarriage with the Indians. Although not opposed in principle to miscegenation, the crown increasingly opposed the Spaniards' informal domestic arrangements with Indian women. Laws were repeatedly passed to forbid married men to emigrate without special license and to repatriate emigrants whose wives remained in Spain. Sometimes a governor's wife would bring to America an entourage of wellborn ladies, who were easily married off. To many expeditions of conquest the wife or mistress of a leader added a special dash of romance. Yet by and large the female emigrants were few. Between 1509 and 1533 they numbered only four hundred and seventy of the forty-six hundred recorded passengers to the Indies. Three centuries later, at the close of the colonial period, Humboldt found only two hundred and seventeen European women in Mexico City as against two thousand one hundred and eighteen European men.

The universality with which Indian and Negro women

129

served as wives or concubines for the white men leads one to suspect the transmission of lasting psychological tonalities to the New World society. To be sure, many stable and legal interracial unions occurred from the earliest years, especially between the Spaniards and Indian women. Such marriages were even of social benefit to the lowborn European if his wife was of Indian nobility. The offspring in these cases tended to become thoroughly Hispanized in their upbringing. More frequently the interracial conjugal liaison was unstable, sexually exploitative, and scarcely conducive to the psychological composure of the offspring. Possibly this type of union between the conquering and the subject races permanently affected the tone of male-female relations throughout Latin America. On the sugar plantations of Brazil and the Antilles, for example, the Iberian woman came to represent for the white man a chivalric ideal of purity bordering on frigidity, quite divorced from the sensuality of the slave girl.

In the formative years of the new societies mixed offspring tended either to be absorbed into the class and culture of the mother or, if recognized by the father, to become Europeanized, that is, to become creoles. By the seventeenth century separate categories of the social schema were developing to accommodate mixed-blood types. At the same time the diversification of economic life created marginal or intermediate avenues of release from servile status. A cultural consequence of miscegenation was that in the long run the mother, the principal transmitter of culture during childhood, could impart her Indian or African heritage only fragmentarily to her mestizo or mulatto children. This contributed to strip down the cultural legacy, to make the mixed-blood generation creatures more of environment than of tradition.

Historically the mestizo or mulatto has been viewed as having a wandering, unreliable spirit with no fixed allegiance. His ambivalent station at the threshold between two culture groups, whatever its penalties, evoked a sharp talent for pragmatic accommodation. This was acknowledged in the saying that northern Brazil was "a hell for blacks, a purgatory for whites, and a paradise for mulattoes." Eric Wolf

130

calls the mestizo the ancestor of that "multitude of scribes, lawyers, go-betweens, influence peddlers, and undercover agents" who are the *coyotes* of modern Middle America, a term once applied to the mixed-blood, now designating the whole tribe of the socially and culturally disinherited who spend their days blinding the eyes of the law. Wolf goes on to posit an antithesis between Indian and mestizo. The Indian was community-rooted, the mestizo rootless. The Indian clung to group norms, the mestizo could change his behavior like a mask. One was saturnine, introverted, closed in a local universe, the other outgoing, adroit, and worldly. One valued land and manual work, the other valued personal power and the talent for manipulating people and situations. The Indian was bound to routine and reality, the mestizo was estranged from society, caught up in fantasies of personal domination and plagued at the same time by fears of his own worthlessness.[6]

In the nineteenth century, when Latin-American intellectuals felt called upon to apologize for the economic and political backwardness of their countries, many had recourse to newly fashionable theories of social evolution which deplored the deleterious effects of race mixing. The mestizo image just presented lent credence to such views. Yet this same image has positive components which under the pressures of insurgent nationalism serve self-congratulatory ends. Our own century has heard militant declarations about an emergent "cosmic race" in Latin America. Revolutionary movements, notably the Mexican, have accorded the mestizo a central cultural identification. For public purposes stress may now be given to the creative cultural composite which the mestizo is alleged to represent rather than to his psychological ambivalences and roguish talents for accommodation. Whatever the new mythology may lack in sociological accuracy is compensated by the vigor of its political appeal.*

* Octavio Paz, however, notes the ultimate irrelevance of any racial propaganda in modern Mexico: "The Mexican does not want to be either an Indian or a Spaniard. Nor does he want to be descended from them. He denies them. And he does not affirm himself as a mixture, but rather as an abstraction: he is a man. He becomes the son of Nothingness. His beginnings are in his own self." *The Labyrinth of Solitude* (New York, 1961), p. 87.

Given the extent of miscegenation, and the extent to which the successive Spanish and republican regimes have weighed upon the Indian burden bearers, it may well be wondered how the Indian peoples themselves and their culture traits have been preserved over large areas of the Middle American and Andean highlands. If the proportion of Indian-speaking citizens has decreased to fifteen per cent in Mexico, it is still over fifty per cent in Guatemala and Bolivia. Aspects of the Indian labor system under the Spaniards will be treated later. Suffice it for now to observe that it depends wholly on one's point of view whether Spanish colonizing policies be deemed a success or a failure for the extreme gradualism with which large groups of Indians are still being assimilated into Western culture. Similarly, how do we evaluate the fact that the monuments in modern Mexico are to Cuauhtémoc and not Cortés, or that Indian prayermakers of Guatemala still chant to their own gods in their own tongue in the Catholic cathedral of Chichicastenango?

By most criteria the Indians were exploited under Spain. Indeed, they were virtually exterminated in the Antilles, while in Middle America the aboriginal population dropped within a century from a preconquest total of twelve to fifteen million to perhaps two million—a decline attributable, however, more to the white man's diseases than to out-and-out maltreatment. Only in our own time has the population of central Mexico recovered its pre-Cortesian density. Yet throughout this long and traumatic confrontation of cultures, the plight of the Indian and the remnants of his civilization were always present to the Spanish state and to the church. Even when the Indian became a "forgotten man" under the ostensibly egalitarian constitutions of the nineteenth-century republics, members of his "race"—a Carrera in Guatemala, a Júarez in Mexico—might become national chief executives. It is in fact a truism that "race" has socioeconomic, not biological, meaning in Latin America, and an adage that an Indian who puts on shoes ceases being an Indian.

In our century the presence of the Indian is once again deeply felt. The symbols of his culture are invoked in nationalistic or demagogic appeals, both within and independently of the mestizo composite. They are reimbodied, militantly or nostalgically, by the artist. Social scientists lavish more analysis on the process of the Indian's acculturation, or Westernization, than on the pivotally important role of the emerging middle classes. All this may have only meager benefits for the Indian in equivalent social justice. If so, it is partly because the current stage of economic development and capital accumulation implies upheaval and sacrifice for the whole of the proletariat. The image of the Indian is still a cultural force to be conjured with. So lastingly did Spain identify this force that J. C. Mariátegui, a Peruvian Marxist of the nineteen-twenties, expressed guarded admiration for the "socialistic" Jesuit missions of colonial Paraguay, and some agrarian reformers of our own day are known to take Spanish colonial legislation as a model for their proposals.

If the mountain backbone of Latin America from Mexico south to Bolivia and Paraguay can be thought of as Indo- or Mestizo America, it is justifiable to think of the Antilles (especially Haiti and the non-Hispanic islands) and the Caribbean-Atlantic coastal zone from Mexico south to northern Brazil as Afro-, Negro, or Mulatto America. In this area, and also in the coastal valleys of Peru and the hot lands of Mexico, the Europeans organized afresh a system of intensive tropical or semitropical agriculture rather than, as in the highlands, taking over and adapting an existing regime of production. As the early missionaries witnessed the rapid disintegration of Indian society in the Antilles they recommended, as a solution *faute de mieux,* the importation of African slaves. Later some, like Las Casas, had second thoughts about the advice. But by 1520 the African slave trade was well under way.

The characteristic rural employment for the Negro was on the sugar plantation, a more clearly "modern" or capitalistic agricultural system than the Indian encomienda to be described later. The Negro was imported as a capital investment and was bought and sold as chattel. Within the Iberian tradition, however—notably in the *Siete Partidas,* the thirteenth-century Spanish law code—the slave was still accorded a position in society which assured him certain minimum

133

guarantees. He was not considered infrahuman. Spanish laws for the Indies contained no such comprehensive protective code for the Negro as for the Indian. Yet there existed stipulations for his treatment and education which were tardily brought together in 1789.

It is generally from a contemporary vantage point and in contrast to situations in the United States or South Africa that the history of Negro-white relations in Latin America is termed "mild." It does seem true that manumission, both by masters and through co-operative efforts of the slaves themselves, was a fairly general practice in Latin America. It also seems true that Negro freedmen enjoyed reliable assurances of their status as free Christian subjects, even though they may have been denied many perquisites of personal dignity (ostentatious dress, firearms, et cetera) or had difficult access to education. The case can perhaps be made that the elaborate nomenclature applied in the colonial period to scores of the possible biological combinations of Negro, Indian, and white reflected less a morbid preoccupation with racial "purity" ("purity" could in fact be legally purchased, even by the slightly "impure") than a classificatory, Catholic habit of mind representing acceptance of a diverse and unwieldy order of the world.

Two contrasting interpretations of the antecedents of Negro-white relations in the New World are those of Frank Tannenbaum and Eric Williams. Tannenbaum holds that the Negro in Latin America, as slave and freedman, has always been recognized to have a legal and moral personality. This he attributes to the long, precapitalist experience of the Iberian peoples with the institution of slavery, to safeguards embedded in their law and custom, to the tolerant and humane ethos of the Catholic church. That is, their inherited experience and wisdom place the Latin Americans *ahead of* North Americans.[7] Williams argues from a Marxist viewpoint that an ostensibly milder slave regime in a Latin country simply meant that it was *behind* in its institutional development. If, for example, slaves were less oppressed in Cuba than in Jamaica in the eighteenth century, this signified that the sugar industry did not reach its exploitative, fully capitalistic phase in Cuba till a later period.[8] A more recent analysis, pitched on psychosocial rather than historico-institutional grounds, suggests that racial attitudes are partly governed by differing "somatic norm-images" of the dominant groups. The Iberian norm-image, it is held, is "darker" than the northwest European one, thus allowing the mulatto, but not necessarily the Negro, greater mobility in an Iberian society.[9] This argument has at least the merit of addressing the question of race relations without detouring to establish a comparative index of slaveowners' malevolence.

Perhaps as important to the tone of contemporary race relations as the nature of the institution of slavery is the process of emancipation. Much of Jim Crowism in the United States originated in the fears, resentments, and trauma consequent upon a bloody fratricidal war. Abolition in mainland Spanish America was declared as part of the movement of national independence (Mexico, Central America, Chile, Argentina) or peacefully a generation later as an expression of liberal nationalism (Andean countries). For Puerto Rico (1873) and Cuba (1880) it came through domestic and international political pressures upon the mother country. In Brazil emancipation did not come until 1888, when it was enacted with a stroke of the pen, by which time alternative sources of immigrant labor had been found in Europe and the coffee planters themselves were forming abolition societies. The most dramatic case was that of Haiti, whose independence (1804) was the result of a mass revolt against a slave-owning oligarchy. With the expulsion of the French, a new "mulatto" elite of those who had previously been freedmen faced the Negro masses. Haitian society and politics today still gravitate around this polarity, which has aspects too complex for explication by conventional paradigms for "race relations."

In the panorama of colonial Spanish American society it was the Indians, Negroes, and a growing class of half-caste laborers and artisans who accomplished the toil of economic production. Here and there existed groups of white farmers, grazers, or artisans, but they were uncharacteristic. At the same time the creole, or American-born white, was practically excluded from high civil and ecclesiastical offices and from important commercial enterprises. This was despite the fact that both creoles and mestizos from legitimate unions enjoyed theoretical parity with Spaniards under the law. It has been calculated that only four of all the viceroys were creoles (all sons of Spanish officials), fourteen of the six hundred and two captains-general, governors, and presidents, and one hundred and five of the seven hundred and six bishops and archbishops. Paradoxically, the breed of conquerors and colonizers became a marginal group with respect to economic production and administrative responsibility except on a local and subordinate scale.

In the sixteenth century all whites, whether American- or Spanish-born, were called "Spaniards." Inevitably the career expectancies, life styles, and even personalities of these groups began to diverge. As a way of asserting self-identity the "Americans" appropriated the term "creole," hitherto applied, somewhat disparagingly, only to Africans born in America. The early creole elite were the conquerors who secured encomiendas of Indians and their direct descendants who enjoyed them. Most of the conquerors were of humble origin, and the crown, fearing creole autonomy and separatism, never bestowed titles of nobility on Americans. By the late seventeenth century this informal aristocracy was broken up because of the unproductiveness or the revocation of many early encomienda grants. There consequently occurred a circulation of the creole elite as new landed oligarchies arose and those once privileged drifted into lesser bureaucratic, commercial, or openly parasitic occupations. The creole group therefore ranged widely on the social scale, yet internally it was fluid and demarcated neither by formal titles of nobility nor by gradations of fiscal privilege. The Indians paid tribute, whites did not. As the creole element grew in size and in self-awareness, their disparate composition failed to prevent them from sharing, by and large, feelings of resentment toward the peninsular Spaniard and of hauteur toward the Indians and *castas*. Their pride of origin and status, their inclinations toward leisure, indolence, and luxury, their man-

136

nered elegance and verbalism engaged the notice of more than a few travelers from the mother continent.

After independence it was the creoles who took over the organization and leadership of the new republics. Although habituated to the attitude of command, they had been accorded no generously defined functions and responsibilities in the colonial world. They had been born into a vast, tradition-bound, seemingly permanent Hispano-Catholic society, highly layered and compartmented, in which status, after the conquest years, was a matter more of definition than of achievement. Yet in the anarchic fragments of that society there was suddenly thrust upon them the role of forging new nations. It is largely the ideals, attitudes, ambitions, confusions, and compulsions manifested by this group which, in constellation, have become the cultural determinants for society and personality in Latin America: their medieval, Catholic concern with hierarchy, with honor and personal loyalty, with rhetoric, with casuistry, with expressiveness, with the wholeness of things; their creole ambivalences, sensitivities, self-denigration and braggadocio, habits of command and of deference; and their stock of half-absorbed ideas from the arsenals of Anglo-French "enlightened" thought.

The intricate structure of the mixed-blood *castas* which interposed between the creoles and the servile races reached its apogee in the eighteenth century. By the end of that century it was in dissolution, and the functional boundaries between creole and mixed-blood, particularly between creole and mestizo, became more and more permeable. The mestizo became creolized socially and culturally; the creole was increasingly absorbed into the racial mix. In our own century it has become clear that the homogenizing process will not be stayed even at the threshold of the "exotic" enclaves of Indian and African culture which still remain. These remnants will in the long run leave coloration rather than structure in the creole patterns of life and society. Those who plan the social and economic "development" of modern Latin America must therefore reckon primarily with the creole cultural fix which it long ago took.

POPULATION OF LATIN AMERICA c. 1570

	Whites (or so considered)	Negroes mestizos, mulattoes	Indians (Tribute-paying)	Total Indians	Total population
Mexico, Central America, Antilles	52,500	91,000	(893,370)	4,072,150	4,215,650
Spanish South America	65,500	139,000	(980,000)	4,955,000	5,159,500
Brazil	20,000	30,000	——	800,000	850,000
Totals	138,000	260,000	(1,873,370)	9,827,150	10,225,150
Per cent	1.4%	2.5%		96.1%	100%

POPULATION OF LATIN AMERICA c. 1825
(Era of independence)

	Whites (or so considered)	Negroes, mestizos, mulattoes	Indians	Total population
Mexico, Central America, Antilles	1,992,000	4,641,000	4,580,000	11,213,000
Spanish South America	1,426,000	2,913,000	3,250,600	7,589,600
Brazil	920,000	2,660,000	360,000	3,940,000
Totals	4,338,000	10,214,000	8,190,600	22,742,600
Per cent	19.1%	44.9%	36.0%	100%

Source: Angel Rosenblat, *La población indígena y el mestizaje en América* (2 vols., Buenos Aires, 1954), I, 36, 88.

2   The Institutional Order

The impression which many may have of the Spanish colonization of America is that it was the work of relatively free-acting conquistadors and their followers, avid for products of soil and subsoil, in particular gold and silver, and for the servile labor to be used in extracting them. Others, who applaud the "individualism" of the self-reliant settlements of British North America, criticize the Spanish regime in America for having stifled colonial development with statism, bureaucracy, and discrimination against creoles. It

Richard M. Morse

is therefore important to distinguish the roles played by private and public initiative and to appreciate the connotations of each in the Spanish American context.

The early institutional history of Spanish America is conventionally divided into a preliminary period of exploration and conquest, when individual enterprise loomed large; a period of institutional organization, lasting for a generation or more after the arrival of the first viceroy of New Spain in 1535; and a long period of institutional stability lasting until the eighteenth-century Bourbon reforms.

This periodization has been challenged by Mario Góngora, who argues that exploration, conquest, and colonization were intermingled and alternating processes. He therefore posits a combined phase of settlement lasting from 1492 to 1570. Although the state's resources were insufficient to underwrite and manage the vast colonizing operation: "Neither the conquests nor the colonization are private enterprises, undertaken at the margin of the Castilian state." [10] Apart from a few important voyages subsidized by the crown (Columbus, Pedrarias Dávila, Magellan), the recruitment and financing of most expeditions were left to private initiative. Permission was given for such undertakings, however, only if they conformed to the broad policies of the state.

Góngora reminds us that although the Spanish state had acquired a strong administrative nucleus by the sixteenth century, it was not yet, as it later became, "a unitary and rationalized whole, dominated by the 'monism of sovereignty.' " Political jurisdiction and other rights brought together in the king were exercised through the bureaucracy. But they might be delegated or conceded as privileges that could be defended juridically against the king himself.[11] The categories of the public and private spheres, established under revived Roman law, were still in process of elaboration. Thus the conquistador was not a "free" entrepreneur under a private contract. He was under continuing obligation to ask the crown for privileges, such as grants of Indian labor. His contract (*capitulación*) linked "freely assembled [social] forces with the power of the state" and "converted them into political elements."

139

The state, then, is a colonizing state (*Estado Poblador*), operating through laws, customs, and judicial and administrative decisions. Grants of soil (farm and ranch) and subsoil (mines) are founded in royal concession, not in private law. Colonization implies the organizing of a congeries of civil and ecclesiastical jurisdictions and hierarchies; a regime of defense, taxation, and tribute; systems of schools and universities. Not only do economic life and claims to the land have their origin in the state, but also the whole colonizing process is conceived as having the "politico-civilizing" function of transmitting Western Christian culture. Some political and philosophical implications of the foregoing will be examined later. For now, the critical point is that the sixteenth-century Spanish conception of the state was in many respects still medieval. The state was an "institutional equivalent of temporal human life in all its fullness." [12] It contained only in embryo such possibilities as the rationalistic "statist" state of seventeenth-century mercantilism, the bourgeois free-enterprise state, or the nineteenth-century "imperialist" state.

From Columbus onward the discoverers and conquistadors took possession of new lands and new oceans in the name of the crown. The Indians were considered crown vassals to be protected and Christianized—and to be taxed. An expeditionary leader might be given a liberal contract for life (or for two or more lives, *i.e.*, generations) to distribute and settle land, found towns, engage in commerce, use Indian labor, and so forth. But his expedition was accompanied by royal officials and ecclesiastics, representing the broad political, fiscal, and spiritual interests of the crown.

Gradually there emerged as an embedding context for the *capitulaciones:* (1) an elaborate casuistry distilled from the polemics of jurists and theologians which justified the Spanish title to the Indies and set down principles for treatment of the native Indians, and (2) a multiform series of hierarchies, civil and ecclesiastical, that exhibited both functional overlap among agencies and coalescence of function (especially administrative and judicial) within given agencies. These hierarchies culminated in the arbitrating crown, which delegated its power hesitantly and erratically. The legal apparatus for empire betrayed its medieval origins. It was *informed by* the broad Christian principles of the theologians and jurists, and it frequently *took the form of* trifling administrative detail. The various legal codifications such as the 1573 colonizing ordinances and the 1680 Laws of the Indies were essentially compilations, rather than systematizations that might have brought natural-law principles and administrative decrees into a single rationalized frame.

That this form of government signified deprivation of autonomy for Spanish America and meager preparation for independent nationhood is often pointed out. Nevertheless, the theoretical premise for royal centralization was not colonial subjection of the Indies, but the assumption that the New World viceroyalties were realms coequal with those of Spain, having equal claims to redress from the crown. The Council of the Indies was not a mere colonial office, but had ministerial status. The viceroy of New Spain or Peru was the king's proxy. He and the lesser crown-appointed officials were under elaborate regulations not to acquire local interests, economic or personal, in their jurisdictions, and they underwent judicial review at the end of their terms. In the case of both Spanish America and Brazil one can argue that it was only under the "enlightened" peninsular monarchies of the eighteenth century and the "liberal" revolutionary regimes of the Napoleonic era that a status, "colonial" in the modern sense, was adumbrated. The differences between Hapsburg rule, under which Spanish American institutions were established, and Bourbon rule, which tried somewhat ineffectually to reform them, has been called the difference between absolutism and despotism.

The insistence upon the neo-medievalism of Spanish American colonial institutions reflects no intent to romanticize them. It looks toward identifying an institutional model which the first eighty years of Spanish rule left implanted in the Indies. This model, which has sociopsychological as well as sociostructural implications, was to conflict with many administrative directives of the Bourbon period. It was to conflict even more sharply with the ideas and ideals, constitutions and reforms, which swept in on the independent

Spanish American nations after 1830. It continues to conflict at many points with twentieth-century programs of
"development"—political, social, and economic.

There was, of course, a practical motivation for the Spanish
monarchs' concern with the Christian treatment of the Indian
and for the sixteenth-century debates as to his rationality
and the propriety of enslaving him. This was the threat to
the crown's income and political control posed by the conquistadors once they were established in their new domains.
The centrifugal movement of settlers out into farm, ranch,
and mining lands, far removed from seaports and administrative centers (with these in turn distant from Spain by a long
and arduous sea voyage), created the danger of virtually
sovereign satrapies, each enjoying absolute control of Indian
workers who, in the Mexican and Andean highlands and in
Paraguay, offered relatively slight resistance to their new
masters. As a result, and:

. . . in the face of the excessive privileges granted by the monarchs themselves to the first discoverers and their descendants, the
officials of the Court and the *Audiencias* reacted by retrieving all
the grants of the Crown in the discovered lands, through long
suits, tenaciously sustained.[13]

Since Tocqueville the growth of the centralized state in
Western Europe has been described as a process which under-
mines local autonomy and initiative and which, by equalizing
all citizens before the law and the state bureaucracy, weakens
the protection afforded them by community ties and customs.
In Spanish America under the Hapsburgs the role of the
state was in some respects precisely the opposite. Central to
its function was the preservation or creation of Indian communities which would maintain their own way of life, be
protected against excessive exploitation, and have independent access to royal justice and to spiritual guidance and
consolation. The Laws of the Indies contained extensive
tutelary legislation which respected the Indians' cultural
identity. Indian tongues were taught in the universities.
Indians were not subject to the Inquisition. Spaniards,

142

Negroes, and mulattoes were not permitted to live in Indian villages, nor were mestizos who had not been born there. Even the Spanish encomenderos were not to live among the Indians from whom they received work. A traveling Spaniard could stay in an Indian community only "the day he arrived and one other"; merchants could stay only three days.

In short, the cultural assimilation of the Indian, as distinct from his formal religious conversion, was conceived as a long-term process during the course of which he was to be protected from exploitation, degradation, and slavery at the hands of encomenderos, merchants, and bureaucrats. Some have called the Laws of the Indies the most comprehensive and humanitarian code ever devised by an important colonizing power. Few would deny, however, that their enforcement was greatly wanting. As the occasion demanded and circumstances permitted, ways were found in which to exact grueling forced labor of Indians, notably in the mines and in the *obrajes* (textile factories). The corregidors of Indian towns, who exercised political and juridical authority, regularly exploited their wards for personal gain, often in conspiracy with the priests and Indian caciques.

It serves little purpose, however, to assess out of context the degree of the Spaniards' cruelty toward or exploitation of the conquered Indians. In an age which saw the predatory forces of commercial capitalism unleashed, and the face of Europe ravaged by religious persecution and the havoc of the Thirty Years' War, it would be fatuous to expect the conquest of a new continent and its millions of pagans to have lacked ferocity and trauma. What concerns us are the implications which the particular premises and patterns of colonization held for the long-run "set" of New World institutions. Before specifying some of these implications, we should examine more closely the actual assault upon the land and resources of America, from which local interests and social structures flowed as an undertow to the wave of formal colonizing policy and missionary purpose.

We have suggested that there was much which was medieval to the apparatus, operation, and rationale of the Spanish state. Such traditional characteristics, however, as the Christian, tutelary purposes of the state, the multiform hierarchy culminating in a mediatorial monarch, and the scholastic intellectual orientations served as an armature to a core of relations between man and land and between privileged and underprivileged groups that was largely defined by place and circumstance. Mario Góngora has said that the system of estates, in the strict sense of social orders having rights of representation, did not exist in the Indies because no Cortes (*i.e.,* parliamentary body) was established.

In a period when the granting of subsidies or pecuniary assistance to the King and the accompanying request for privileges was at the heart of the internal life of the State, the Indies—relatively free of tribute and paying the King the royal fifths and other perquisites which did not require consent—did not exhibit the political density and the pronounced King-Kingdom dualism characteristic of Europe in this era.[14]

Only in the broader sense of groups "having common jurisdictional privileges" can estates be said to have existed in Spanish America. The state was of a corporate character. Within it, there were independently defined privileges and jurisdictions for broad groups (Indians, Europeans, ecclesiastics, Negroes) as well as for smaller component groups, such as: Indians in missions, *pueblos de indios,* Indians on encomiendas; merchants, university students, artisans; regular clergy, secular clergy, inquisitorial officials; Negro slaves, colored freedmen, and so forth. The medieval imprint which the system as a whole bore was not that of parliamentary representation, but that of pluralistic, compartmented privilege and of administrative paternalism.

Sánchez-Albornoz argues persuasively that the institutions of classical feudalism had never fully developed in Spain itself.[15] In summary his argument runs as follows. During the reconquest of the central tableland from the Moors, roughly A.D. 850-1200, cities and castles served as the advance points of resettlement. From these nuclei the work of colonization was undertaken only with maximum guarantees of personal liberty and freedom of movement. Few colonists were tied permanently to the soil or to a lord. Society had, relatively speaking, a fluidity which worked against the solidifying of a complex net of vassalic relations or the emergence of a stable, conservative bourgeoisie. The commoner who could equip himself with arms and a steed was valuable to the crown and could become a lesser knight or, in the almost contradictory phrase, a *caballero villano*. He might even owe fealty directly to the king rather than to a blood noble.

The importance of the central authority to the reconquest meant that the strength of the crown and the organization of the state never faded out, as in the Carolingian realm. Even when the centralizing process was temporarily checked in the tenth century, the crown never recognized the usurpations of nobles. The flood of feudal ideas and practices which entered Spain in the eleventh century with warrior or pilgrim knights from Northern Europe, and with royal marriages to French princesses, was not accompanied by the juridical formulae of feudalism. Thus in Castile-León lay lords had not the privilege to coin money; a vassal could not acquire contractual relations with two or more lords; the ties between all subjects and the state were never displaced by personal ties between vassals and lords.

The advancing frontier periodically renewed the spoils and prebends which the crown could distribute, thus renewing its economic and military potential. The towns were strong and numerous, and not merely islands dispersed in a feudal sea. They were an active counterweight to the church and the nobility; to keep pace with them the nobles were forced to beg additional lands, honors, and prebends from the crown. When in the thirteenth century a struggle developed between crown and nobles, it was not one by which the crown strove to break feudal power (as in France) or by which the knights strove to restrict royal power (as in Germany), but a contest by both to control an extant state apparatus.

With respect to organization for economic production, as distinct from sociopolitical organization, the following factors should be borne in mind as militating against the emergence of a manorial regime in the Spanish Indies:

(1) Spain itself never witnessed a flowering of the classic manorial pattern of other parts of Europe because of the seven centuries of strife between Christians and Moors, and because of the privileges, prejudicial to agricultural development, acquired by the medieval sheep raisers' guild.

(2) A manorial system implies that lord and worker share a common culture and a traditional legal regime of mutual obligation. Clearly, such a context was lacking for Spaniard and Indian, to say nothing of Spaniard and African. As suggested above, the tutelary state or the "universal" church (usually through its regular orders) was the ultimate protector of the Indian worker, not the local agrarian unit.

(3) The manorial system takes form in vegetative, decentralized fashion in a nonurban economy, generating and perpetuated by local tradition, reflecting stability and balance both social and ecological. The initial settlement of America was accomplished by a mere handful of men, not simply avid for gold as is sometimes said, but certainly in quest of status and fame as these might be embodied in specie (however fleetingly retained), land, and a situation of authority free of manual toil. In vast land areas with immeasurable natural resources and native labor potential, it was inevitable that honor, status, and possession should be factored out of the medieval social complex. Henceforth, for example, status might be acquired by control of land rather than the relation to land being a function of status. Or, honor and status might be achieved through heroism, rather than heroism being assumed as an attribute of status.

The role of the city must be seen as pivotal to the Spaniards' assault upon the land. The preliminary institution of settlement was customarily the chessboard town or city with its spacious central plaza surrounded by substantial buildings for municipal, imperial, and ecclesiastical administration and for worship. When a town was laid out, the founders each received an urban lot, a grant of outlying farm or ranch land, and rights to lands set aside for common use. Possession of land was contingent upon occupation and cultivation of it, often for five years. In effect, vast tracts of the royal domain were alienated with no operative restriction.[16]

Before the end of the sixteenth century the usurpation of public lands and Indian community lands had become general. As land values rose, the crown became interested in putting unclaimed lands up for sale, and it began to wage intermittent warfare against improper land titles. Finally in 1754 the *audiencias* were empowered to make land grants and were given jurisdiction over questions of title. But all lands that had been occupied since before 1700 were adjudged held by prescription and, if they were under cultivation, their titles were unchallengeable. It was by then too late to arrest the formation of a landed elite whose holdings surrounded the towns and had often made large inroads upon the commons and upon Indian lands. This elite, often of humble or socially marginal origin, was the colonial creole aristocracy. It had extensive social power, especially in the regions distant from the viceregal capitals of New Spain and Peru, although its political participation was generally limited to town government. After Spanish American independence this elite became free to assert its political, economic, and social hegemony on a national scale.

The distribution of land was a process distinct from the distribution of Indian labor. It was a principle early established, though not conscientiously adhered to, that the only enslaveable Indians were cannibals or Indians who refused to acknowledge the Spaniards' sovereignty and were therefore taken in a "just war." In the early years of the occupation of the Greater Antilles, however, the natives, many of them quite submissive, were in effect parceled out for labor. Their culture offered no resistance to the conquering one, and they were soon virtually extinguished. Although the encomienda was used in name in the Antilles, it received institutional definition and development only with the settlement of the mainland.

An encomienda was a distribution and entrusting of a community of Indians to a Spanish colonist who collected from them various forms of tribute and was obliged to protect them and assist their assimilation into Christian civilization. After 1542 the exaction of personal services was expressly, if not effectively, forbidden. The encomienda took its classic form among the more advanced, sedentary Indian societies of the Mexican and Andean highlands, although it gave new and enduring organization to less advanced Indian communities, such as those of Paraguay. The purposes of the encomienda were several: (1) as recompense to deserving conquistadors and their descendants, (2) as a source of tribute to colonist and crown, (3) as a means of utilizing and safeguarding a vast and ready-to-hand labor supply, and (4) as an agency for bringing the aborigines into Spanish Christendom.

The encomienda was not a grant of land. An encomendero had only limited rights to acquire holdings within his encomienda, and these were not to encroach upon Indian community lands. The encomienda further differed from a land grant in that: (1) it was a grant for a limited number of lives and not a permanent alienation, (2) it was a grant conferred by the crown and not locally (although governors and viceroys of Peru enjoyed more delegation of authority in this respect than those of New Spain). Because the encomienda bore only limited resemblance to the medieval manor Góngora prefers the term "patrimonialism" to "feudalism" or "manorialism" for describing the system it represented. His reason is that the conquistadors in their urgency to acquire land and sources of wealth were at the same time bearers of royal authority. They conceived of the state as a mass of lands, tributes, offices, benefices, grants, and honors, belonging to the royal patrimony but legitimately claimed by those who had made them available to the crown.

The specifically vassalic relation of loyalty evaporates before general loyalty of subjects to King; the link between conquistadors and King assumes a new aspect, not through a personal bond distinct from what they have as subjects, but through the relation which they have with the lands, won for the royal domain.[17]

Having distinguished between the medieval manor and the encomienda, we must also differentiate the encomienda from the subsequent hacienda and plantation of Spanish America. By the early eighteenth century encomiendas were becoming less desirable for their holders because of the crown's heavier tributary exactions. Then, in 1718-21, royal decrees ordered the reversion of encomiendas to the crown upon the death of the holders. The institution lingered on for a century more, but only in certain outlying areas.

There may have been regions where encomiendas became converted into haciendas through the years, as the holders asserted claim to Indian lands and virtual authority over Indian workers. There may have been other regions where control of both land and workers was asserted from the start, perhaps in the form of the *estancia*. But more typically, the hacienda seems to have grown out of the municipal land grant and not the encomienda. By offering them manufactures, liquor rations, and prepayment of tribute, landowners could attract Indian communities into bondage through debt. The process began as early as the mid-sixteenth century in Mexico, although it was in the nineteenth century that the hacienda achieved its classic form. In these main respects the hacienda differed from the encomienda: (1) The proprietor held title to the land. (2) The Indian workers had little or no land, and were bound to the hacienda through debt peonage. (3) The Indians enjoyed no tutelage from the state and in effect were under the jurisdiction, and at the mercy, of the *hacendado*. Although the Spanish crown was largely ineffectual in controlling the abuses of the hacienda system, it was only when the Indian workers became nominal citizens of independent republics that they suffered the full impact of the predatory social and economic forces unleashed by the conquest, three centuries earlier.

Even in the nineteenth century, however, the hacienda was not a depersonalized, cash-nexus unit of production. The Indians lived community lives in their own cultural ethos, preserving personality traits quite different from the whites and Westernized mestizos. Although victims of the arbitrariness and enforced submissiveness of an overbearing paternalism, they had access to land for their own use and were not subjected to capitalistic demands for maximizing production.

Organized for commercial ends, the hacienda proved strangely hybrid in its characteristics. . . . Geared to sell products in a market, it yet aimed at having little to sell. Voracious for land, it deliberately made inefficient use of it. Operating with large numbers of workers, it nevertheless personalized the relation between worker and owner. Created to produce a profit, it consumed a large part of its substance in conspicuous and unproductive displays of wealth.[18]

It is permissible to think of the hacienda (which occurs mainly in livestock and cereal zones) as a form of agrarian organization intermediate between the encomienda and the plantation. (The term *latifundio* is applied to both haciendas and plantations.) Of the three, the last is most nearly a "capitalistic" institution. The plantation specializes in intensive single-crop production for a world market; it tends to be heavily capitalized and to rely on slave or immigrant labor, utilized more or less efficiently to minimize labor costs. Mechanization, as it becomes available and economical, tends to be introduced on plantations, not on haciendas.

The classic plantation systems were those of the Caribbean sugar islands—the French and British ones in the seventeenth and eighteenth centuries, the Spanish-speaking ones in the nineteenth and twentieth. In Brazil the colonial sugar fazendas, although slave-based, had some features in common with the hacienda. The Brazilian coffee plantations of the past hundred years or so—at first slave-based but soon immigrant-labor-based—more closely follow the plantation model.

In contemporary Latin America the ideal of land reform receives wide support and well-nigh universal lip service. The program of an actual agrarian revolution, however, is importantly determined by whether it affects an hacienda or a plantation economy. In the former case, a revolution such as the Mexican or the Bolivian encounters the problems of expropriating inefficiently used land and redistributing it to peasant communities. At this stage the education of the peasantry to more productive methods—a difficult task in itself—may merely increase production for local consumption and for betterment of the subsistence level. The next step may have to be the encouragement of industrialized or plantation agriculture, for suitable crops in suitable regions, as a means of improving the national export balance.

150

When revolution comes to a plantation economy, as it has to Cuba, the agrarian phase is also difficult to accomplish. For if production of the leading crop is already rationalized, reasonably efficient, and best served by large landholdings, loss of efficiency is almost inevitable when control of the plantations passes to the state or to co-operatives. If lands planted to a single cash crop are replanted to other crops, the nation's foreign trade position probably suffers. If unused lands are programmed for diversified agriculture, it will be difficult to recruit labor for them from an already "industrialized" rural proletariat, and even more difficult to recruit from the cities.

In these ways the agrarian heritage of four centuries weighs heavily upon contemporary Latin America, and the contagious slogan of "land reform" gives little clue to the diversity and complexity of the situations where it is to be effected.

3   Political Foundations

Having stressed the adaptation and mutation of Spanish culture and institutions in the New World, it is important that we examine more closely the premises and structure that are common to the parent society and to its New World offshoots. Just as there are political and psychological assumptions which characterize Protestant societies and transcend, or underlie, the circumstances of time and place, so may we expect there to exist a common ethos within which Catholic societies find their historical development.

For conveying the spirit of Protestant colonization there is no more revealing statement than that made by Martin Luther in his *Open Letter to the Christian Nobility:*

If a little group of pious Christian laymen were taken captive and set down in a wilderness, and had among them no priest consecrated by a bishop, and if there in the wilderness they were to agree in choosing one of themselves, married or unmarried, and were to charge him with the office of baptizing, saying mass, absolving and preaching, such a man would be as truly a priest as though all bishops and popes had consecrated him.

151

This passage contains two suggestions important for our purposes. The first is that a land uninhabited, or inhabited by heathen, is a "wilderness," a no man's land outside the pale of society, civilization, and church. The second is that the world is composed not of *one highly differentiated society* for which certain common forms, acts, and ceremonies are a needed binding force, but of a *multitude of unrelated societies,* each of them a congregation of similar persons which is finite in time and place and ordered by the declarative terms of a compact rather than by common symbolic observances. As Kenneth Burke puts it:

[In] contrast with the church's "organic" theory, whereby one put a going social concern together by the toleration of *differences,* the Protestant sects stressed the value of *complete uniformity.* Each time this uniformity was impaired, the sect itself tended to split, with a new "uncompromising" offshoot reaffirming the need for a homogeneous community, all members alike in status.[19]

If, then, Christendom was for the Spaniard "universal," this meant that his overseas settlements were not truly "colonies," whether orthodox or heterodox, that had been spun off from the mother country into a "wilderness." [20] Nor was Spanish expansion properly a "conquest" insofar as this means the acquisition of alien lands and peoples. In fact the word itself, which Las Casas called "tyrannical, Mohammedan, abusive, improper, and infernal," was banned from official use in favor of *pacificación* or *población.*[21] The term frequently used to designate the extension of Spanish political rule to America is "incorporation," as for example "the incorporation of the Indies to the crown of Castile." What is implied is not the annexation of terra incognita but the bringing together of what should rightfully be joined.[22]

To say this much is not to idealize the motives of those who erected the Spanish empire in America. Fortune-seeking, aggrandizement, fanaticism, escapism were all in evidence. Economically and otherwise the Spanish Indies were exploited. The point is that they were incorporated into Christendom, directly under the Spanish crown, by a specially

designed and carefully legitimized patrimonial state apparatus. Oppression certainly occurs within such a realm. But
subjects tend to attribute it to bad information, misunder-
standing, incompetence, and selfishness originating at lower
administrative levels. The system itself is not seriously challenged, nor is the authority of the symbolic and irreplaceable
crown.[23]

These principles of society and government help us not
only to understand Spanish rule in America, but also to assess
the impact of the Enlightenment on Spanish America, to
analyze the process by which the Spanish American nations
became independent, and to interpret their subsequent political careers. There are scholars who emphasize the relevance of the ideas of such postmedieval Spanish thinkers as
Vitoria, Molina, and Suárez to the later institutional development of Spain and Spanish America.[24] Others, however, are
impatient with any suggestion that the mists of the medieval,
Catholic heritage of Spanish America cannot be, or are not
being, evaporated by the rays of the Enlightenment. As we
see it, the critical question is not the rather empty one as to
whether the neo-Thomist Suárez or the Jacobin Rousseau
was the intellectual lodestar for the sovereign Spanish American juntas of 1809-10 at the dawn of the independence era.[25]
If we accept seriously the notion that Spanish America had
taken a cultural and institutional fix long before this time,
we are interested in identifying a deep-lying matrix of
thought and attitude, not the rhetoric by which it may for
the moment have been veiled.

Francisco Suárez (1548-1617) is generally recognized as the
thinker who most fully recapitulated Thomist political
thought in Spain's age of *Barockscholastik*. This recapitula-
tion was far from being a mere disinterment of Thomism. It
reformulated the philosophic dilemmas of the past in a very
modern search for a metaphysics that would be epistemologi-
cally autonomous. The significance of Suárez for Spanish
American political history therefore does not depend upon
whether or not he provided a Spanish, pre-Enlightenment
precedent for contract theory and popular sovereignty. It
lies, rather, in the fact that his fresh marshaling of scholastic

doctrines, under powerful influences of time and place, encapsulated certain assumptions about political man and certain political dilemmas that pervade Hispanic political life to this day. Some of the points of Suarezian philosophy relevant to this consideration are the following:

(1) *Natural law is clearly distinguished from conscience.* Natural law is a general rule; conscience is a practical application of it to specific cases. Natural law is never mistaken; conscience may be. Society and the body politic are therefore seen as properly ordered by objective and external natural-law precepts rather than by consensus sprung from the promptings of private consciences. (In societies where such an assumption prevails it is unlikely that the free election and the ballot box will ever attain the mystique which is theirs in Protestant countries.)

(2) *Sovereign power originates with the collectivity of men.* God is the author of civil power, but He created it as a property emanating from nature so that no society would lack the power necessary for its preservation. A proposition of this sort allowed the view that most of the pre-Columbian Indians were not savages but lived in societies ordered by natural law. A second implication, important for the period of independence, was that in the event of a collapse of central authority, power would revert to the sovereign people.

(3) *The people do not* delegate *but* alienate *sovereignty to their prince.* Although the people are in principle superior to the prince, they vest power in him without condition (*simpliciter*) that he may use it as he deems fitting. By contract, then, the prince is superior to the people.

(4) *In certain cases the law of the prince loses its force,* namely: (a) if it is unjust, for an unjust law is not a law; (b) if it is too harsh; (c) if the majority has already ceased to obey it (even though the first to cease obeying would have sinned).

(5) *The prince is bound by his own law.* He cannot, however, be punished by himself or by his people, and is responsible only to God or His representative.

In modern times the difficulties that Spanish American peoples experience in erecting constitutional regimes based on wide popular participation are commonly attributed to: (1) inadequate suffusion with Anglo-French democratic principles; (2) disorderly or unwholesome social conditions characterized by ignorance, poverty, disease, and malnutrition; (3) "Spanish" or "Latin" personalistic psychology. Anchored in the scholastic propositions of Suárez, however, we discern precisely those seeming inconsistencies of political attitude which many would attribute to modern Spanish Americans. Paul Janet summarized them as follows:

Such are the Scholastic doctrines of the 16th century, incoherent doctrines in which are united . . . democratic and absolutist ideas, without the author seeing very clearly where the former or the latter lead him. He adopts in all its force the principle of popular sovereignty: he excludes the doctrine of divine law . . . and he causes not simply government but even society to rest upon unanimous consent. But these principles serve only to allow him immediately to effect the absolute and unconditional alienation of popular sovereignty into the hands of one person. He denies the need for consent of the people in the formulation of law; and as guarantee against an unjust law he offers only a disobedience both seditious and disloyal. Finally, he shelters the prince under the power of the laws and sees over him only the judgment of the Church.[26]

We need not say that Suárez himself was a decisive intellectual influence upon Spanish America's institutional development (although the University of Mexico did have a Suarezian chair, and his doctrines won increasing attention in New Spain during the seventeenth century). The evidence does suggest, however, that his writings are symptomatic of a postmedieval Hispano-Catholic view of man, society, and government which is by no means superseded in modern Spanish America.

It is important to grasp that Spanish neo-Thomism was not a blind, obstinate reaction to the Protestant Reformation any more than it was a romantic revival of ethereal religious aspirations. What it did was to offer sophisticated theoretical formulation of the ideals and many sociological realities of the Spanish patrimonial state. In some ways the political philosophy of St. Thomas was more relevant to sixteenth-century Spain and her overseas empire than to feudal, thirteenth-century Europe, in which it was conceived—just as the ideas of John Locke, some say, were better keyed to Jeffersonian America than they were to seventeenth-century England.

The two central principles of Thomist sociopolitical thought, as Ernst Troeltsch states them, are organicism and patriarchalism.[27] First, society is a hierarchical system in which each person or group serves a purpose larger than any one of them can encompass. Social unity is architectonic, deriving from faith in the larger *corpus mysticum* and not from rationalistic definitions of purpose and strategy at critical moments of history. To the social hierarchy corresponds a scale of inequalities and imperfections that should be corrected only when Christian justice is in jeopardy. Thus casuistry becomes more important than human law, because to adjudicate is to determine whether a given case affects all of society or whether it can be dispatched by an *ad hoc* decision.

Second, the inequalities inherent in society imply the acquiescence of each person in his station with its attendant obligations. Such acquiescence is naturally contingent upon public acceptance of the supreme power—king, prince, or pope—who must enjoy full legitimacy to serve as the ultimate, paternalistic source of the casuistical decisions that resolve the constant conflicts of function and jurisdiction throughout the system.

Troeltsch suggests why this majestic philosophic edifice was partly inconsonant with the thirteenth century. He points out that the image of the Aristotelian city-state influenced St. Thomas more strongly than did the constitutional life of his own day. "Catholic theory is, largely, comparatively independent of feudal tenure and the feudal system; the relation between the public authority and subjective public rights is treated in a highly abstract manner." Moreover, St. Thomas displays an urban bias: "[In] contrast to the inclination of modern Catholicism towards the rural population and its

156

specific Ethos, it is solely the city that St. Thomas takes into account. In his view man is naturally a town-dweller, and he regards rural life only as the result of misfortune or of want." [28]

Previously we stressed the weakness of the feudal tradition in Spain and the important role of the medieval Spanish city. We are now in a position to appreciate that it was for sociological rather than mere doctrinal reasons that Thomist theory struck such resonances throughout the Spanish empire in the sixteenth and seventeenth centuries.

It remains to cast the model of the patrimonial state in terms that allow us to trace its persistence unequivocally in modern Spanish America. This task was accomplished by Max Weber when he distinguished "patrimonialism" as one of the forms of "traditional domination." [29] The patrimonial ruler is ever alert to forestall the growth of an independent landed aristocracy enjoying inherited privileges. He awards benefices, or prebends, as a remuneration for services; income accruing from benefices is an attribute of the office, not of the incumbent as a person. Characteristic ways for maintaining the ruler's authority intact are: limiting the tenure of royal officials; forbidding officials to acquire family and economic ties in their jurisdictions; using inspectors and spies to supervise all levels of administration; defining only loosely the territorial and functional divisions of administration so that jurisdictions will be competitive and mutually supervisory. The authority of the ruler is oriented to tradition but allows him claim to full personal power.[30] As he is reluctant to bind himself by "law," his rule takes the form of a series of directives, each subject to supersession. Thus problems of adjudication tend to become problems of administration, and the administrative and judicial functions are united in many different offices throughout the bureaucracy. Legal remedies are frequently regarded not as applications of "law," but as a gift of grace or a privilege awarded on the merits of a case and not binding as precedent.

This typology of the patrimonial state describes with surprising accuracy the structure and logic of the Spanish empire in America. It also assists us to understand why chaos ensued when the ultimate authority for the system, the Spanish crown, was suddenly removed.

Until the moment that Napoleon's troops took Ferdinand VII of Spain into custody in 1808, there had existed throughout the Spanish empire a relative lack of concern with the remoter framework of society and general acquiescence in the ultimate authority. A study of those dispersed and sporadic uprisings against authority which did occur in Spanish America before independence classifies them as: revolts by the original conquistadors, uprisings of the subject races, and creole movements of protest. If we except seditious revolts caused by a single leader's personal ambitions for power, we find all the three kinds of uprising to have common characteristics. They are precisely the characteristics one could define as "legitimate" for revolt within the framework of the Thomist, patrimonial state.

Those movements were spontaneous, in the double sense of indigenous (that is, not determined by any foreign influence, although subsequently certain foreign elements might be employed for their development and legitimation) and accidental (that is, they did not respond to an organic plan or to a doctrine elaborated *ex professo*).

They were in embryo energetically local, produced by a crisis affecting the region or zone and directed to regional needs. When various movements broke out simultaneously at various points, this was a sociological and chronological coincidence, not a planned prior agreement.

Lastly, in the cases when abstract principles are invoked to encourage revolutionary activity, the latter never occurs as a mere ideological outburst; it tends always toward the immediate resolution of a severe and urgent crisis.[31]

In the second half of the eighteenth century Enlightenment ideas and writings circulated freely in Spanish America among intellectual, professional, and clerical groups, within the universities, in the new economic societies, and, with restrictions, in the public press. Yet their effect was to stimulate reformist criticism, not to engender programmatic opposition to the regime or revolutionary Jacobinism. The traditions of the Spanish system itself in fact allowed possibilities for greater autonomy for the colonies and parity for the creoles. It has been argued that the main shortcoming of the "enlightened" reforms of the most notable Bourbon king, Charles III (1759-88),[32] was that they were alien to tradition in being too rationalistic and technocratic, that they failed to develop initiative, self-rule, and human resources *in loco*. His expulsion of the Jesuits in 1767 (accompanied by a ban on the teachings of Suárez!), to the dismay of many creoles and Indians, deprived the Indies of important intellectual, pedagogical, and even economic leadership. It is an example, not without relevance to modern Latin America, of how "progressive" administration can stifle internal sources of potential progress.

4   Independence

The best historical analogue to the Spanish American wars for independence is the Protestant Reformation. Both movements occurred within a far-flung, venerable Catholic institutional order which was exhibiting decadence at its upper levels. Both movements developed as unco-ordinated patterns of dispersed and disparate revolt. Neither was heralded by a coherent body of revolutionary doctrine, and each improvised its multiple "ideologies" under pressure of events. Indeed, each movement at its inception betrayed a strong conservative or fundamentalist character. Each was the final cluster of a centuries-old series of random and localized heresies, uprisings, or seditions; and, in the case of each, world events were finally propitious to transform the impromptu outbreak into a world-historical revolution.

On the South American continent it was not until a number of years after Napoleon's deposition of the Spanish king that the goal of independence became clearly defined and was pursued in the military campaigns conducted separately by Simón Bolívar and José de San Martín. Even then the mass of the people played no role in the movement. The independence of the Spanish South American countries was achieved under the auspices of the creole elites in the more outlying regions. The impetus for the two main campaigns was imparted from Venezuela in the north and Buenos Aires in the south. Both of these regions were offering fresh promise for agricultural and commercial development. After independence, both Venezuela and Argentina fell under strongman rule. This served to entrench the somewhat reconstituted creole oligarchies, which were now unhampered by the presence of Spanish bureaucracy.

If we except the special case of Saint Domingue, where a massive slave revolt produced Haiti's independence from France, Mexico is the only Latin-American country where there occurred substantial popular uprisings. Under Hidalgo an inchoate crowd of humble Indians and mestizos in central Mexico was led to fight for land, for Mexican autonomy, and for an end to the caste system (1810-11). Under Morelos they were led to fight for independence (1813-15). Both leaders were liberal parish priests. Both were captured and executed. Well-to-do creoles resisted identification with the rebellion or with a French revolutionary spirit. Some creoles even suspected the Spaniards themselves of being tainted with freemasonry and Illuminism. The army, church, and landowners remained loyal to the crown during the Napoleonic interregnum and after the establishment of reaction and despotism under the restored Ferdinand VII (1814). The Mexican insurgent movement was flickering out when suddenly, in 1820, liberal, constitutional reforms were forced upon the Spanish monarchy. At this point, fearing for their privileges, the Spaniards in Mexico and the upper creoles joined to embrace the separatist cause, setting up the short-lived emperorship of Agustín de Iturbide. Mexican independence was an act of counterrevolution.

It cannot be said, therefore, that "nationalism" was an ingredient of the Latin-American independence movement. Simón Bolívar, the *líder máximo* of independence, was torn between the generous vision of a transnational amphictyony of the Hispanic American peoples and a keen perception of the feuding local oligarchies and earthbound peasantries from which only phantom nations could be formed. One surmises that Bolívar's use of the term "amphictyony," dictated by the Enlightenment fashion of neoclassicism, was a surrogate for his instinctive sense of a Hispanic unity rooted in a political and religious heritage having medieval coloration.[33] A modern Colombian writes, "Had Bolívar not feared to be Napoleon and had he abandoned the paradigm of George Washington, perhaps our national destiny would have been saved." The independence of the United States caused a bonding through compact of autonomous colonies. The independence of Spanish America caused the decapitation of a realm that had ever been, if not unified, at least unitary. In one case *e pluribus unum,* in the other *ex uno plures.* The Panama Congress of 1826, while it served as a first utterance of the Pan American ideal, symbolized the abandonment of attempts to regulate the internal affairs of the Spanish American peoples on a continental scale.[34]

The extent of the politico-administrative crisis faced by the independent Spanish American nations of 1830 can be appreciated when we recall our model of the Thomist-patrimonial state. The lower echelons of administration had operated by the grace of an interventionist, paternal monarch, thoroughly sanctioned by tradition and faith. His collapse straightway withdrew legitimacy from the remnants of the royal bureaucracy. It was impossible to identify a substitute authority that would command general assent. Decapitated, the government could not function, for the patrimonial regime had developed neither: (1) the underpinning of contractual vassalic relationships that capacitate the component parts of a *feudal* regime for autonomous life; nor, (2) a rationalized *legal* order not dependent for its operation and claims to assent upon personalistic intervention by the highest authority.

Although legitimacy was withdrawn from the hierarchies of government and society by independence, no revolutionary change occurred. "Thus the social and spiritual structure of the past is preserved under new forms; its class hierarchy, the privileges of special bodies . . . the values. of the Catholic religion and Hispanic tradition are maintained. At the same time its political and legislative forms and its international

161

status change." [35] To state the case more fully, political or social revolution was neither cause nor concomitant of the independence wars. Once independence was achieved, however, the bureaucracy found a new role thrust upon it. Whereas the mission of the colonial bureaucracy had been to protect and uphold a traditional order, the republican one took on just the contrary function. As Villoro puts it:

[The new bureaucracy] has arisen from the destruction of the old political order, and it has *raison d'être* only as a force to transform society. Far from finding itself, like the colonial functionaries, at the summit of the established power, it must for its preservation oppose the economically privileged classes. The decrees it applies, the institutions it creates, do not repeat old models but are fated to deny those that exist and provoke the transformation of society. From the moment this task is over, its bureaucratic function also ceases. The colonial bureaucracy, tied to preserving the past, was necessarily antirevolutionary. The creole bureaucracy, sprung from a negation of the past, is condemned to be revolutionary for its own preservation.[36]

The collapse of the supreme authority activated the latent forces of local oligarchies, municipalities, and extended-family systems in a struggle for power and prestige in the new, arbitrarily defined republics. These telluric creole social structures were direct heirs of social arrangements proliferated in the conquest period but held in check by the patrimonial state. Now again they seized the stage. The *caudillo* of the independence period, controlling a clanlike or an improvised retinue through charismatic appeal, was the latter-day version of the conquistador. In the absence of developed and interacting economic interest groups having a stake in constitutional process, the new countries were plunged into alternating regimes of anarchy and personalist tyranny. The contest to seize a patrimonial state apparatus, fragmented from the original imperial one, became the driving force of public life in each new country.

There is abundant testimony that Spanish America universally suffered a collapse of the moral order during the early decades of independence. The face of anarchy was somewhat masked, however, by that ancient habit of legalizing and legitimizing every public act which had been so important a cement to the former empire. Each new country duly produced its constitutional convention and one or more Anglo-French-type constitutions. The political mechanism which emerged was generally a biparty system. Party programs faithfully reflected the rhetoric of Western parliamentary politics, though not without occasional shrewd adaptation to local situations. Although only an elite was politically active (as was the case in the England of 1830, for that matter), party adherence frequently reflected an alignment of "conservative" landed and monied interests, high clergy, and former monarchists against the "liberal" professionals, intellectuals, merchants, and those with a creole, anticlerical, and anticaste outlook. Given a static rather than a dynamic social system, however, the game of politics became a naked contest for power.

Chile was an example perhaps unparalleled of a Spanish American country which managed, after a twelve-year transitional period, to avoid the extremes of tyranny and anarchy with a political system unencumbered by the mechanisms and party rhetoric of an exotic liberalism. Despite its outlandish contour the country had a certain ecological cohesion around its central agricultural zone. Because the landholding class had been infiltrated by mercantile groups partly composed of recent immigrants from northern Spain, the elite represented a spectrum of moderately diverse economic interest. A Valparaiso businessman, Diego Portales, was shrewd enough to identify and co-ordinate those interests within a constitutional system having an aura of native legitimacy. The centralizing 1833 Constitution which bore his influence created a strong executive without stripping the congress and courts of countervailing powers. The first president had the aristocratic bearing which Portales himself lacked; a staunch Catholic and brave general who stood above party factionalism, he helped to legitimize the office itself. The first several presidents each served double five-year terms. The official candidate was generally victorious and hand-picked by his predecessor. Thus the structure of the Spanish patrimonial state was re-created, with only those minimum concessions to Anglo-French constitutionalism that were necessary for a nineteenth-century republic which had just rejected monarchical rule.*

From our broad premises and from the specific case of Chile we may infer that for a newly erected Spanish American political system to achieve stability and continuity it had to reproduce the structure, the logic, and the vague, pragmatic safeguards against tyranny of the Spanish *patrimonial state.* The collapse of monarchical authority meant that this step required the intervention of strong *personalist* leadership. The energies of such leadership had to flow toward investing the state with suprapersonal *legitimacy.* The ingredients of legitimacy, in turn, were native psychocultural *traditions,* leavened or perhaps merely adorned by the *nationalism* and *constitutionalism* which had become watchwords of the age.

The usual political trajectory of a Spanish American nation can be plotted as one or another form of breakdown or short circuit in this model. The most notorious form is personalist leadership that constitutes its own untransferable legitimacy. In a telluric setting of moral and institutional collapse, the instances of personalism ranged from the superb, intellectually informed, yet tragically frustrated political genius of a Bolívar all the way to careers dominated by sheer enactment of impulse, such as those of the Argentine *caudillo* Facundo described by Sarmiento; or the Bolivian president who commanded his aides to play dead like poodles, and who had his ministers and generals troop solemnly around the table on which his mistress stood naked.

It is beyond our purposes to present even a perfunctory account of the careers of the twenty Latin-American nations during the past century and a half. At this point we will merely suggest a way of periodizing Spanish American history

* Brazil, which gave refuge to the Portuguese ruling family when Napoleon invaded the mother country, is another example of nineteenth-century political stability. If space allowed the coequal treatment which Portuguese America deserves, the Brazilian case could be used to confirm and refine the arguments here presented. Some of the relevant points are dealt with in my essay "Some Themes of Brazilian History," *The South Atlantic Quarterly,* LXI, 2 (Spring 1962), 159-182.

that allows us to explore the political dilemmas of the modern countries in the light of their Thomist, patrimonial heritage. The historical divisions conventionally used are the following:

Indigenous Period	To 1492
Colonial Period	1492 to 1824
National Period	Since 1824.

Here is our radically revised schema (offered chiefly for heuristic purposes):

Indigenous Period	To 1520
Spanish Period	1520 to 1760
"Colonial" Period	1760 to 1920
National Period	Since 1920.

We extend the Indigenous Period to 1520 because for a generation after Columbus' discovery Spanish colonization was restricted to the islands and shores of the Caribbean Sea and conducted on a trial-and-error basis, with commercial exploitation rather than effective colonization usually in the ascendant. Hernando Cortés, who conquered the Aztec empire in 1519-21, was the first of the explorers and conquistadors to make clear to the crown the full scope of the colonizing and civilizing venture upon which Spain had embarked.[37]

The rationale for the Spanish Period was set forth above in Sections 2 and 3. It was the time of "incorporation" of the Indies into Hispano-Christian civilization.

The term "Colonial" (used hitherto in this essay in the conventional meaning) serves in the new schema to characterize the period when the creole, Catholic culture and institutions of Spanish America lay open to influences and pressures of the Western world which were on the whole ineffectually mediated to the ethos of the formative Spanish Period.

The National Period is still today in its inception. It is a time when political arrangements are being devised, erratically and painfully, which directly accommodate the traditions, structures, and psychology of the patrimonial state to the imperatives of a modern industrial world. It is a time when Spanish Americans are beginning to contemplate their countries' first sustained involvement with each other and with the world as autonomous nation states.

The start of the "Colonial" Period we set at 1760, the eve of the most important Bourbon reforms. As Octavio Paz sums up the case for it:

The reforms undertaken by the Bourbon dynasty, particularly Charles III, improved the economy and made business operations more efficient, but they accentuated the centralization of administrative functions and changed New Spain into a true colony, that is, into a territory subject to systematic exploitation and strictly controlled by the center of power.[38]

As Paz goes on to make clear, the critical matter is not quantitative exploitation. It would be hard to make the case that the financial enrichment of Spain at the expense of the Indies, or the cruelty to Indians and Negro slaves, was greater in 1780 than it had been in 1680 or 1580. The primary sense of "colonial" as here used designates not a unilaterally exploitative relationship, but a discontinuity of structure and purpose between two systems. The fact was that the "enlightened," rationalistic, technocratic Bourbon policies were an overlay upon and not a radical reform of Spanish American institutions.

Bourbon economic reforms aroused antagonism from creole merchants in Mexico City, Caracas, and Buenos Aires who were thriving under the old monopolistic system. It can even be concluded that "while Spain evolved toward [economic] liberalism, there were interests in America which obstructed those new currents." [39] Administrative reform, and specifically the creation of the intendant system, "revealed a fatal lack of integration in Spanish policy." New officials were underpaid without being allowed the traditional extralegal fees and exactions. The division of authority between the intendants and the viceroys was unwisely or vaguely stipulated. The activities of the intendants aroused the town governments to greater activity without their receiving a commensurate increase of authority. "[The] reforms of Charles III, both in their administrative and in their commercial aspects, helped to precipitate the collapse of the imperial regime they were intended to prolong." [40]

The assumptions and programs of Western liberalism continued to be a bone in the throat of Spanish America, whether their guise was enlightened despotism, Manchester economics, or Anglo-French constitutional democracy. The tendency of doctrinally liberal reforms was to withdraw legitimacy from the patrimonial state, to dismantle its apparatus, and to cancel the shadowy, paternalistic safeguards of status for the inarticulate masses. Since, however, the stimuli to economic change came from without—from the Western world—and not from within, there did not occur even among the new oligarchies that competitive differentiation of economic function which gives liberalism its *raison d'être*. Mexico's liberal Constitution of 1857 was informed by the vision of a prosperous independent peasantry. But its enactment merely hastened the delivery of traditional Indian communities to systems of debt peonage that were beyond the tutelage of church and state. A similar process occurred in the other Indian countries south to Bolivia. It gave to the landowning oligarchies a measure of absolute local power that would have exceeded even the dreams of the conquistadors.

The anti-Spanish rallying cries of Democracy! Liberalism! and Civilization! provoked by the Spanish American independence wars contained hopes which were persistently undermined by the drift of the nineteenth century. This trend is implied by the "two stages" into which Leopoldo Zea divides the period's intellectual history.[41] The first was a romantic, eclectic phase when such diverse and often contradictory currents as Cartesianism, sensationalist psychology, physiocratic economics, Saint-Simonianism, utilitarianism, Scotch realism, and French traditionalism were all commingled in a multiple attack on the Hispanic, scholastic legacy. The second phase saw many of these streams of thought, and some new ones, merge to form a unified intellectual position, that of positivism.

Positivism occurred in many versions throughout Latin America, sometimes with an Anglo-Spencerian rather than a Franco-Comtean emphasis. Whatever its guise, it appeared to offer a unitary, constructive, systematic, scientific approach to the problems of stratified societies, stagnant economies, and archaic school systems. In practice, however, the watchwords of positivism could be used to justify systems of vested interest and entrenched privilege. Frock-coated bourgeois *caudillos* had replaced the soldier *caudillos* of the postindependence era. Their regimes were secured less by charismatic leadership and military prowess than by creation of orderly conditions for attracting foreign trade and investment in this heyday of European capitalism. Liberalism tinctured by social evolution could justify limiting economic freedom to those who already possessed it. Tinctured by nineteenth-century anthropology it acquiesced in the continued exploitation of Indians, Negroes, and those of "mixed race."

It might be imagined that Latin America's intellectual drift from romanticism to scientism, from eclecticism to determinism, merely reflected the general European movement. Zea offers us two caveats to correct this impression. One is that the acceptance of positivism in Latin America represented a search for the inclusive doctrine and instrument of order which might replace scholasticism. Seen thus, positivism appears to serve familiar casuistical purposes more importantly than those of speculative scientific inquiry.

Secondly, at the same time that the Latin-American, especially the Spanish American, mind groped unconsciously to recover a habitual mold of thought, it was explicitly attacking the civilization within which that mold had been shaped. Spanish Americans were condemned to the impossible task of denying and amputating their past. Yet Spain was always with them. Unable to deal with their past by a *dialectic logic* which would allow them to assimilate it, they rejected it by a *formal logic* which kept it present and impeded their evolution. The Conquest, Colonialism, and Independence were problems never resolved, never placed *behind*. They are still alive in our own century.

The Hispanic American continued as if no change had taken place. And in truth none had. Nothing real or conclusive seemed to have been gained. The political freedom which had been attained was only a formality. . . . Every Hispanic American sought only to take the place left by the conquistador. From the dominated man which he was, he aspired to be the dominator of the weakest. . . . Meanwhile the rest of the world marched forward, progressed, and made history. Hispanic America continued to be a continent without history, without a past, because the past was always present.[42]

Not only did ideas from nineteenth-century Europe assume new coloration and use in the Latin-American setting, but some were screened out before reaching it. Marxism, for example, made virtually no impact whatsoever. A philosophy which identifies an engine of political demolition in society will scarcely win general acceptance among a people groping to recover and legitimize an overarching patrimonial state. The clarion call to a single solidary and militant class echoes weakly in a society where all groups look separately to a patrimonial structure for accommodation, tutelage, and salvation. The model toward which the Thomistic society tends must be formulated in statics, not dynamics. Its ultimate law is natural and moral, not scientific and sociological. These strictures were for the most part overlooked in nineteenth-century Latin America. But they continued in clandestine operation.

5 Contemporary Latin America: Five Political Premises

The date 1920 was suggested as the start of Latin America's truly "National" Period. Some nations have not yet entered it, and none has fully emerged from "colonial" status and outlook. But within the decade or so preceding and following 1920 one can say that certain key countries produced political regimes, social programs, and cultural statements which evinced a new fealty to historical realities. Mexico's was the classic Latin-American national revolution because of the decadence and corruption of the bourgeois-*caudillo* regime which it overthrew and because of the outright theatricality with which it was conducted and perpetuated. Its many facets and phases, however disconnected in actuality, are bonded in a rhetorical and emotive mystique.

The fact that the Mexican Revolution was, among other things, fiercely anticlerical does not mean that it was not deeply consonant with Hispanic tradition. Traditions which are matrices of social action and not mere ceremony retain vitality precisely because they accommodate to many guises and purposes. This same anticlerical revolution had as its martyr-hero the spiritualistic (and literally a practitioner of spiritualism), "Christ-like" Madero. Revolutionary teachers sent among the poor and the Indians went as "missionaries," sometimes too as martyrs. Revolutionary painters revived the tradition of monumental public art, spreading the walls of government buildings with murals depicting the Indian's exploitation through the centuries like so many stations of Calvary leading toward chiliastic redemption.

After the long Porfirio Díaz interregnum, the subsoil was declared to be the patrimony of the state, as it had once been of the Spanish crown. The *ejido* system, by which the soil itself was redistributed to rural workers on a quasi-communalist basis, took its name from the town commons of the old Spanish municipality. Reawakened interest in the Indian, his problems and his culture, restored him to his former position of special tutelage. Groups hitherto neglected politically, the rural and urban workers, were brought into national prominence through paternalistic institutions established or heavily influenced by the new patrimonial state. Laborers, capitalists, managerial and commercial groups, syndicates of professionals and teachers, tend to relate primarily to the strong politico-administrative core of the central government, only secondarily to each other. State and regional conflicts are often referred to the central government for resolution, except where a local *caudillo* manages to establish a temporary satrapy.

The Mexican Revolution is customarily described as a dynamic, protean movement that is not yet ended. As evidence one can point to the shifting emphasis over the decades upon successive programs of education reform, trade unionism, anticlericalism, land reform, oil expropriation, industrialization, and public works. This apparent dynamism conflicts with our static model for the patrimonial state. On closer inspection, however, it turns out that the Mexican Revolution differs from the "permanent revolution" of a capitalist society. Mexico's official and, in practice, single political party changed its name in 1946 to the Party of Revolutionary Institutions. Revolutionary institutions, above all the institutions of a particular revolution, are hardly the same as a revolutionary process or a dynamic interplay among institutions.

The Magna Charta of the revolution, its Constitution of 1917, does not primarily serve as a social compact or set of ground rules for the conduct of public life. This lengthy codification, which like the old Laws of the Indies mixes general precepts and regulative specifics, is characteristically viewed as a document to be put into effect. No one was concerned that many provisions of the Constitution were in abeyance for years after its promulgation. In the Hispano-Thomist tradition there is no urgency to enforce law if enforcement is for good reasons unfeasible and if the community at large shows no great concern. Once having attained legitimacy, the Revolution was regarded as something to be permanently institutionalized, not as point of departure for open-ended process.

This view of the Mexican Revolution is highly schematic. It takes no account, for example, of Bourbon survivals (such as, perhaps, overcentralization and technocratic tendencies) or positivist tendencies (such as, perhaps, the "socialist education" of the nineteen-thirties). It suggests little of rapid socioeconomic change (much of which, however, appears to be triggered by the external industrial world, not generated internally). What it does attempt is to identify a historical matrix of social action and attitude, now recovered sufficiently to endow the eclectic solutions of the moment with legitimacy and partial coherence.

Earlier we said that the first political problem of a Latin-American country is the routinization of charisma. We now suggest that the ideal form toward which this routinization gravitates is the patrimonial state. Once a version of this state is achieved, however imperfectly, the second great political problem is how, in the twentieth century, to reconcile the static, vegetative features of the patrimonial state with the imperatives of a dynamic industrial world. This problem is one of accommodation and not, as many liberal Western minds would have it, one of transcendence—not even perhaps, in its ultimate terms, a problem of "development."

At this point we may summarize some of the presuppositions, limiting conditions, and possibilities for political change in the Latin-American countries as they advance into the genuinely "national" phase of their history. However heavily the Western, industrial world—or, for that matter, the Communist, industrial one—may impinge upon these countries, quickening their pace of life, engendering new hopes, wants, and fears, introducing new programs, equipment, technology, and wares, it seems probable that any changes wrought will in some way eventually accommodate to a number of enduring premises that underlie Latin-American political life.

The first point is that *now as in the past the sense that man makes and is responsible for his own world is less deep or prevalent than in many other lands.* The Latin American may be more sensitive to his world, or more eloquently critical of it, or more attached to it. But he seems less concerned with shaping it. The natural order looms larger than the human community. The old tradition of "natural law" has not atrophied as it did in the United States. The individual conscience is presumed more fallible, the process of voting less consequential than in the northern democracies. The regime of voluntary, rationalized political association, of seesaw bi-party systems, of quasi-rational legislative procedure has a fitful existence after almost a century and a half of "republican" life.

These characteristics, some will argue, are generic to all "underdeveloped" countries. Scales of political maturity have been devised for ranking the emergent nations of Latin America, Africa, and Asia. Granted that Latin America has much in common with other "developing areas," the point stressed in this essay is that Latin America is subject to special imperatives as an offshoot of postmedieval, Catholic, Iberian Europe which never underwent the Protestant Reformation. In its shaping of the present, such a past differs substantially from a Confucian or a Mohammedan or an African tribal past.

To Spanish American society Talcott Parsons applies the rubric "particularistic-ascriptive pattern" and in so doing differentiates it explicitly from, for example, Chinese society. In Spanish America, he observes, the larger social structures, beyond kinship and local community, tend "to be accepted as part of the given situation of life, and to have positive functions when order is threatened, but otherwise to be taken for granted."

Such societies tend to be individualistic rather than collectivistic and non- if not anti-authoritarian. . . . The individualism is primarily concerned with expressive interests, and hence much less so with opportunity to shape the situation through achievement. There tends to be a certain lack of concern with the remoter framework of the society, unless it is threatened. Similarly, there is no inherent objection to authority so long as it does not interfere too much with expressive freedom, indeed it may be welcomed as a factor of stability. But there is also not the positive incentive to recognize authority as inherent that exists in the cases of positive authoritarianism. The tendency to indifference to larger social issues creates a situation in which authority can become established with relatively little opposition.[43]

The second point, implied in the quotation just given, is that *the Latin-American peoples still appear willing to alienate, rather than delegate, power to their chosen or accepted leaders,* in the spirit long ago condoned by sixteenth-century Hispano-Thomist thought. Yet the people retain also a keen sense of equity, of natural justice, and their sensitivity to abuses of alienated power. It may be that the classic image of the Latin-American "revolution" is the barracks coup by an insurgent *caudillo* against an incumbent whose authority lacks legitimacy. But the more significant if more infrequent uprising is that having a broad popular base and no clearly elaborated program beyond reclamation of sovereignty that

173

has been tyrannically abused. Socioeconomic change of a truly revolutionary character which may occur in the wake of such movements tends to be improvised under leadership that desperately seeks to legitimize its authority.

The third point, therefore, is that *the present "National" Period is marked by a renewed quest for legitimate government*. The regimes of the last century did not, by and large, attain legitimacy. Most have not yet done so. A "legitimate" revolution in Latin America needs no sharp-edged ideology; it need not polarize the classes; it need not produce an immediate and effective redistribution of wealth and goods. The regime it produces need not be conscientiously sanctioned at the polls by a majority vote. (The difference between popular political support in Latin America and in the United States recalls Rousseau's mystical distinction between the general will and the will of all.)

On the other hand, a legitimate revolution probably necessitates generalized violence and popular participation, even though under improvised leadership and with unprogrammed goals. It needs to be informed by a deep even though unarticulated sense of moral urgency. It needs to be an indigenous movement, unencumbered by foreign support. It needs charismatic leadership of special psychocultural appeal. Even with all their bluster and blunder, Perón and Fidel Castro have such appeal. So may gentler, saintly types, especially if martyred at an early stage as were Martí and Madero. Mere tyrants are not acceptable revolutionaries.

Liberal North Americans are congenitally unable to deal with charismatic Latin Americans—precisely because they project upon the latter their own criteria for leadership. One might almost venture that the shape and feel of politics in the southern United States equips the Southern conservative better than it does the Northern liberal to understand the political life of Latin America. However much a Lleras Camargo may be respected by Latin Americans as a reforming, law-abiding, conscientious democrat, his sort does not inspire revolution. And it is a revolutionary as well as a national era which Latin America now enters.

Why is a somewhat vague legitimacy so important in mod-

174

ern Latin America? It is because the lawmaking and law-applying processes in Latin America do not in the last instance receive their sanction from popular referendum, from laws and constitutions, from the bureaucratic ideal of "service," from tyrannically exercised power, from custom, or from scientific or dialectical laws. As Gierke said of the Middle Ages: "Far rather every duty of obedience was conditioned by the rightfulness of command." [44] That is, in a patrimonial state, to which command and decree are so fundamental, the legitimacy of the command is determined by the legitimacy of the authority which issues it. Hence the importance of sheer legalism in Latin-American administration as constant certification for the legitimacy, not of the act, but of him who executes it. Hence too the unsatisfactoriness of the personalist regime which fails to take the extraordinarily difficult step of institutionalizing leadership.

Fourthly, *the innate sense of the Latin-American people for natural law is matched by a more casual attitude toward man-made law.*[45] Human laws are frequently seen as too harsh or impracticable or inequitable or simply as inapplicable to the specific case. Hence the difficulty of collecting income taxes; the prevalent obligation to pay fees or bribes to officials for special or even routine services; the apathy of metropolitan police toward theft and delinquency; the thriving contraband trade at border towns; the leniency toward those who commit crimes of passion—all the way down to the nonobservance of "no smoking" signs on buses and in theaters.

One of the impediments to nation-building in Latin America appears to be precisely the fact that natural law most effectively guides judgment either at the international level or at the level of the family and the smallest communities and villages, not at the national level. It is no accident that Latin Americans are so often prominent as international jurists, or that "community development" figures so importantly in modern plans for reform in Latin America. In confrontation with the complexities, abstractions, and compromises of policy-making for the nation-state, instinctive moral sentiments tend to be weakened or suppressed. Understandably therefore, North Americans with their strong and viable nation structure show moral ambivalence in international affairs and in domestic family relations.

From the point being made flow two conclusions. First, as Latin-American countries in the new National Period shrug off the long-standing tutelage of the United States, they may be expected to develop relations—economic, political, cultural—with all nations of the world, particularly the non-Western. Informed by traditions of Catholic universalism, they will do so with greater ease and understanding than characterize United States overtures in such directions. Second, it appears essential that the architects of social and economic reconstruction in Latin America challenge those models which overstress the organizational and depersonalizing aspects of "development." Plans for the largest factories, the largest bureaucracies, even the largest metropolises must somehow build in the small, revitalized face-to-face group as the nodal element.

Finally, it seems scarcely less true now than in the sixteenth century that *the larger society is perceived in Latin America as composed of parts which relate through a patrimonial and symbolic center rather than directly to one another.* A national government operates not as a referee among dynamic pressure groups, but as a source of energy, co-ordination, and leadership for occupational groups and syndicates, corporate units, institutions, social "estates," and geographic regions. In the absence of powerful internal pressures generated by competitive institutional life, and lacking strident ideological imperatives or world power aspirations, there is a tendency for political regimes to vegetate after the enthusiastic seizure of power. Many Mexicans say this today of their "revolutionary" government. Vegetative political regimes, however, are intolerable in the twentieth century. Thus the patrimonial state model, in some ways so viable under the Hapsburgs, becomes revolution-prone in twentieth-century Latin America.

If a last reckless prophecy may be permitted, it is this: that the salvation and energizing of the Latin-American patrimonial state cannot be expected to occur merely in rational response to the demands of a fast-moving technological world.

176

They may not even be significantly advanced by massive education programs, industrialization, higher economic production, better living standards, and free elections—though all these, with their ambivalent effects, are bound to come. What may more significantly change the tendencies of the Latin-American state are the thrusts of nationalism from within and the impingement of world politics from without. These will disrupt the hemisphere's somewhat unhealthy Pax Monroviana and bring the Latin-American nations increasingly into intense, sustained involvement with the nations of the world, and with each other. The first steps will be erratic, sometimes timid, sometimes melodramatic. But eventually they may lead to greater maturity and to national self-images of deeper coherence. A Protestant civilization can develop its energies endlessly in a wilderness, as did the United States. A Catholic civilization stagnates when it is not in vital contact with the diverse tribes and cultures of mankind.

Chapter Six

The South African Dilemma

by Leonard M. Thompson

1 Distinctive Features

Some of the ingredients of South African history are similar to those of Canadian. The histories of both countries are concerned with two successive fragments of European societies, and the relations between them. In the seventeenth century French settlers established themselves along the St. Lawrence River in North America and Dutch settlers at the Cape of Good Hope. By the end of the eighteenth century the latter had become so thoroughly adapted to the South African environment that they had undergone a cultural mutation. The Afrikaner people had been born. Thereafter, following the British conquest of the Cape Colony during the Napoleonic wars, a fragment of the society of industrialized and post-Enlightenment Britain was superimposed upon the Dutch fragment; and while it, too, became adapted to South African conditions it did so less completely and less uniformly than its predecessor.

As in Canada, this succession of one European fragment by another led to tensions between them; but the outcomes differed greatly. In Canada the British fragment became larger than the French, and in 1867 a modus vivendi was reached under a federal constitution which diminished the area of conflict. In South Africa the British fragment was

178

always smaller than the Dutch, and although Great Britain gained a military victory in 1902 the subsequent withdrawal of imperial authority paved the way for an Afrikaner triumph. Thus South African history provides a variant of the two-fragment situation. The first fragment generated enough power to survive military defeat, to gain control of the political machinery, and to master and, indeed, to begin to absorb the second.

But South African history is not merely a variant of Canadian. Its two-fragment character was always distorted by the presence of large numbers of people who did not originate in Europe. The cultural adaptations of both fragments were affected by this fact; the relations between them were to a great extent determined by this fact; and the triumph of the first was promoted by this fact. Today the Afrikaner nationalists, victorious over Great Britain and the British South Africans, find the fruits of their victory being challenged by Africans.

On a longer view, therefore, the chief ingredients of South African history are more like those of Latin America. The succession of one European fragment by another and the relations between the two fragments are secondary phenomena in South Africa. The primary phenomenon is that both have been established amidst more numerous peoples of non-European origin.

In Latin America tendencies toward the creation of a horizontally stratified system of endogamous classes, distinguished by skin color, were offset by other factors and the dominant trend has been the interpenetration of Iberian, Amerind, and Negroid cultures and peoples. In South Africa such factors were always weaker, and the country has become an absolute pigmentocracy. So in 1961 the Afrikaner Nationalists severed South Africa's last political links with Europe and steeled themselves to suppress internal opposition and to fend off foreign pressures.

2   Holland and the Afrikaner

The Afrikaner people are the product of fragmentation from Dutch society in the second half of the seventeenth century. The Dutch Republic, triumphant from its war of independence from Spain, was a loose agglomeration of oligarchic corporations, municipalities, and provinces. In the inland provinces the feudal nobility were still powerful; but in the more populous and dynamic maritime provinces a new class of merchant princes had risen to the top, and it was they who were dominant at the national level. Dutch society was the most mobile and competitive in Europe. It offered great economic opportunities to a man of talent and industry; and he who seized them could, regardless of his origins, acquire social standing and even, if a member of the Reformed church, a share of political authority; but the majority of the Dutch people remained ignorant and poor. It was also an absorptive society, continuously enriched by refugees—Protestants from Germany, France, and England, and Jews from Spain and Portugal. It was an outward-looking society, drawing most of its wealth from the herring fisheries, the sea-carrying trade of Europe, the slave trade from Africa to America, the spice and textile trade from Asia, and the investments of foreigners in the Amsterdam banks. It was a Christian society, for the Reformed church had provided the initial spur to independence and possessed considerable influence. Disputes within the church had resulted in the victory of the primitive Calvinists, who had worsted the liberal Remonstrants at the Synod of Dort, imprisoned Grotius, and encompassed the judicial murder of Oldenbarneveldt. But the church had not managed to inspire the civil authorities with its own intolerance, nor to curb the expression of the genius of Rembrandt and Vondel, Descartes and Spinoza, nor to eliminate the humanistic tradition of the Brethren of the Common Life and Erasmus from the schools and universities. Indeed, the republic was a seedbed of the rational spirit which was to flower in the European Enlightenment of the eighteenth century. Such was the society from which the Afrikaner people was born.

In 1602 Dutch traders who had been competing with one another to exploit the sea route to Asia combined their resources to form the Dutch East India Company, which was given a monopolistic charter by the States-General. By 1652 the company had built up a most profitable trade with Asia, but it suffered heavy human losses from scurvy on the long voyage to and from Batavia, so it founded a refreshment station at the Cape of Good Hope. To the end of its existence, the company valued the Cape settlement for this purpose and this purpose only. South African produce was worth little in Europe in comparison with Eastern spices and textiles, and the Cape pages in the company's ledgers almost always showed a deficit.

In 1657 the company freed nine of its sailors and soldiers from their contracts and gave them land in Rondebosch, hoping it would be cheaper to buy their produce than to continue to be directly responsible for agriculture. Thereafter over the years a considerable number of company servants took their discharge at the Cape. On occasion the company also sent groups of settlers to the Cape from the Netherlands, including a few orphan girls to make wives for the men and about one hundred and sixty Huguenots (men, women, and children), who were among those who fled from France after the revocation of the Edict of Nantes. In 1691 there were about a thousand "free burghers"—men, women, and children—by 1795, about seventeen thousand. Today's Afrikaner people (who may be defined as white South Africans whose mother tongue is Afrikaans) are descended very largely from the thousand of 1691 and almost entirely from the seventeen thousand of 1795.

According to Theal, the thousand of 1691 were approximately two-thirds of Dutch origin, one-sixth of French, and one-seventh of German, and most of the remainder were Swedes, Danes, and Belgians; and the proportions were much the same in 1795.[1] This cannot be far wrong, though it is probable that the German element was somewhat stronger than Theal estimated. However, except for the small minority who came as assisted emigrants, virtually all of them had a period of service in the Dutch East India Company before becoming free burghers. The fragment was primarily Dutch in origin.

Men with the ability to make good in the Netherlands rarely entered the service of the Dutch East India Company, where the pay was bad and the death rate high. Rewards were better and life was more secure in the Netherlands. As O. F. Mentzel put it, referring to his own experience when he enlisted in 1732, "Men who enlist as soldiers or sailors under the conditions offered by the Company are as a rule down at heel and practically destitute." [2] Many of them were completely illiterate, and few could have had more than a rudimentary education. Of the fourteen free burghers who petitioned Governor van Riebeeck for improved conditions in 1658, only seven were able to sign their names.[3] The Huguenots had been stripped of their property owing to the intolerance of the French Government, but they were a more cultured and talented group, and they alone of the South African settlers were actuated by a religious idealism comparable with that of New England. With that exception, the progenitors of the Afrikaner people were drawn almost exclusively from elements which had failed to prosper in the free, competitive society of the Netherlands.

The South African fragment, therefore, was not a microcosm of seventeenth-century Dutch society. It was an inferior, partial selection from it. The cultural attainments and interests of Dutch society—the art, the literature, the spirit of scientific enquiry—were almost completely absent from the fragment. What were present were the toughness of the peasant and the unsuccessful townsman, their capacity to endure adverse circumstances, and their receptivity to a simplified version of the gloomy doctrines of primitive Calvinism. Those qualities were invaluable in their struggle to adapt themselves to a harsh environment, where wild animals were a constant menace, Bushmen and Hottentots were liable to steal their property, the rainfall was unreliable, the soil was generally poor, crops and livestock were subject to strange diseases, and the government was not much concerned with their welfare.

182

The company sought to mold the free burghers into a Dutch community. No language but Dutch was officially recognized. No church but the Dutch Reformed church was allowed to exist until 1780, when a Lutheran congregation was formed. No schools were allowed to exist other than those controlled by the church. The result was that the Germans and Scandinavians were easily assimilated. And so, after some initial resistance, were the Huguenots. On their arrival they had been scattered among the Dutch farmers, from Stellenbosch to Drakenstein, and within a generation they abandoned the French language and even pronounced their French names in the Dutch manner. Notwithstanding their diverse national, linguistic, and religious origins, the free burghers became a single community. But it was not a Dutch community. Not only were many ingredients of seventeenth-century Dutch society absent from the South African settlers, but also the settlers themselves experienced a profound cultural mutation in the South African environment.

During the time of Jan van Riebeeck, the first governor, the company began to import slaves to the Cape from tropical Africa and Madagascar, Indonesia and India, and many of them were acquired by free burghers, who also made use of Hottentots and Bushmen as shepherds and cattle-herds. Therefore the free burghers were never an autonomous community, but a community dependent on nonwhite labor. Like other slave-owning communities, they despised manual and domestic work as servile work; and they did not generate an artisan class. Indeed, with the exception of those who lived in Cape Town, virtually all the free burghers were farmers, so that in the course of time the name of an occupation, *Boer* (farmer), became applied to the entire Afrikaner people. Moreover, since their government was a trading corporation with a monopoly of the external trade of the colony, they turned their backs upon the sea, which was the lifeblood of the Netherlands; and since it was concerned with profits for its shareholders and not with the welfare of its subjects, the free burghers developed no sense of obligation to political authority. Already by the end of the seventeenth

183

century these factors were creating a gulf between the free burghers at the Cape and their kinsfolk in Europe.

The gulf widened in the eighteenth century. Previously the company had sought to confine the burghers within a distance of about fifty miles from Cape Town, hoping, like the government of New France at the same time and the government of New South Wales at a later stage, to create a compact and easily controllable agricultural settlement. This policy led to an economic crisis. The company was virtually the only buyer of colonial produce. Its needs were limited to provisioning the garrison and ships in harbor, for there was little cargo space available for the transport of Cape produce to Europe or Asia. Furthermore, the company fixed the prices for burgher produce and company servants themselves farmed for personal profit and had privileged access to the limited market. By 1700 the burghers were producing an unmarketable surplus. They therefore had a strong incentive to reduce their dependence upon the company and become, as nearly as possible, subsistence farmers; and that is what they did. Beyond the agricultural settlement lay a vast expanse of land, sparsely populated by weak Hottentot tribes and small Bushman bands, much of it suitable for extensive pastoral farming. The company gave way, allowing burghers to take occupation of large tracts of land in return for small annual licenses, which were not in fact always enforced. Consequently from 1700 onward many burghers moved from the original area of settlement to the north and the east, to become *trekboers*—seminomadic farmers. By 1795 they were thinly spread over a vast area, extending nearly to the Orange River in the north, where they were checked by aridity, and to the Fish River in the east, where they were checked by a formidable human barrier—the Bantu-speaking African tribes. It cannot be said that they had tamed this wilderness: they had merely occupied it. In the eighteenth century the *trekboers* were relatively unobserved. Their importance lies in the fact that they were the ancestors of most of the *Voortrekkers* of the eighteen-thirties and eighteen-forties, and of the republican Boers of the second half of the nineteenth century; and it is the *trekboer* and *Voortrekker* tradition that has become the heroic element in the modern Afrikaner national mythology. This was the second phase in the differentiation of the Afrikaner from the Hollander.

The company was always concerned to maintain its hold over the Cape peninsula, with its Table Bay anchorage sheltered from the southeast wind which prevails in summer and its False Bay anchorage sheltered from the winter north-wester; and to extract what revenue it could from the external and internal trade of the colony. Its administrative system was a mixture of autocracy and negligence. Nearly all its employees were concentrated in the peninsula. Its supreme local authority—the Council of Policy—consisted exclusively of officials. As a matter of convenience it allowed a few burghers to sit on the High Court when burgher cases came before the court, and it became customary for the Council of Policy to consult these "burgher councillors" when it was considering burgher affairs. These men were not elected. When a vacancy occurred, the existing burgher councillors submitted two names to the council, which nominated one of them. That was all that was done to give the burghers a say in central administration. Dutch colonists were given no more training for the assumption of political responsibilities than were the colonists of Spain, Portugal, or France. Local administration away from the Cape peninsula was another matter. There the company had no interests and it provided scarcely any services. As the frontiers of settlement advanced, it created districts—Stellenbosch (1679), Swellendam (1746) and Graaff-Reinet (1786)—and to each of them it sent a landdrost—an all-purpose official—and perhaps a clerk and a handful of soldiers. In theory each district was administered by the landdrost in collaboration with unpaid heemraden and veld cornets drawn from the burgher community. In practice they were scarcely administered at all, for the districts were vast and the means of communication primitive. For example, the only court with criminal jurisdiction in the entire colony was the High Court, which sat in Cape Town. The result was that most crimes went unpunished and a high proportion of the land tax was unpaid. There was a similar situation in military affairs. All burghers were subject to conscription to help the garrison defend the peninsula against seaborne invasion; but beyond the peninsula the burghers were left to improvise their own defense against Bushmen and Africans, which they did by forming commandos. In these circumstances the impact of the rule of law diminished in proportion to the distance from Cape Town. The farmers, and more particularly the *trekboers,* were a law unto themselves. The company did little for them, and expected little of them.

The burghers who lived in Cape Town were intimately involved in the cash nexus. Petty traders and innkeepers, their prosperity rose and fell with the size of the garrison and the number of ships in harbor. No fortunes were accumulated, and Cape Town produced no *haute bourgeoisie* comparable with that of the Netherlands or the English colonies in North America. The agricultural farmers in the Cape peninsula and the settlements of Roodezand (Tulbagh), Zwartland (Malmesbury), Drakenstein, and Stellenbosch were less involved in a money economy. Though they sold their surplus wine, wheat, and vegetables as best they could, they learned to guard against the unsatisfactory market conditions by producing most of their needs on their estates. The *trekboers* were still less dependent on the market. Unlike the Australian pastoralists of the nineteenth century, they had no connection with a European industry. Their needs were few. If possible they kept regular supplies of sugar, tea, coffee, and, above all, ammunition; and once or twice in a lifetime they bought a gun and a wagon. They obtained these things from traveling traders, and paid for them in cash received from the sale of cattle and sheep on the hoof to agents of the men who held the monopoly of the colonial meat trade.

The Dutch Reformed church played a more positive part in shaping the Afrikaners than the civil administration. Reformed congregations were constituted at Cape Town (1665), Stellenbosch (1686), Drakenstein (1691), Roodezand (1743), Zwartland (1745), and Graaff-Reinet (1792). The Reformed ministers were employees of the company. The president of the church council of each congregation was a senior company official, and the elders were appointed annually by the Council of Policy from a double list submitted by the outgoing church council. Consequently, the ecclesiastical establishment was a branch of the government. In matters of faith and discipline, however, the colonial churches were subject to the classis of Amsterdam, which was jealous of its prerogatives and prevented a colonial classis from developing. Its doctrine was primitive Calvinism as embodied in the Heidelberg catechism and the decrees of the Synod of Dort. This doctrine—with its emphasis upon the Old Testament and predestination, its rejection of emotionalism, and its embryonic nationalism—was peculiarly suited to the taste of the white community in South Africa, struggling to survive in a stern environment and accustomed from birth to treating nonwhite peoples as slaves, or serfs, or enemies. In South Africa, unlike Holland, its influence was not moderated by other influences. South Africa knew nothing of the eighteenth-century Enlightenment, scarcely anything of the evangelical movement. The image which the Afrikaners had of themselves, of their place in the world, of their relations with others, was a primitive Calvinist image.[4]

By 1795 the European roots of the white South African community were almost completely severed. Most of its members were South Africans of at least the third generation. Very few of them had ever visited Europe, or were in communication with anyone in Europe. They were white Africans. Sheer distance and the dangers and discomforts of the voyage to Europe were not the only causes of this separation. Within two years of their emancipation the first free burghers were protesting to Governor van Riebeeck that "instead of being helped, we are oppressed."[5] In the first decade of the eighteenth century there was a vigorous protest against the administration of Governor Adriaan van der Stel. In the seventeen-seventies "patriots" of the southwestern Cape signed a petition and sent delegates to protest to the directors and the States-General. And in 1795 the *trekboers* of Graaff-Reinet expelled the company's representative and declared their district to be an independent republic, and so did the *trekboers* of Swellendam. These were merely the high points in a relationship which was always essentially disharmonious.

187

The company was a commercial enterprise. Its directors were concerned with the interests of the shareholders, which were inexorably opposed to those of the colonists. Consequently no loyalty to the Dutch East India Company developed within the white South African community, and there was nothing to preserve a sense of kinship with the people of the Netherlands.

The divorce of the South African fragment from the society from which it originated is illustrated by the changes that took place in the spoken language in South Africa. Deviation from Dutch began early in the eighteenth century and continued unchecked. O. F. Mentzel, who was there from 1733 to 1741, noted "The language of the Country people is . . . far from being pure Dutch." [6] Henry Lichtenstein, there from 1803 to 1806, wrote of the "African Dutch language." [7] Many of the inflections disappeared from the article, the adjective, the pronoun, and the verb. Dutch words which were not related to the needs and experience of the people fell into disuse, and words of Portuguese, Malay, and Hottentot origin were adopted. A new language, Afrikaans, came into being; and, with it, the Afrikaner people.

In other respects, too, the Afrikaners differed remarkably from the Hollanders. To the end of the eighteenth century the Afrikaners produced no literature, no painting, no music. The one distinguished art form in the colony was the architecture of some of the public and private buildings, but they were designed by Europeans, notably L. M. Thibault (who arrived at the Cape as an officer in a Swiss mercenary regiment in 1783), and executed by slave artisans. The Afrikaners looked inland to the dry karroo, not outward to the sea. Cape Town was the only place remotely resembling a city in the colony, and *trekboers* rarely if ever visited it. The educational facilities of the colony were very meager. A solitary high school was founded in 1714, only to cease in 1725 for lack of support, and it had no successor.[8] A very few of the most prosperous colonists sent their children to Europe for schooling. Nearly everyone had to rely on the elementary schools, or employ tutors, or teach his children what he could himself. The elementary schools were controlled by the church councils and at best they provided a rudimentary knowledge of the three R's. The tutors were mostly men who had come to the colony in the service of the company; and while some of them were highly literate, the majority had no more than a smattering of knowledge and were ne'er-do-wells who gave the name "meester" a pejorative meaning which endured in South Africa until the twentieth century. Consequently, although most Afrikaners in Cape Town and the agricultural belt could read and write, there were various shades of semiliteracy and illiteracy among the *trekboers,* and in all South Africa there was nothing approaching an intellectual circle. The Afrikaners were poorly educated in comparison with the settlers in Spanish America and in the English colonies in North America.

The social unit within the frontiers of white settlement was the patriarchal white family and its nonwhite dependents. On the agricultural estates this was sometimes a large unit, since there were as many as a hundred slaves on some estates. Among the *trekboers* the unit was much smaller, comprising the white family, perhaps a slave or two and a captured Bushman or two, and probably a few Hottentots. Rarely was a white family a self-sufficient entity.

Within the Afrikaner community there was much social mobility. With no opportunity to accumulate great wealth, and with land available for the taking, there were no clear-cut class distinctions. A young white man lacking inherited resources could become a *knecht*—a farm manager—and build up his own flock of sheep, and then set out on his own as a *trekboer.* One man was as good as another, provided his skin was white. Nevertheless, there were gradations within the community. At the top a few people benefited from the company's system of auctioning exclusive rights to deal in key commodities. Late in the eighteenth century Dirk Gysbert van Reenen, the grandson of a German immigrant, frequently held a share in the wine and meat contracts as purveyor to the company, and he also had a monopoly of

189

beer production. On that basis he owned or had the use of eleven farms at a time—from the Cape peninsula to the Swellendam district. He was a progressive farmer, interested in breeding improved strains of horses, sheep, and cattle, and an agreeable companion to visiting travelers from Europe. But van Reenen's prosperity was a by-product of the company's monopolistic system, and it collapsed with it. When he died in 1828 he was "notoriously bankrupt." [9] At the other end of the scale were the most remote *trekboers*. These were the people who persuaded the government to recall their first landdrost, M. H. O. Woeke, in 1792, and drove out their second, H. C. D. Maynier, in 1795, not for any valid reason, but because they were so accustomed to being a law unto themselves that when the company did eventually appoint a landdrost to Graaff-Reinet they were chronically unable to co-operate with him, though his policy was designed to promote their interests. [10] Even if one discounts strictures from British pens, on the assumption that they were moved by bias, [11] one should not ignore Dutch and German assessments. O. F. Mentzel, who was German, deplored their ignorance and dullness, found they had a "kind of secret hatred toward the Europeans," and feared that without a continuous infusion of fresh European blood "the African [sic] nation would degenerate and become uncivilized." [12] After touring the hinterland in 1768, J. W. Cloppenburg, who was the company's official next in rank to the governor, expressed similar views. [13] And in 1803 Henry Lichtenstein, a German in the service of General Janssens, Governor of the colony for the Batavian Republic, reported of the people of Graaff-Reinet:

Selfishness, lawlessness, hardiness, intolerance, and a thirst for revenge, are the reigning vices of their character, which will perhaps hardly be thought atoned by a disposition to be easily satisfied, by a spirit of economy yet united with unbounded hospitality, a firm adherence to truth, and a great respect for religion. But what is most to be deprecated in the character of some among them, is the harshness with which they treat their slaves and Hottentots, and in others, the bitterness and irreconcilable animosity with which they carry on their differences among each other. [14]

190

Thus by the end of the eighteenth century the South African fragment of European society had crystallized into a new community, with a distinctive culture. Ruled by a commercial company which exploited them economically and neglected them in other respects, they had turned their backs upon the sea and rejected Europe. Lacking incentives to accumulate capital or expand production for market, but with land and alien labor readily available, they formed the upper class in a loose-knit multiracial society of subsistence and near-subsistence farmers—a social order for which they found divine sanction in their religion. They had become Afrikaners—white Africans—speaking a new, simple language and conditioned to stark sunlight, unreliable rainfall, and vast distances. They were tough, unimaginative, and isolated—not only from Europe, but also from their government; and in most cases so isolated from one another that they lacked a corporate spirit. To this day there are Afrikaners living in small, remote communities, separated from others by mountain, forest, or desert, who describe their valley as "Onse Wêreld" (Our World). This saying epitomizes the Afrikaner people before the British conquest.

3 The British Impact

It was inevitable that new forces emanating from Europe should impinge upon this backward society during the nineteenth century. The crucial question was whether they would bring it into some sort of harmony with the modern world, or whether the Afrikaner people would generate the will and the power to resist such a process. The reaction of Afrikaners to some of the reforms introduced by the Batavian Republic (1803-1806) showed that the process of modernization would have been difficult, even under a Dutch administration. As it was, in 1795 and again in 1806 the Dutch were ousted from the Cape by the British, who wanted to make use of its harbors and deny their use to France; and Britain retained the Cape at the end of the Napoleonic wars.

The British South African community was founded in the

191

next fifty years, during which Britain was the wealthiest and the most powerful country in the world. Like seventeenth-century Holland, nineteenth-century Britain was a dynamic, outward-looking society. Unlike Holland, Britain derived its wealth not only from maritime commerce, but also from the application of technological advances to industrial production; and the resultant increase in productivity was marred by the sufferings of occupationally displaced people in all parts of the British Isles. If the dominant assumptions had been different, the human cost might have been less disastrous. As it was, free competition was assumed to be the necessary means to material progress and the state did little to mitigate distress. Britain's age of world leadership was also, therefore, a bleak age, which nearly produced an irreparable schism in British society. That it did not do so was due to three factors. One was that the strata in British society never had been separated by impenetrable barriers, and social mobility continued to exist throughout the nineteenth century. Another was that callousness and irresponsibility were checked by a sense of Christian morality, which had recently been reinvigorated by the evangelical movement. Equality before the law, freedom of speech, publication, and assembly, and immunity from arbitrary arrest and imprisonment were regarded as desirable standards, however much they were thwarted in practice. And thirdly, there was always the safety valve of mass emigration.

Between 1815 and 1870 seven million people emigrated from the British Isles. Most of them went to the United States and to Canada, and did so without official aid. In the eighteen-thirties and eighteen-forties Edward Gibbon Wakefield and his associates diverted some of this flood to Australia and New Zealand, and soon afterward gold discoveries attracted an unaided stream to those countries. Before 1870, however, assistance was given only sporadically and on a small scale for emigration to South Africa, and the country exerted no strong attraction to unaided immigrants. Consequently the South African share of the seven million British emigrants was fewer than fifty thousand people.[15]

Before 1820 there were no more than one or two thousand

British settlers in South Africa, most of them in the vicinity of Cape Town.[16] By then, however, the colonial government had become embroiled in the problem of the eastern frontier, where Afrikaner settlement was too sparse to contain the African tribes without the assistance of a large garrison. The government therefore decided to try to establish a compact agricultural settlement of British immigrants in the Albany district west of the Fish River, in the hope that they would stabilize the frontier, and in due course exert a leavening influence upon the Afrikaners and a civilizing influence upon the Africans. Advertisements were placed in the British press calling for applications from men who were able to organize parties of settlers. They were to pay ten pounds for every adult, in return for which their parties would be taken to South Africa and granted land at the rate of ten acres per adult, free of rent for ten years. Applications were received for ninety thousand passages, but only four thousand people were actually dispatched, for Parliament had voted only fifty thousand pounds for the scheme. Another thousand joined the migrants at their own expense, so that the 1820 settlers numbered about five thousand men, women, and children.

The compact settlement did not materialize. The Albany district was not suited to intensive agriculture, and the settlers gradually dispersed; but most of them eventually made good—some as farmers, others as traders, artisans, and professional men—in the eastern districts of the Cape Colony and in "Kaffirland" beyond the Fish River. For the next quarter-century there was little further immigration. In the years 1848 to 1850 another four thousand were assisted to migrate to the colony by the Colonial Land and Emigration Commissioners, and from 1857 to 1863 the colonial government provided funds which brought in another ten thousand. By then the 1820 settlers were well established, and they formed the nucleus around which the later British immigrants cohered.*

* The 1865 Cape Colony census showed 181,600 white people in the colony, of whom 26,300 were stated to have been born in Europe. Of the latter, some 3,500 were German immigrants and most of the rest were from Britain. H. M. Robertson, "South Africa," in B. Thomas, ed., *Economics of International Migration* (London, 1958), p. 176.

Meanwhile Britain had taken possession of Natal in 1843. Most of the Afrikaner *Voortrekkers* recrossed the Drakensberg mountains soon afterward, to what became the Orange Free State and the South African Republic. A few British traders had been at Port Natal since the eighteen-twenties, but until 1849 the British population was minute. In that year J. C. Byrne, a British speculator, made an agreement with the Colonial Land and Emigration Commissioners to transport to Natal emigrants of whom the commissioners approved, in return for the acquisition of large landholdings there. He then offered prospective emigrants steerage passages and twenty acres of land for ten pounds. Intermediate passengers were to pay nineteen pounds and cabin passengers thirty-five. Though Byrne soon went bankrupt, his scheme, a number of smaller similar schemes, and independent settlers made a total British immigration to Natal in the years 1849 and 1850 of about five thousand men, women, and children. There was very little immigration into Natal for the next six years, and when it was resumed it was on the basis of nomination by established settlers of friends and relations for assisted passages.[17] The Natal settlers of 1849-1850 like the Albany settlers of 1820 were the nucleus of a new British colonial community.

These South African fragments of nineteenth-century British society were distinguishable from the mass movement across the North Atlantic to America. Like the New Zealand fragments, they were the product of a selective system. The 1820 settlers were selected from ninety thousand applicants. They were organized in parties, some of which comprised a leader and men who were indentured to him for a number of years, while in others each man paid his own deposit and was personally entitled to his hundred acres. About forty-nine per cent of them had previously been connected with farming, thirty-one per cent had been artisans or mechanics, eleven per cent had been in commerce or trade, five per cent in the army, the navy, or the merchant marine, and four per cent in the professions.[18] There was a similar range among the Natal settlers. The South African fragments came from all parts of the British Isles, all classes of British society, a

194

wide range of occupations, and several different religious denominations. Like the North Atlantic migrants of the same period, however, they were all people for whom, for one or other reason, life had become unpalatable in bleak-age Britain. And like others who had gone to British colonies over the previous two centuries, they considered that they took with them the common law of England, and they aspired to the freedoms which were respected, if not always applied, in Britain.

4   The Great Trek and After

At the time of their juxtaposition in South Africa, there was a wide gulf between the Afrikaner and the British fragments. The Afrikaner fragment was more numerous, self-reliant, and cohesive, but it was preindustrial and deficient in education. The British fragment was the product of an industrialized society and could count upon some support from the imperial government at Westminster, but it still had to adapt itself to the South African environment, it was divided between separate areas of settlement, and it had the internal tensions of the nineteenth-century British class structure.

Initially the British settlers brought a fresh breeze of modernity to South Africa and performed a creative role. They led a successful struggle against the official autocracy for freedom of the press, for the introduction of the jury system, and for representative institutions. They laid the foundations of a modern educational system. They supplied the administrators who gave the civil service of the Cape Colony a distinguished record. They introduced new strains of cattle and sheep, and made wool an important export. They built roads and harbors. They established a commercial and banking network throughout South Africa. And they provided the majority of the missionaries who worked among the colored and African peoples.[19] But outside the economic and educational fields their creative impulse was soon spent, for reasons which will appear.

195

It was not easy for the Afrikaner fragment to adjust to the British conquest of the Cape Colony, especially when the government began to introduce reforms after the end of the Napoleonic wars. The *trekboers,* in particular, were dismayed to find the rule of law being applied to them, and with it the concept of equality before the law; and also by the failure of the government to subdue the African tribes who were pressing upon the eastern frontier of the colony. The result was that in 1836 and the succeeding years some twelve thousand Afrikaners—most of them *trekboers*—moved out of the colony with their wagons, their sheep, their cattle, and their servants, to escape British control. Britain soon annexed Natal—the first *Voortrekker* republic—but recognized the independence of the *Voortrekkers* in the Transvaal (1852) and the Orange Free State (1854). South Africa was thus partitioned between Britain and the *Voortrekkers*. But the partition did not separate the fragments: most of the Afrikaners remained in the Cape Colony, where they continued to form a majority of the white population; and British and Jewish traders established themselves in the republics.

During the intervening years, there have been periods when the gulf between the two fragments has appeared to be closing. Intermarriages have taken place; the fringe of the Afrikaner fragment has become Anglicized and the fringe of the British fragment has become Afrikanerized. There are Smiths who are Afrikaners and van der Byls who are British South Africans. Nevertheless, there has always been a hard core of each fragment which has regarded the other with suspicion and hostility and which forms a virtually endogamous community, distinguished by its language, its religious and secular associations, and its loyalties.

Before the Great Trek the loyalty of the Afrikaner was focused upon his parochial community in the Cape Colony. The *Voortrekker* was loyal to his trek party and its leader, later to his republic and its president; and today most Afrikaners are dedicated to the cause of the Afrikaner people and its instruments, notably the Afrikaner Nationalist Party and its leader. At this point Afrikaner loyalty has ceased to expand; but it has become exceptionally intense. The Afrikaner people have become a nation, in reaction to the challenge presented by Great Britain and the British settlers. Its loyalty has become monolithic. The British South African, on the other hand, has not been prone to concentrate his loyalty upon a single object, but has found room for a plurality of loyalties, including the British Empire and Commonwealth. The British fragment has certainly not become a nation. In a world where the nation-state has been in the ascendancy, the Afrikaner has been able to claim a virtue in the territorial limitation of his own loyalty and a vice in the extraterritorial loyalties of the British South African; whereas the British South African has been able to claim a virtue in his greater comprehensiveness and a vice in the exclusiveness of the Afrikaner, whose nation comprises only three-fifths of the white population and less than one-eighth of the total population of the state.

In the absence of common loyalties the relations between the cores of the two fragments have been continuously competitive and intermittently hostile. In this struggle for supremacy, the integrity of the Afrikaner core has been threatened by three main factors: immigration, economic change, and education. The Afrikaner has always been anxious lest his numerical superiority over the British South African should vanish. It was not seriously endangered before the last quarter of the nineteenth century. Then, however, large numbers of immigrants came from Britain and other parts of Europe to operate the diamond mines of Griqualand West and the gold mines of the Witwatersrand, and around the turn of the century it seemed as if the issue was in doubt. But in the twentieth century European immigration has been kept down to a level where, in conjunction with the greater reproduction rate of the Afrikaner and the far greater emigration rate of the British, the Afrikaner advantage has been preserved and increased. Consequently, the Afrikaner fragment has survived the peril of being swamped by the British fragment and is now secure in its numerical superiority.[20]

Secondly, the Afrikaner has faced the danger that economic change might destroy his cohesion, which was originally a function of his singleness of occupation in a preindustrial

197

economy. Already in the eighteen-thirties the continuity of the *trekboer* mode of life was threatened by human barriers on the eastern frontier and aridity on the northern. The Great Trek then made fresh land available for Afrikaner occupation on the high veld in the Orange Free State and the Transvaal, but by the end of the nineteenth century the *trekboer* mode of life had ceased to be attainable, because no more fresh land was available. This produced a class of poor whites, who used small portions of other men's farms and lacked the will or the training to pursue another occupation. However, as a result of the expansion of secondary industries, especially after 1936, the poor white became an industrial worker, protected by a color bar. Since the urban economy was initially controlled by the British fragment, this raised the further danger that the urban Afrikaner would be denationalized by the individualistic pressures of a predominantly British ethos. But the danger was successfully surmounted through the agency of the Dutch Reformed churches, Afrikaner social, cultural, and economic organizations, and the Nationalist Party, and eventually Afrikaners gained control of many of the trade unions and founded their own industries, building societies, insurance companies, and banks. So, while continuing to dominate the rural sector of the South African economy, the Afrikaner also went to town and acquired a significant share of the industrial sector. Moreover, although this process produced a class stratification, the Afrikaner nation retained much more cohesion than the British fragment ever had.

Thirdly, modern education threatened to undermine the Afrikaner fragment from within, since its original character was largely the product of isolation and ignorance. The first systematic education that the Afrikaner people received was provided in the public schools of the nineteenth-century Cape Colony, where most of the teachers were British and the English language was the principal medium of instruction. The result was that among the nineteenth-century colonial Afrikaners there was a broadening of horizons and a discernible trend toward Anglicization. By the end of the century, however, predikants had initiated a reaction in the Cape Colony,

198

and the colonial trend was being offset by a distinctively Afrikaner emphasis in the schools of the two republics. In the early twentieth century, following the South African war, Afrikaner resistance to Anglicization stiffened throughout South Africa. The Afrikaans language, hitherto merely a vernacular, began to replace Dutch as the literary medium of the people; nationalistic writings began to appear in it; and Christian National schools were founded in opposition to the public schools. More recently, the public schools of the Orange Free State, the Transvaal, and the Cape Province have come under Afrikaner control and provide Afrikaner youth with free and compulsory education in a thoroughly nationalist atmosphere; and Afrikaner universities at Stellenbosch, Pretoria, Potchefstroom, and Bloemfontein have become centers for the propagation of cultural and intellectual nationalism. So modern education has not undermined the Afrikaner fragment. On the contrary, it has become a vehicle for preserving and refining the Afrikaner tradition and transmitting an intense national spirit.

There have been three main phases in the relations between the fragments: a phase of British ascendancy, ending in 1905; a phase of approximate balance, ending in 1948; and a phase of Afrikaner ascendancy, still in progress.[21]

Throughout the nineteenth century the British fragment was assured of survival and of a general superiority throughout southern Africa by the power of Great Britain. The Great Trek and its aftermath did not destroy this position. To an extent, it is true, the *Voortrekkers* achieved their ambition of renouncing British rule and establishing their own governments; but Great Britain never ceased to regard their republics as falling within its sphere of influence and paramountcy. It cut them off from independent access to the sea and from expansion to the north, the west, and the south; it prevented them from uniting; and from 1877 to 1881 it ruled the Transvaal itself in an abortive attempt to coerce South Africa into a federal dominion on the Canadian model. Later, when the republics, strengthened by the proceeds of the Witwatersrand gold reef, did strive to make their formal independence a reality, Britain intervened, because it was not

199

willing to tolerate the growth of a truly autonomous center of power in southern Africa. It conquered the republics, reduced them to the status of crown colonies, and tried to destroy Afrikaner nationalism once and for all by swamping the Afrikaner fragment with British immigrants, by forcing the rate of economic change, and by educating the Afrikaners in a British mold. But, as we have seen, the Afrikaner fragment survived this onslaught. Indeed, the attempt boomeranged, because it stiffened the Afrikaner will to resist.

It must be emphasized that throughout this period nearly all the decisive initiatives came, not from the British fragment in South Africa, but from the British Government—its colonial secretaries such as Lord Carnarvon and Joseph Chamberlain, and its high commissioners such as Sir George Grey and Lord Milner. The only significant exception was Cecil Rhodes, who operated through the Cape political system. But Rhodes spent the first seventeen years of his life in England and thereafter he was always something of an exotic in South Africa, standing above rather than within the British South African community. By and large, the British South Africans, including the Transvaal *uitlanders,* were but pawns in the struggle for supremacy at the turn of the century. It was essentially a struggle between Great Britain and the Afrikaner republics. This meant that the British South Africans acquired the habit of looking beyond their own ranks for leadership and failed to develop a sense of ultimate responsibility for their own destiny. Consequently at a later stage, when the power of Great Britain ebbed from South Africa, they lacked the ability to make an independent appraisal of their role. Moreover, from their association with an attempt to denationalize the Afrikaners, they acquired a guilt complex which diminished their capacity to resist Afrikaner domination when the wheel turned full circle. Upon the Afrikaners, on the other hand, the period of British ascendancy left an indelible Anglophobia, directed not only against Great Britain, but also against its accomplice, the British fragment in South Africa.

The second phase started in 1905, with the accession to power in Britain of the Liberal Party under Sir Henry

Campbell-Bannerman. In varying degrees Campbell-Bannerman and most of his colleagues had been critical of their predecessors' South African policy, and they sought to make amends to the Boers by abandoning coercion, and thus to elicit their support for the Empire. They therefore gave the former republics self-government, with constitutions which enabled Afrikaner parties to gain power. For a time it seemed that this gamble would succeed. Louis Botha and J. C. Smuts, the Transvaal leaders, responded to the olive branch, pursuing a policy of conciliation between Boer and Briton, South Africa and England, and founding the Union of South Africa on that basis in 1910. In their view the two fragments were to coalesce into a single white South African nation, which would freely co-operate with the evolving British Empire. That they were sincere was demonstrated on the outbreak of the First World War, when they complied with a British request that South African troops should occupy German South-West Africa. This action gained them the confidence of the British fragment; but it was their undoing with their own people. J. B. M. Hertzog, the Orange Free State Afrikaner leader, had already seceded from Botha's party and founded an Afrikaner Nationalist Party. He differed from Botha and Smuts in two respects. Firstly, he was determined to preserve the integrity of the Afrikaner people, and he believed that the conciliation policy would not do this. He therefore stressed the need for protecting the Afrikaner from absorption, by educational and economic measures, until he could safely stand on his own feet in free competition with the British. Secondly, he was determined to remove all vestiges of the power of Great Britain over South Africa and to pursue a foreign policy designed exclusively and narrowly in the interests of South Africa. He gradually weaned the majority of the Afrikaners to his side, making Botha and Smuts increasingly dependent upon British support, and in 1924 he became prime minister. He then devised protective measures for the Afrikaner and promoted the decentralization of the British Empire into the Commonwealth. By 1933 he considered that his objectives had been achieved—that the Afrikaner fragment could safely afford to co-operate with the

British fragment without endangering its own survival; and since his party was losing ground on account of the depression, he formed a coalition with Smuts, leading to a fusion of parties. A large majority of the voters of both fragments endorsed the new United Party, and it seemed that the old tensions were at last subsiding. The honeymoon ended, however, on the outbreak of the Second World War, which Hertzog regarded as another war between rival European imperialisms, of no concern to South Africa, and Smuts as a conflict between good and evil, whose outcome would determine South Africa's future. Smuts's view prevailed by a small majority in Parliament, and he was able to form a government to wage war with the Allies against Nazi Germany. But the Second World War, like the first, exposed the deep cleavage between isolationists and internationalists in South Africa.

The third phase was inaugurated by the victory of the new Nationalist Party, led by D. F. Malan, in the general election of May, 1948. Afrikaner nationalism had not been eliminated in the honeymoon era. Malan and a few others had refused to follow Hertzog into fusion with Smuts and proclaimed their loyalty to the principles of Afrikaner nationalism. Even when they fared ill at the polls, their views had been cherished in ecclesiastical and academic circles, which, by 1948, had elaborated the traditional national mythology and brought it up to date. God had created the Afrikaner people and given them the mission to carry out His will in South Africa. Britain and her accomplices, the British South Africans, had persistently obstructed the Afrikaner. Botha and Smuts had been downright traitors in pursuing a policy which endangered the integrity of the nation. Hertzog, notwithstanding the value of his earlier contributions to the cause, had erred egregiously in co-operating with a man who had become an unrepentant jingo. The new Nationalist Party was the only political instrument for the expression of the true Afrikaner will. It was its function to gain control over every aspect of life in South Africa, to establish a second and greater South African Republic, and to sever all links with the Commonwealth. Compromise would be of no avail, for it would allow Britain to outwit the Afrikaner nation, as it had done in the past. Later on, once the position had been secured, it might be possible to admit the British South Africans to membership in the Afrikaner nation, but only provided that this was done without sacrificing one iota of principle. That is to say, the neo-Nationalist spirit was as far from the nationalism of Hertzog as the neoimperialism of Chamberlain and Milner had been from the "imperialism of free trade" of Palmerston and Gladstone.

Since 1948 a revolution has taken place in South Africa: a reactionary revolution, designed to ensure the survival of the Afrikaner nation, pure and unsullied; and a creeping revolution, which advanced step by step, in due constitutional form, by the enactment of laws, the placing of loyal men in key positions, and the silencing of opponents. Its relentless advance toward authoritarianism was marked by changes of leadership, from the ponderous Malan, to the shallow Strijdom, to the inflexible Verwoerd.

The extent of the revolution was obscured by the fact that South Africa's parliamentary institutions had been more closely modeled on the British example than those of the United States, Canada, or Australia. Since 1910 South Africa had been a legislative union, so that there were no insuperable legal obstacles to intervention in provincial affairs by the central government; and the constitution had been almost fully flexible, so that the will of bare parliamentary majorities was sufficient for the enactment of valid legislation in nearly every field, including amendments to most sections of the written constitution. These factors eased the path of the Nationalists. The conventions of the constitution were some embarrassment, insofar as they enabled opponents to delay legislation and created an expectation of a change of government. Consequently, the legal basis of parliamentary government was retained, but the conventions and the spirit were abandoned. Debate was abbreviated when expedient by the use of the guillotine, the kangaroo, and the closure; and Parliament became a rubber stamp for the legislative expression of the will of the party caucus. Laws were passed to ensure that elections should not threaten the regime: the white

203

voters of South-West Africa, predominantly of German and Afrikaner origin, were given seats in Parliament and more seats than their numbers warranted; Smuts's immigration scheme was scrapped; the Cape Colored voters were removed from the common roll and given the right to elect four white representatives to the House of Assembly; the Africans were deprived of their parliamentary representation; and the minimum age for white voters was reduced from twenty-one to eighteen. These measures, in conjunction with a districting system which had always favored the rural over the urban voters, destroyed any chance which the United Party might have had of ousting the Nationalists. Furthermore, the judiciary and the upper echelons of the armed forces, the police, and the civil service were largely Afrikanerized, in some cases by overt or covert dismissals, in others after normal retirements; Afrikaner youths were corralled into schools where they were indoctrinated; and opponents were intimidated by threats to withhold passports and import licenses and by arbitrary arrests. Beyond the range of direct governmental action, a plethora of organizations, from the secret Broederbond to the Jeugbond and the Dutch Reformed churches, enforced conformity upon Afrikaners. Then on May 21, 1961, the Afrikaner Nationalists attained their most precious objective: South Africa became a republic and left the Commonwealth.

The creeping revolution was experienced by a helpless and ineffective British fragment. Gone were the dreams of British domination which had been aroused by Milner. Gone was the hope of an equal partnership which had been offered by Botha and Smuts and Hertzog. Gone were the final political links with Britain.

In their place was a bleak prospect of permanent subordination to the Afrikaner nation. As the revolution unfolded, some talked of revenge, or of the secession of Natal, but they lacked the means to achieve it. Others continued to pin their hopes upon an electoral victory for the United Party, but it suffered increasingly severe defeats. And others again became numbed into apathy, or even found pretexts for supporting the Nationalists. So the British fragment began to amalgamate with the Afrikaner, on Afrikaner terms.

5   Racial Complexity

The presence of superior numbers of nonwhite peoples within the frontiers of white settlement in South Africa has always been a major determinant of the performances of both the white fragments.[22]

In their cradle days in the second half of the seventeenth century, the Afrikaner people used slave labor, imported from tropical Africa, Madagascar, and Asia, and local Hottentot labor. As the *trekboers* expanded north and east in the eighteenth century, they assumed occupation of land previously used by Hottentots and Bushmen, and as they did so they took some of the survivors into their service as shepherds and cattle-herds. The *Voortrekkers* of the nineteenth century acted similarly toward the Africans in the Orange Free State and the Transvaal, defeating them, permitting some of them to continue to live on their farms in return for labor services, and confining the surplus to attenuated tribal areas. The British settlers in the Cape Colony and Natal did much the same thing; and those who produced sugar along the Natal coast also imported Indians as estate laborers. Consequently, neither white fragment in South Africa ever was a self-sufficient community.

Nor, however, were they to any decisive extent biologically mixed communities, although miscegenation between whites and nonwhites inevitably took place in all periods of South African history. Many of the male partners in miscegenation were European soldiers and sailors, who were only temporarily stationed in South Africa; but others were Afrikaners and British South Africans. Formerly, young Afrikaner men frequently indulged in sexual experimentation with slave, Hottentot, or African women before they married, and some of them recorded the names of their illegitimate offspring on the rear flyleaves of their family Bibles and their legitimate offspring on the front flyleaves. Nevertheless, in the eighteenth and nineteenth centuries the Afrikaners waged intermittent warfare, first with Bushmen and then with Africans, to gain secure possession of land. Consequently, they regarded non-whites as enemies as well as servants and casual sexual partners, but never as equals. To them, nonwhiteness itself became a badge of inferiority; and they found religious vindication for this attitude in a perversion of the Calvinist doctrine of the elect and in selected texts from the Old Testament. Mixed marriages were therefore frowned upon and the offspring of mixed unions out of wedlock were generally rejected by the white community. Hence, for example, the emergence of the people originally known as the Bastards, later as the Griquas, who are the product of miscegenation between eighteenth-century *trekboers* and Hottentot women. The British settlers were not slow in acquiring a pride in color comparable with that of the Afrikaners. Those who came to the Cape Colony in 1820 did not know that they were settling on land which had long been in dispute between Afrikaners and Africans, and when they bore the main brunt of the frontier wars of the middle of the nineteenth century they became Negrophobic. Those in Natal were always conscious of the vast numerical preponderance of the Africans around them. In both cases, they rationalized their Negrophobia in terms of the evolutionary ideas which were current in Britain at that time.

In the preindustrial age, therefore, South African society within the frontiers of white settlement was a racially stratified society of white landowners and African, Colored, and Asian people, who owned little or no land themselves, but performed labor services in return for a subsistence.*

* Four main racial groups are now recognized in South Africa: (a) "Whites" or "Europeans," meaning people of, or reputed to be of, exclusive European descent, including Jews; (b) "Africans" or "Bantu" or "Natives," meaning the Bantu-speaking people whose ancestors entered southern Africa from the north by land; (c) "Coloured People," being the descendants of local Hottentots and Bushmen and of imported African and Asian slaves, with, in most cases, some European admixture; (d) "Asians," meaning people who came to South Africa from Asia (mostly from the Indian subcontinent) in and after 1860, and their descendants. For some purposes "Malays," Muslim descendants of Asian slaves, are distinguished from the "Coloured People" as a separate group.

Mining industries developed rather suddenly in South Africa in the late nineteenth century, following the discoveries of diamonds in Griqualand West (1867) and gold in the Transvaal (1885). Thanks to later gold discoveries in the Orange Free State, South Africa still produces nearly half of the world's annual supply of gold, which gives it a powerful position in international trade. In the present century, and more particularly since about 1935, South Africa has added a wide range of manufacturing industries, and her economy is now self-sustaining and by far the strongest and the most modern in Africa.

From the first the labor force in the mining and manufacturing industries was organized on a basis of color stratification. The industries are operated by white managers and skilled workers, and by nonwhite skilled workers who are drawn from all over southern Africa; and there is an exceptional gap between the wage rates of the whites (which are comparable with skilled rates in the United States) and the wage rates of the nonwhites.

Today South African society is horizontally stratified into endogamous classes. The dominant class has the lightest skin color, the middle class has an intermediate skin color, and the lowest class has the darkest skin color. Such a structure has points of conjunction with both European feudalism and the Indian caste system. But since the essential criterion of status in South Africa is skin color, which is absent from European feudalism and is not the essence of caste, South African society requires a different label. The word pigmentocracy seems most adequately to describe it. Many societies which were produced by European settlement in the last few centuries have had pigmentocratic features: the Republic of South Africa is an ideal pigmentocracy.

The republic contains three categories of territories, each of which has its roots in a particular historical culture: the "Bantu Areas," rooted in African tribalism, are scattered lands in the eastern half of the republic, forming what is left to the Africans of their original tribal holdings and amounting to about one-eighth of the total area of the republic; the "White Rural Areas," rooted in preindustrial pigmentocracy, comprise most of the arable and pastoral land in the republic; and the "Urban Areas" have emerged within the White Rural Areas as an industrial pigmentocracy. There is considerable mobility among the three categories of territories —mainly a movement of South Africans of all races from the country to the towns. Many Africans work as migrant laborers in the White Rural Areas and the Urban Areas for a number of years and then end their days in the Bantu Areas; but the number of Africans who have completely severed their connections with the Bantu Areas is continuously increasing. In 1960 the inhabitants of the republic were distributed as follows:[23]

POPULATION OF THE REPUBLIC OF SOUTH AFRICA (MILLIONS)

	Bantu Areas	White Rural Areas	Urban Areas	Total
Whites		0.5	2.6	3.1
Africans	4.0	3.4	3.5	10.9
Coloreds		0.5	1.0	1.5
Asians		0.1	0.4	0.5
Total	4.0	4.5	7.5	16.0

In the Cape Colony before the second quarter of the nineteenth century, the pigmentocratic structure was supported by law as well as by custom. Slavery was a legal institution from the time of van Riebeeck, the first governor, and the Hottentots were virtually outside the pale of the law until 1809, when they were given a serflike legal status. In 1828, however, "free persons of color"—*i.e.*, nonwhites who were not slaves—were given the same legal status as the whites in the Cape Colony; and in 1834 slavery was abolished throughout the British Empire, with the result that the Cape slaves immediately acquired the benefits of the 1828 ordinance, and so, later, did large numbers of Africans, who were incorporated in the colony when the Ciskeian and Transkeian territories were annexed in the second half of the nineteenth century. When the Cape Parliament was founded in 1854, the franchise was made available to any man, irrespective of race, who possessed specific economic qualifications. Thereafter, although some discriminatory laws were enacted, including laws which made it difficult for Africans living in their tribal areas to acquire the franchise, relations between the races within the frontiers of white settlement in the Cape Colony were determined by custom more than by law and were fairly relaxed and humane. Some colored and African men surpassed some of the least successful whites, but generally speaking the social order remained pigmentocratic.

The *Voortrekkers* left the Cape Colony in the eighteen-thirties and eighteen-forties largely because they were not prepared to submit to the elimination of legal barriers against nonwhites. As the constitution of the South African Republic put it: "The people are not prepared to allow any equality of the nonwhite with the white inhabitants, either in Church or State." [24] This principle was rigorously maintained in both the Afrikaner republics; and in the British colony of Natal also, there was a considerable amount of legal discrimination.

The result was that when they founded the Union of South Africa in 1910 white South Africans were generally agreed that they should preserve their position of dominance, but they differed as to the means of achieving this. Most northeners, British as well as Afrikaners, wished to keep legal barriers between themselves and nonwhites; most southerners, Afrikaners as well as British, were content to rely mainly upon custom, even though that permitted an occasional breach of the pigmentocratic order. They therefore founded the Union upon a compromise: they left the colonial laws, including the colonial franchise laws, as they were, pending their alteration by the Union Parliament; but on the one hand they debarred nonwhites from becoming members of Parliament, and on the other hand they protected the franchise rights of nonwhites in the Cape Province by providing that they should not be amended without the consent of two-thirds of the members of both houses of Parliament.

At that time, however, there was no conspicuous challenge to white supremacy in South Africa. The last African tribes had been conquered, the last tribal rebellions quelled, and not many Africans had become permanent inhabitants of the towns. Furthermore, only a few nonwhites were seriously concerned about politics, and they were asking only that those of them who were "civilized" should be admitted, as individuals, to the privileges of the whites.

After 1910, as the preindustrial pigmentocracy became increasingly overladen by the industrial pigmentocracy, the situation became more tense. Until 1948 the successive governments of South Africa responded by applying a policy which they called Segregation. In practice this amounted to improvising additional legal barriers against nonwhites in areas where the pigmentocratic order seemed most vulnerable. The Cape Colored people, who did not present a serious challenge, were left as they were, "an appendage of the white population." Further Asian immigration was prohibited and the existing Asian community was subjected to severe restrictions. Africans were by law debarred from obtaining fresh land outside the existing reserves, confined to unskilled work in the mining industries, and subjected to stringent controls in the towns. Those Africans who were voters in the Cape Province were taken off the common roll and given the right to elect three whites to represent them in the House of Assembly; and Africans throughout the Union were given the right indirectly to elect four senators, and a Natives' Representative Council, which the government could consult when it wished.

This segregation policy was promoted, rather than impeded, by organized white labor. British immigrants had brought trade-unionism with them to South Africa toward the end of the nineteenth century, but once they were there most of them concentrated upon securing privileges for their own group: better working conditions, the right to collective bargaining, and, above all, the maintenance of a white monopoly of skilled employment. The benefits of pigmentocracy overshadowed any broader socialist principles they might have had. Leading trade-unionists founded the South African Labor Party in 1910, with membership confined to whites and a frankly segregationist program. White workers also organized the first industrial disturbances. The most serious of those disturbances—the Witwatersrand "rebellion" of 1921, with a death toll of two hundred and forty-seven—was precipitated because the gold-mining corporations had decided to rationalize the industry by opening up more advanced types of work to nonwhites. The Smuts government proclaimed martial law and suppressed the rebellion, whereupon the Labor Party made an agreement with Hertzog's Nationalists and became the junior partner in his government of 1924 to 1929. Thereafter power in many trade unions began to pass into the hands of Afrikaners, who were being drawn to the towns in increasing numbers, and most of them found their natural political home in the Nationalist Party, first of Hertzog and later of Malan, while most British urban workers were drawn into Smuts's party after the outbreak of the First World War, leaving Labor with dwindling support. The only political party that transcended the color bar was the Communist Party, which was founded by secessionist trade-unionists in 1921. But the Communist Party of South Africa was the victim of successive directives from Moscow, reflecting the shifts of Russian policy, and it made no headway among the white electorate. So socialism, whether of the Russian or the Western variety, fell upon stony ground among white South Africans.

Nevertheless, by the end of the Second World War it had become apparent that it was extremely difficult to maintain a pigmentocratic order in a society which had become highly industrialized. Frustrated by the government's failure to accept its advice, the Natives' Representative Council adjourned sine die. The African National Congress, founded in 1912, was becoming a powerful and experienced organization. Notwithstanding legal impediments, it had managed successful strikes and, encouraged by the events of the Second World War and the ideology of the victors, it was demanding the abolition of all forms of racial discrimination. Colored and Asian organizations were beginning to co-operate with it. And a number of whites sympathized with African aspirations in varying degrees, including Jan H. Hofmeyr, cabinet minister and heir apparent to Prime Minister Smuts. It seemed possible, indeed, that the pigmentocratic order was beginning to collapse beneath the pressures of industrialization and that a freer type of society was in genesis.

This was profoundly disturbing to many white South

Africans, especially to Afrikaner traditionalists, who faced the possibility that the fruits of their resistance to the alien British conqueror and his British South African accomplice might be garnered by the nonwhites. The differences between the human races, they declared, were fundamental and ordained by God, and it was the duty of man to preserve them by keeping the races apart. The segregation policy was woefully inadequate, because it was piecemeal and unsystematic. What was wanted was a policy of apartheid, under which white supremacy should be enforced absolutely in the Urban Areas and the White Rural Areas, the Colored people and Africans should be allowed to develop along their own lines in their own areas, and the Asians should be sent back to Asia. Only through apartheid, they said, could the integrity of the white race be preserved against the sea of color in South Africa.[25] Thus was born the policy which played a large part in bringing the Afrikaner Nationalist Party into power in 1948 and giving it increased majorities in the elections of 1953, 1958, and 1961.

The Nationalist governments have been trying to preserve the pigmentocratic order in the Urban and the White Rural Areas by creating legal barriers where they did not exist, and to revive and control the tribal system in the Bantu Areas; but very few Asians have left South Africa, scarcely any land has been provided for the Colored people, and not much land has been added to the Bantu Areas. Furthermore, industrial expansion has remained the lifeblood of the South African economy and has continued to draw more and more people of all races into the urban vortex, so that the realities are set forth in the statistics given in the table on page 208 above.

Legal color bars now pervade almost every conceivable aspect of life in South Africa. The racial category of every inhabitant is determined by law. No African, no Asian has any say in the composition of the sovereign Parliament; and the say of the Colored people is limited to four elected whites in the House of Assembly, and one white senator nominated by the government. Africans are forbidden to become skilled workers or to strike, and they play no effective part in the determination of wage rates. The towns are zoned into uni-

212

racial residential and trading areas. Miscegenation, in or out of wedlock, is a crime. All schools and universities are uniracial, and the schools for Africans and the so-called university colleges for Africans, Asians, and Colored people are strictly controlled by the government. The color bar continues after death, when one is carried in a uniracial hearse to a uniracial burial ground.

The Bantu Areas are administered through chiefs, who are appointed and dismissed by the government. In the Transkei, the most compact part of the Bantu Areas, embryonic parliamentary institutions were introduced in 1963. There is a Legislative Assembly consisting of sixty-four chiefs and forty-five elected members, with the power to make laws on local matters, subject to the approval of the government.[26]

Since white settlement has taken place in South Africa over a longer period and on a larger scale than anywhere else in the continent, and since industrialization is more advanced in South Africa than anywhere else in the continent, the traditional social bonds of the Africans in the republic have been most completely disrupted. Yet it is they who have seen their freedom drastically curtailed at the very time when Africans farther north have been advancing to independence. Consequently, they are a peculiarly frustrated people. But all their efforts to produce a change of heart in their rulers have failed. The Afrikaner Nationalist regime is deeply committed to its policy, and it has developed efficient and ruthless techniques of control. In 1960 a passive protest against the pass laws became a blood bath when the police opened fire and killed over seventy Africans at Sharpeville, and resistance to the tribal authorities in Pondoland was forcefully suppressed. The African National Congress and its offshoot the Pan-Africanist Congress have been banned. Opponents of apartheid of all races have been systematically harassed and intimidated by arbitrary arrests, bannings, banishments, house arrests, and charges of treason.

Afrikaners are becoming politically more united than ever behind the Nationalist Party. Prime Minister H. F. Verwoerd, a man of strong will and great ability, has conveyed to them his conviction that apartheid is essential to secure the greatest good for the Afrikaner people and all white South Africans—the preservation of their racial integrity. Some Afrikaners doubt whether apartheid can be made to succeed, and some are dubious of its moral foundations; but the number of Afrikaners who oppose the party is decreasing, because to do so is to incur the drastic sanction of ostracization. Most British South Africans, too, are tending to accept the principle of apartheid, though they prefer to call it by some other name and may oppose its application in particular cases. Consequently, the United Party, which is supported by a minority of the Afrikaners and the bulk of the British, has moved continuously closer to the Nationalist Party, using slogans such as "White Leadership with Justice." This is not to deny the existence of white opponents of apartheid, whose courage in adverse circumstances is greatly to be admired. They include a number of distinguished Afrikaners, and they are influential in most of the churches—they even have a foothold in the Dutch Reformed churches—and in the English-medium newspapers and universities. They are convinced that apartheid is an evil thing and they hope that South Africa will soon become a co-operative multiracial society. But they have never been able to muster effective support at the polls, and in 1961 the white electorate returned only one outright opponent of apartheid to Parliament.* The upsurge of nonwhite expectations, at a time when African nationalism has been marching from victory to victory farther north with the approval of nearly every nation in the world, is promoting unity between the two white fragments—a unity based on common interests, common fears, and common isolation. For nearly every pigmentocrat of either stock, life in South Africa today dulls the edges of sensitivity and corrodes the spirit. At the same time as Africans throughout the continent are transcending tribal backgrounds in the creation of broader units, white South Africans, paradoxically, are becoming tribalists.

* Election results of 1961: Nationalist Party, 105; United Party, 49; National Union, 1; Progressive Party, 1. The National Union was a splinter from the Nationalist Party. The Progressive Party is opposed to the principle of apartheid; so is the Liberal Party, which won no seat.

Conversely, white unity in defense of pigmentocracy is forging nonwhite unity in opposition to it. So far as one can gauge nonwhite opinion in South Africa when its overt expression is banned or curtailed, it would seem that the Africans, the Asians, and the Colored people are drawing closer, and that the politically conscious Africans have abandoned the traditional policy of the African National Congress, which confined itself to nonviolent methods and looked forward to a multiracial goal, in favor of violent methods and an antiwhite goal.

The polarization of white South Africans behind the Afrikaner Nationalists and nonwhites behind the African Nationalists seems likely to continue; and with it, intermittent violence. So long as there is no external intervention, it seems probable that the pigmentocratic order will be preserved. Sooner or later, however, the antipigmentocrats inside the republic are likely to be provided with substantial aid from outside, in which case a combination of internal and external forces may eventually overthrow the pigmentocratic order.

6 Lessons of the South African Experience

The history of the Afrikaner people is a striking illustration of the conservatism which may encrust a fragment of European society after its transplantation to a new environment. Although the Afrikaners have now mastered modern educational, industrial, and military techniques, the basic ideas of the majority, including their political leaders, remain those which crystallized in the seventeenth and eighteenth centuries. Bred in isolation from the main stream of Western thought, they have rejected three of its dynamic modern impulses—liberalism, socialism, and democracy. A fourth—nationalism—they accepted; but they have perverted it because, unlike other nations, they do not form a majority of the inhabitants of their country. Today their position

215

vis-à-vis a hostile outside world and a restless internal proletariat is based upon sheer physical power. But they themselves
are the victims of their past. So tyrannical is tradition over
them that they are left with no room for effective maneuver,
no means to genuine reconciliation. The last and most dan-
gerous of the tribes of Africa, they are an anachronism in the
second half of the twentieth century.

The South African example also suggests certain conclusions about the nature of the two-fragment situation. One
is that the first of two fragments acquires a great advantage
from its priority in time. As the only white community upon
South African soil for almost two centuries, the Afrikaner
fragment regards itself as *the* South African nation, and allows
the British fragment no ultimate justification except as a
potential part of itself; whereas the British fragment has never
quite succeeded in getting firm bearings in a terrain already
occupied by the Afrikaner. The case of Canada supports this
conclusion, for there the French fragment became a minority
over a century ago, and yet it remains a strongly established
nation within the Canadian nation.

Secondly, in two-fragment situations the competition between the fragments may determine political alignments to
the exclusion of all other factors. Since 1910 all parties which
have ruled South Africa, or have been official oppositions,
have been founded upon some logic of interfragmentary relations. The Afrikaner parties of Hertzog and of Malan,
Strijdom and Verwoerd, and Jameson's British party were
one-fragment parties; and the South African Party of Botha
and Smuts and the United Party of Hertzog, Smuts, Strauss,
and de Villiers Graaff were founded to unite the fragments.

Thirdly, the South African example shows the shortcomings
of a unitary and flexible constitution in a two-fragment situation. Lacking assured control over any field of government
in any part of South Africa, each fragment has had to struggle
with the other for all or nothing. The mediating role of
federalism is well shown in Canada. Nevertheless, federalism
would not have been as effective a mediating device in
South Africa as it is in Canada, because neither of the South

African fragments is concentrated in one geographical area. The Afrikaners are spread throughout the country, and the British are scattered between a few pockets of urban and rural settlements and there would have been intense inter-fragmentary conflict in several areas under any conceivable division of the country.

The South African example also demonstrates the distortions which fragments undergo when they are in the presence of more numerous alien peoples. If the Afrikaner fragment had been truly self-sufficient, its claim to an enduring and exclusive place in the South African sun would have had more substance, and its idiosyncrasies would not have become perverted to the stage where it ignores the ethical convictions of mankind; and if the British fragment had been truly self-sufficient, its struggle with the Afrikaner might have been a straightforward contest of modernity versus archaism. Alternatively, if both fragments had been willing to relax their racial pride and gradually to mingle their blood with the alien peoples without being ashamed of the consequences, as was the general trend in Latin America, their long-term prospects might have been more propitious. As it is, the most important thing about the Afrikaner fragment is that it became irretrievably committed to a pigmentocratic order when it crystallized in the seventeenth century, and the most important thing about the British fragment is that its modernity became corrupted by its participation in pigmentocracy; with the result that both fragments now stand together in a laager, commanded by Afrikaners, defying the world.

Perhaps, however, the historian of a future generation, who will have the advantage of a longer perspective, will conclude that South Africa, after all, was not a two-fragment situation: that the British fragment was abortive, because it failed to generate the power to stand on its own feet once the authority of Great Britain had been eliminated. Such a historian may even conclude that both fragments were abortive. The present posture of the white community is that of King Canute. In trying to stem the tide of African nationalism, it is being driven by its own racial logic to stoop to meth-

217

ods which are incompatible with the ideals of the Western Christian civilization from which it sprang and which it claims to uphold, it is providing communism with its best prospect in all of Africa, and it is inviting upon itself a terrible denouement.

Chapter Seven

The Structure of Canadian History

by Kenneth D. McRae

1   The Building of New France *

Canada offers almost a classic instance of a two-fragment society. A French fragment, planted and nurtured over a century and a half of continuous settlement, was firmly established before France ceded Canada to Britain at the end of
the Seven Years' War. An English fragment,† though its roots
in the Atlantic provinces go back earlier, was built up primarily in the years following the American Revolution.

Both sectors grew rapidly, but the combined English-
speaking population of the scattered colonies of British North
America remained smaller than the compact French-speaking
population of Lower Canada until it was substantially rein-

---

* For informative discussion and helpful criticism during the preparation
of this essay I should like to thank Professors Michael Oliver, of McGill University, and Pierre Elliott Trudeau, of the University of Montreal, as well as
several of my colleagues in the History Department of Carleton University,
without implicating any of them in any of the more controversial conclusions
that I have reached.

† Here and later the word "English" means "English-speaking" rather than
"derived from England." As we shall see, the roots of this fragment are complex and are not derived primarily from England itself, nor even exclusively
from English-speaking countries.

forced by immigration from the British Isles after the Napoleonic wars. Since the federation of the colonies in 1867, the population of French origin has remained at every decennial census within the narrow range between twenty-eight and thirty-one per cent of the total, despite immigration, emigration, differential birth rates, and the addition of six new provinces to the original four. From the standpoint of numbers—and the very exactitude of the counting is a testimony to the distinctness of the fragments—the balance between the two cultures has been stable for the past century. But it is advisable to begin by examining each fragment separately.

Concerning the French colonial experience, the question of timing is crucial. The significant date is not 1535, when Cartier explored the St. Lawrence to Montreal and wintered in Quebec, nor is it 1608, when Champlain established the first permanent settlement, but rather 1663, the year in which a struggling and still-insignificant colony was transferred from the Company of New France to direct royal control. For the earliest developments are in some respects at variance with the later character of the colony. Under a succession of chartered trading companies, colonization and settlement had been thoroughly subordinated to the fur trade, despite undertakings to the contrary. Several of the earliest concessionaires had been Huguenots, a far cry from the religious uniformity of later years. There was, then, an initial fleeting, commercial, bourgeois—even semiliberal—phase to the French experience in Canada, but this tendency was soon superseded. In the long run New France bore the imprint not of the age of Henri IV, but of the age of Louis XIV and his great minister Colbert.

By the sixteen-sixties the doctrines and practice of absolutism in France had reached their highest peak. The Fronde, that last, futile assertion of feudal particularism by a politically decadent nobility, had been suppressed. The King himself took full control of all aspects of government. His position was acknowledged with adulation by a society imbued with absolutist principles. The veneration for royal

220

authority shown by Bossuet, the great apologist of divine right, is hardly less evident in the Huguenot divines, whose correligionists were to suffer so drastically when that authority was turned in full force against them. Like the Tudor monarchs of a century earlier, the French monarch had the solid backing of the bulk of the bourgeoisie, and the royal bureaucracy was drawn chiefly from their ranks. Absolutism was a progressive force, a unifying force, a successful and powerful instrument of a dynamic state. Its universal popullarity lay in the fact that, to all appearances, it had made France by far the greatest nation in the world.

The effects of absolutism were felt in every branch of public policy. In the economic sphere a vigorous mercantilist policy was the counterpart to political centralization. The army was reorganized and reshaped into a highly efficient instrument of state policy. Religious orthodoxy was made complete by the total revocation in 1685 of the Edict of Nantes. In the light of the disasters that plagued the final decades of Louis XIV's long reign, his political system may appear more a façade than a reality, but this perspective is inappropriate here. In Canada the first and most active phase of royal government, the phase that stamped the character of the colony, occurred in the years immediately following 1663, when the star of absolutism was unmistakably in the ascendant.

It is necessary to pause briefly to insist on the significance of this point. New France was a projection—a deliberate and official projection—into the New World of a dynamic, authoritarian society at the zenith of its power. This does not mean that the colony became an ideal model, or even a mirror image, of the mother country; the rough conditions of a colonial society prevented that. But it does mean that in its law and institutions the colony reflected the prevailing ethos of authoritarianism to an even greater degree than did the more complex and less malleable society of old France. If it is basically true, as has been argued of the English colonies, that "America was settled by men who fled from the feudal and clerical oppressions of the Old World," [1] such a generalization cannot hold true for French Canada. In this fact lies the first and most fundamental difference between the English and the French traditions in North America. The early English colonies were liberal, heterodox offshoots of a society already deeply divided within itself. French Canada was the closely controlled projection of a highly centralized regime. Though both societies might believe in principle that colonies should exist for the benefit of the mother country, though both might be mercantilist in economic policy, there was yet room for considerable divergence as to the latitude to be permitted to the colonists.[2]

If the English colonies were by the very circumstances of their foundation born free, that is, born with a prevailing ethos of religious dissent, individual freedom, and limited government, it is equally clear that freedom in New France —and it existed incontestably in substantial measure—was a matter not of doctrine, but of circumstance and accident. First and foremost, it arose from the geographical environment, from the long and uncertain delay in communication with France, from the physical inability of officials to control the vast geographic empire that was French America. Second, it arose from conflicts within the institutional structure, from the differing and occasionally clashing interests of church and state, from rivalry between governor and intendant. Finally, it arose from neglect. The magnitude of France's involvement in Europe relegated colonial affairs to insignificance for long periods.

It is this theme of theoretical absolutism—albeit a paternalistic and well-meaning absolutism—tempered by practical difficulties in its application that provides the most comprehensible conceptual framework for the study of New France. In the political and administrative sphere it can be documented in the roles of the governor, the intendant, and the Sovereign Council. In a military sense absolutism brought badly needed security, for the arrival of royal troops in 1665 rescued the infant colony from the menace of extinction at the hands of the Iroquois. In economic policy the doctrine can be seen in the regulation of prices, in the sponsoring of secondary industries, and in control of the fur trade, the colony's only staple export. Economic control was facilitated by geography; there was no seacoast fit for smuggling, and the monopolistic nature of the St. Lawrence route meant easy control of imports. In the fur trade, however, regulation could not be pushed too far, owing to competition of traders from Hudson Bay and from the English colonies to the south. In the religious sphere, the early missionary work of the Jesuits and the tireless organizing talents of François de Laval, first Bishop of Quebec, rapidly laid the foundations for a strong ecclesiastical authority. After 1627 few Huguenots reached New France, and the handful who did were carefully watched. The occasional trader might visit the colony briefly, but Protestants were forbidden to winter there unless engaged in the king's service. At the end of the French regime, Masères could record the presence of only three Protestant families.[3]

The most striking illustration of the theme of absolutism is the seigneurial system of land tenure. An edict of 1664 established the Custom of Paris as the legal system of the colony, and in the land law this meant that New France possessed what would appear at first glance to be an exact replica of the feudalism of Europe, a feudalism already in decline. Lands were granted *en seigneurie,* as indeed had been the case since the earliest grants during the sixteentwenties. Seigneurs swore fealty and homage to the Crown on taking possession of their seigneuries. Minerals were reserved to the Crown, as were oak trees for shipbuilding. Seigneuries transferred otherwise than by direct descent were subject to the *droit de quint,* a tax of one-fifth of their value.

Similarly, the habitant owed a series of feudal obligations to the seigneur. There were the *cens et rentes,* paid annually, and the *lods et ventes,* an irregular mutation fine corresponding to the seigneur's *quint.* There were the *banalités,* of which the *droit de mouture,* or seigneur's milling right, was the principal one exercised in Canada. The *droit de four banal,* or right of oven banality, was rarely attempted in Canada. The *corvée* required the habitant to work several days each year for the seigneur, the exact number being fixed by custom. Other minor rights, such as the reservation of wood, sand, and stone, or the levy on fish, or the right of ferry, are worth a passing mention if only to complete the picture. Many of the seigneurs were granted judicial rights, often with full powers of *haute, moyenne, et basse justice,* but high jurisdiction was infrequently exercised, and in any case appeals were always open to the royal courts.

Yet closer examination will show that when feudal tenure was transplanted its spirit was necessarily transformed. Certain of the seigneurial payments, such as the *cens et rentes,* were little more than nominal, and others were seldom enforced. The *corvée* seems to have been imposed lightly, seldom more than six days per year, often only three. In a small pioneer settlement the seigneur frequently found that the milling banality was more of a financial burden than a boon, but it was his obligation no less than his right. Justice, administered informally by the seigneur in person, was certainly never the source of revenue that it was in France.

On behalf of the habitants the royal administration intervened vigorously to check attempted abuses and extortion by the seigneurs, as well as to enforce fulfillment of their obligations. Far from being an unchecked source of oppression for an overburdened peasantry, as they were in France, the seigneurs in Canada became in effect the unsalaried agents of the Crown for the settlement of the colony. In France feudalism merely supported a privileged order that had lost its social function; in New France seigneurialism, not unlike the European feudalism of an earlier age, regained some of its primitive rationale in providing elements of security, order, and social cohesion in an environment ringed about with potential dangers. It is possible to regard Canadian feudalism as a mere anachronism, accidentally carried to the New World. Some aspects of it undoubtedly were vestigial, but behind the façade there stands at least one towering reality: the continuing concern of the central authorities for regulating even the minor details of rural life.

The essence of Canadian feudalism is its mildness, its relaxation, its absence of systematic harshness or oppression. The proof of this lies in the almost incredible survival of seigneurial tenure long after the end of the French regime, despite increasing difficulties owing to population pressure and subdivision of holdings. Feudal dues and obligations were not terminated until 1854, and even at this date the rights of the seigneurs were merely converted into fixed annual rentals which the habitant could pay off in a lump sum capitalized at six per cent. But few chose this alternative; the majority continued to pay the annual rental. Only in 1935 did the Quebec legislature incorporate a syndicate to borrow funds at low interest and buy out the remaining rights of the seigneurs.[4] The farmers were then to repay principal and interest to the syndicate at a rate equal to the former annual rental. In this way it is now expected that these last vestiges of feudal tenure will disappear sometime in 1969 or 1970.

It was the very mildness of feudalism and indeed of the whole structure of absolutism that preserved the institutions of French Canada from revolutionary overthrow. The ultimate reason for this mildness lies in the conditions of the frontier. The structure of absolutism in French Canada was rather like a sieve: as soon as pressure was applied, there was an escape through the meshes to freedom outside the settlements. The tighter the web of control, the more appealing became the life of freedom in the forests. From the very beginning the *coureur de bois* emerged as a distinct social type, embracing Indian ways and living off the fur trade, a continuing source of concern to both secular and ecclesiastical authorities. In this easy alternative to absolutism lies an important clue to the moderation of government policy in general, to the mildness of feudal obligations, to the light incidence of ecclesiastical tithes,[5] to the chronic ineffectiveness of the system of economic controls. If an open, nonhostile frontier provides an escape valve in any new society, it becomes proportionately more troublesome and more debilitating to the extent that the colony is built upon authoritarian foundations.

The flow of immigration to the colony was disappointingly small. The one significant wave came during the early years of royal rule under the brief but all-important *intendance* of Jean Talon (1665-1672). The population increased from 3,215 at the census of 1665 to 6,705 in 1673, and to 9,677 in

1681. After this date immigration declined very sharply, and one severely limiting factor was an almost morbid reluctance of the French authorities to depopulate France in order to build up the colony. All in all, though only rough figures can be devised, it is estimated that total immigration to Canada during the entire French regime was at most 10,000 persons, and about one-quarter of these came during the brief Talon period. The immigrants were carefully selected in France and rigorously inspected on arrival in the colony, often by the intendant in person. Physical robustness, youth, unimpeachable religious orthodoxy, and—for the women at least —good moral character were the principal qualifications demanded.

Despite the strong element of government control and screening, the colonization of New France was overwhelmingly a voluntary one. Though large numbers achieved passage to the colony by means of a system of indenture for three years, these obligations were undertaken willingly in the hope of personal betterment. For more than a century, the transportation of convicts was unknown in Canada. Only in 1723 did the home authorities, over strenuous protests from the colony, send a first small contingent of minor lawbreakers, mainly smugglers and poachers, to strengthen the desperately small trickle of immigrants. Characteristically, even the convicts were carefully selected *"bons hommes"* drawn from the royal prisons. On arrival they were enrolled in the ordinary indenture system and quickly absorbed into the life of the colony. The experiment was relatively successful, and protests soon faded, but at this late date the small number of deportees left no visible impression on a society whose main outlines were already firmly established.[6] What is significant is the prolonged hesitation in sending prisoners. The reason is one that can be illustrated time after time: in the framework of absolutism, the colony was to represent the quintessence of the virtues of the parent society; its vices were to be filtered out in the process of fragmentation.

Since immigration became negligible after the sixteen-eighties, later population growth depended very largely upon natural increase. In an environment already highly favorable, governmental policy imported young girls to balance the sexes, paid cash premiums for early marriages, fined bachelors and denied them trading rights, and provided liberal pensions for families of ten or more children. Under these stimuli New France achieved a fertility rate among the highest ever recorded, and with only modest assistance from immigration the population increased to 13,815 in 1698, to 24,434 in 1720 to 42,701 in 1739, and to 55,009 in 1754, the last census of the French regime.

But it was not enough. The original base of immigrants was too small. While New France was doggedly building her population to 55,000, the English colonies had grown to well over a million inhabitants during the same century and a half of settlement, even though the population of metropolitan France was probably twice that of Great Britain. One basic weakness of France is not difficult to identify. While only a few thousand carefully screened settlers were trickling to Canada, almost simultaneously some 200,000 Huguenot exiles were driven from their homeland after the revocation of the Edict of Nantes, to establish themselves in Germany, Holland, England, South Africa, and even the rival English colonies in America. The effects on France itself were severe enough, but for Canada the consequences were even more profound. Had the colony offered a place of refuge, an escape for dissenters on New England lines, for even a modest fraction of these exiles, the subsequent history of North America might have been vastly different.

It is not easy to portray in a few lines the social structure of the colony, and one should avoid the pitfall of trying to extrapolate backwards from the truncated society that existed under the first decades of British rule. In the rural areas, there was no wide social or economic gap between habitant and seigneur, nor could there be under frontier conditions. Quite a few seigneurs were of modest origins, merchants, officials, or even habitants. Those who tried to live like independent gentlemen soon sank into penury and literal starvation. Only a small number of seigneurs belonged to the nobility, and practically all of these were colonials ennobled in Canada. Even this group did not constitute a legally privileged order. Unlike their counterparts in France, they were free to engage in trade. They had no exemptions from export or import duties (or from the *taille,* since the latter was never levied in Canada), they paid tithes, and they were equal to the habitants before the law.

If New World conditions leveled down the seigneur, they clearly raised the habitant to a condition well above that of the French peasant. Though life was hard and luxury non-existent, there is abundant testimony from European visitors as to the rude sufficiency and even comfort of his life, his fine physique, politeness, dignity, cheerfulness, and attachment to religion. Not all of the testimony is favorable. There are references to vanity, laziness, wastefulness, stubbornness, improvidence. But these merely prove the point, for these are the vices of the man who feels himself well off.

The urban population is far more difficult to characterize, and it was not a negligible element. In the census of 1698 Quebec accounted for almost 2,000 and Montreal almost 1,200 of a total of 13,815. Together they represent much the same proportion in 1754, nearly 13,000 in a total of 55,009. As might be expected under a paternalistic regime, a large sector of this population was made up of civilian officials, garrison troops, and workers in government enterprises such as the naval shipyards at Quebec. Commerce was a significant element in the colony's economy, but it is difficult to discern any sizable independent bourgeoisie.[7] Small merchants and retailers and a few wealthy fur traders were certainly in evidence, but even in the prosperous years of the eighteenth century the colony had only a handful of reasonably prosperous families, and these few tended to develop close links with officialdom. Much of the important export trade was carried on by employees of merchants resident in France, merchants whose connection with the colony remained tenuous. Similarly, although the professional classes were ably represented by a few outstanding individuals, their numbers were small. Even the Catholic clergy, profoundly influential in town and country alike, were surprisingly few in relation to their vast spiritual and educational responsibilities. Thus although

228

urban life was well established, the mentality of an independent middle class with its roots in the colony was not.

Perhaps the best way to comprehend the society of New France is to identify those elements in metropolitan society that were absent from the colony. First, there were no Huguenots, practically speaking. The unity of Catholic doctrine was unchallenged; even Jansenists were all but unknown. Second, there were very few examples of the old French nobility. Third—and most striking—no *avocat* was permitted to practice his profession in the colony, most legal matters being handled by notaries. Nor was there an independent, hereditary judiciary as in France, the principal court being the appointed Sovereign Council. It is no coincidence that the very groups which had held out the longest against the triumph of absolutism in the mother country found no place in the life of the colony. It is also significant that Canada possessed no printing press throughout the entire French regime.

In the eighteenth century there is a visible and widening gulf between French Canadians and Frenchmen from France, a consciousness of separate interests and separate identities. In other words, the traditionalism of the fragment is already asserting itself. The beginnings may be discerned around 1700. By this date immigration had fallen off sharply, and no doubt a considerable majority of the population were Canadian born. The following decades saw economic progress, material comfort, and a growing self-confidence. From the Treaty of Utrecht in 1713 to the War of the Austrian Succession in 1744, New France enjoyed an unprecedented peace, a brief respite which enabled the culture to consolidate itself. For many historians these three tranquil decades constitute the Golden Age of New France, and they could not have come more opportunely, in view of the ordeal that lay ahead.

The evidence of this hardening of identity is not difficult to find. In 1725 the Governor, Vaudreuil, commented that a "spirit of rebelliousness and independence" permeated the whole colony. The intendant Hocquart comes even closer to the mark: "They are," he writes of the Canadians in 1736, *"naturellement indociles."* [8] This general intractability forced the modification or even abandonment of many an ill-considered official policy, yet it occurs in a society that remains technically absolutist.

There is a relationship here that deserves careful analysis. Legally speaking, the absolutist ethos continued, but the character of the colony checked its excesses and prevented it from slipping into despotism, thereby assuring for Canada an eighteenth century far different from the eighteenth century in France. For absolutism in Canada remained inescapably a moderate absolutism, a doctrine that could evoke no such stark antithesis between the real and the rational as inspired the Enlightenment in France. The main writings of the Enlightenment were not unknown in the colony, though their circulation was restricted by ecclesiastical censorship. But the crucial point was that they lacked explosive potentiality. Though the fuse might be available, there was no keg of powder to explode. The whole issue may be reduced to a simple series of propositions. Because legal absolutism found natural limits in the conditions of the new society, there could be no despotism. If no despotism, there could be no revolution. If no revolution, then the absolutist ethos was bound to persist, however subtly it might be transmuted, in some form or other, as in fact it does even to the present day.

Probably the most dramatic event in Canadian history is Wolfe's capture of Quebec in 1759. Its political sequel was France's cession of Canada to Great Britain by the Treaty of Paris in 1763. To the two European powers, the transfer was a straightforward political settlement reflecting the fortunes of war. To the American colonies, it was the final destruction of an ancient enemy. To the Canadians, it was a cataclysm beyond the power of the mind to grasp. To a devout Catholic culture, it was totally incomprehensible that Providence should decree its subjugation to an alien and Protestant power.* The fact of conquest was for French Canada a searing and scarring psychological experience that manifests itself even today in a hundred different ways. It

* There is an interesting contrast here with South Africa, where the initial transfer of sovereignty seems to have occasioned no comparable psychological shock.

230

is a treacherous, hidden rock that constantly troubles the smooth flow of French-English relations, no matter how carefully it is camouflaged.

It is significant that many French Canadians have written not of the Conquest, but of the Cession. There is more here than the simple masking of a painful fact, more than the search for a scapegoat for the catastrophe. There is an almost Freudian transfer of a deep resentment from the outsider to the parent. For in this view French Canada was left in 1763 like a lonely and fearful child, not removed by force from its mother's arms, but callously abandoned.

The Treaty of Paris permitted unhindered emigration to all French subjects, but the proportion who chose to retire from Canada was very small. For how could generations of New World history be reversed? Those who left were those whose ties were weakest and most recent, especially the French military forces and administrative officials. Of the Canadians, perhaps a hundred whose interests were primarily mercantile or military retired to France. The remainder of the middle class and practically all the clergy chose to remain.[9] But the bourgeoisie soon found its position seriously threatened by a new English-speaking mercantile community, while the status of the clergy was subtly enhanced. Throughout the French regime the church, while independent in doctrinal matters, had been subject to stringent control by the state, but this relationship broke down under British rule, and once certain unfamiliar problems such as episcopal consecration had been settled the church enjoyed a far greater degree of independence than before. It is scarcely surprising that the episcopacy became one of the strongest supports of the new regime.

Beyond its religious functions, the church acquired a special significance as a rallying point for the defense of French Catholic culture. The strategy of survival called for a closing of ranks, a united front against the intrusion of alien ways, a clinging to the past as the clearest landmark of cultural identity. Thus the main tendency of the Cession was to harden still more the conservatism and traditionalism of the fragment and to concentrate in the hands of the clergy, as the only effective remaining elite, the full force of an authoritarian heritage previously shared with secular officials. It is this enlarged role of the church, political and social as well as religious, that is the key to its continuing central position in French Canada.

For more than a decade British policy toward the new colony wavered uncertainly. In the end it was largely shaped by the governors on the spot, Murray and Carleton, both career army officers, both aristocratic, both Tory, the one the son of a Scottish peer, the other from the Anglo-Irish squirearchy. Significantly, both men ran into their greatest difficulties from the English-speaking merchants who arrived in the wake of the army, mainly from the American colonies, a group for whom they could feel only cold contempt. The policy that gradually emerged was prompted by external strategic and political considerations as well as by their own aristocratic temperament: in essence, the perpetuation of the *ancien régime*. It found its main legislative embodiment in the Quebec Act, 1774, which confirmed the free exercise of the Roman Catholic religion, retained French civil law and seigneurial tenure, and denied the colony a representative assembly.

As events were soon to show, however, Carleton's interpretation of the French regime rested upon a misconception. He thought he saw in Canada a replica of European society, and tried to preserve it. In fact he was attempting to create an Old World aristocracy of a sort that New France had never known. The Canadian tradition might be authoritarian, but paradoxically it was also far more egalitarian than Carleton suspected. Even as in the American colonies, any attempt at a rigidly hierarchical class structure on the European model was bound to antagonize the masses. Under the French regime their position had been protected by constant governmental oversight of the seigneurial system. With British rule the delicate balance of forces, resting upon a labyrinthine web of custom, inevitably broke down, necessitating considerable readjustment. But the crucial point was that despite the protests of the English-speaking minority, the main foundations of the old society had been preserved.

Once confirmed and consolidated during these first decisive decades of British rule, they were not easily to be displaced, no matter what political institutions might be superimposed.

The course of French-Canadian history since the Cession reveals three distinct but unsuccessful challenges to the established social tradition. The first is seen during the American invasion of 1775 in a wave of habitant disaffection against the seigneurs and the British authorities, the result primarily of Carleton's misjudgment of the seigneurial system. The second is a ripple of unrest that arose in the seventeen-nineties in response to the French Revolution. Both these challenges, however, were instigated primarily by outside forces and they left no serious or lasting imprint on the colony. Indeed, the ultimate effect of the French Revolution was to reinforce strongly the sense of separate identity and to widen the gulf between colony and metropolis until it became unbridgeable.

A third challenge, more prolonged and more serious, arose from the gradual emergence of a more indigenous stream of French-Canadian radicalism in the Rouge movement of the mid-nineteenth century. Led by Louis Joseph Papineau, it reached ideological maturity under the stimulus of the European revolutions of 1848. Its program combined demands for a more thoroughgoing political democracy, some elements of anticlericalism, and an intransigent nationalism, the most pervasive and universal element of all French-Canadian movements of protest. In the eighteen-fifties the Rouges had some strength in the provincial legislature, but their fate as a political force was sealed by the rising tide of ultramontanism in the church in the eighteen-sixties. Yet even in political eclipse a thin thread of social radicalism has remained as a continuing minor theme of French-Canadian intellectual history, never strong enough to dominate the political scene but never wholly absent either. The continuing spirit of *rougisme* is one element in the intellectual ferment that is stirring French Canada today.

The "quiet revolution" that has become visible in Quebec since 1959 is a complex phenomenon. Basically it comprises two distinct but interacting elements. First, it is a revolt of the society against itself, against its tradition and its elite. But simultaneously it is a revolt against the past relationship of French Canada with English Canada, which will be considered in Section 3. Whether in longer historical perspective it will be seen primarily as yet another internal challenge to the French-Canadian tradition or as a question of changing relationships between the two fragments must depend upon the outcome of developments that have scarcely begun to run their course.

2   The Society of English Canada

When we turn to the English-speaking fragment in Canada, there is something about it that is strangely but elusively familiar. At first this feeling of reliving a faintly remembered experience is disturbing, baffling, perplexing, until finally the truth hits home. As the central figure of the English-Canadian tradition we encounter once again the American liberal. To be sure, he is not quite on his home ground, and this accounts for our initial difficulties in recognition. He appears first as an exile, a political refugee from his own land, a fragment torn once again from the original American fragment. He settles in a land where his religious feelings are once again hypersensitized by an attempt, ultimately unsuccessful, at church establishment, and by the presence of a large Catholic majority. He lives through a period of government by narrow colonial oligarchies which aspire to become full-fledged aristocracies. Yet through all this he retains, no matter how far obscured or submerged, much of the original liberal heritage of the American colonies.

It is easy to show that the scanty English-speaking population of Canada-to-be before the American Revolution was fundamentally American in outlook. We have already noted the typical clash that ensued when the fledgling merchant community of Montreal confronted Governors Murray and Carleton. Nova Scotia, an even more forceful example of the same phenomenon, is a new New England whose failure to

234

join the other colonies in revolt was the result of economic, geographic, and military factors rather than of any significant difference in outlook. But can we make the same judgment of the American Loyalist refugees who poured into Upper Canada and the Maritime Provinces in the seventeen-eighties? To do so is to deny traditions which have become cherished myths in both the United States and Canada. For in the American view the Loyalists were unregenerate Tories, placemen, servile monarchists, enemies of the notion of liberty upon which the new republic was founded. In the Canadian view they become heroes who endured exile and hardship to demonstrate their attachment to the Crown and the British connection and their abhorrence of mob violence and democratic excesses. When the emotional content is allowed to boil away, the two traditions are not very far apart.

Before examining the facts, let us consider for a moment the theoretical problem. The key to the puzzle is the interpretation to be placed on the American Revolution. For if the United States achieved its present liberal ethos through the expulsion of genuine preliberal or feudal elements at the Revolution, then it is logical to look for those elements in Canada. But if, as is argued elsewhere in this book,[10] the American experience is fundamentally a liberal one from its earliest origins, and if the American Revolution was not a social revolution, then it is folly to represent the Loyalists as a genuine Tory aristocracy or a privileged class. For how could America cast off a social order that it had never really possessed? And if the American experience was basically a liberal one, how could the main Loyalist heritage be anything else? The logic alone is compelling in its clarity, but behind it stands a wealth of empirical evidence.

The Loyalist influx to Canada flanked the French fragment on both sides, and the two segments differ slightly, the one representing the seaboard, and the other the frontier, of the older colonies. Yet both segments, on analysis, reveal the American liberal. The influx to Nova Scotia considerably outnumbered the prewar population and led to the creation of New Brunswick as a separate province, where some 6,000 heads of families settled, perhaps 15,000 persons in all. Their background is significant. More than ninety per cent were American born, and many came from families settled in America for several generations. About seventy-five per cent, as closely as can be estimated, came from New York, New Jersey, and Connecticut. A sprinkling of gentlemen, esquires, clergymen, physicians, and graduates of Harvard, Yale, and King's (Columbia) is to be found among their ranks, but the numbers are wholly insignificant in relation to the numbers of tradesmen and farmers. It is clear that the New Brunswick group consisted of a fairly representative cross-section of American seaboard society.[11]

In Upper Canada we scent at once the atmosphere of the American frontier. The Loyalist influx is described by one of the commissioners investigating their losses claims as "mostly farmers from the back parts of New York Province," [12] and indeed five-sixths of the claimants were from New York. Their losses had been correspondingly small. The typical claimant might have left behind a hundred-acre farm, either owned or leased, of which ten acres or less might be cleared land. Many of these men were illiterate, or nearly so, as the records of their signatures and marks subscribing to the oath of allegiance show. Perhaps it is also typical of the still-fluid frontier society that of some six hundred whose claims were examined in Canada only about half were American born. Many of the rest arrived in America only a few years before the Revolution.* Only the barest handful of the Upper Canadian Loyalists belonged to the professions, and large landholders seem to have been almost as scarce. But the crowning fact is that this political migration of some 6,000 persons in the late seventeen-seventies and seventeen-eighties was soon far outnumbered by a continuing flow of American settlers moving westward in search of free land. The Upper Canadian Loyalists became simply a phase in the unrolling of the North American frontier, living in harmony with the new arrivals, and indistinguishable from them in any social sense.

* Does the fact of birth abroad mean that the American liberal influence had not begun to operate? This seems unlikely. That these recent immigrants were willing to pioneer a second time under similar conditions indicates an acceptance of the liberal ethos.

All this may seem rather puzzling, but two cardinal facts must be remembered. The first is that there is no simple criterion to explain the incidence of Loyalism during the Revolution. American society split vertically almost from top to bottom. Factors of geography, military campaigning, local politics, and private vendettas all added their weight to political and economic considerations. Many, as the Loyalist claims amply prove, changed allegiance during the war, and families were often split within themselves. All of which demonstrates that we are not dealing here with a simple social revolution of class against class.

The second point is that out of the vast numbers who supported the Loyalist side, which many estimate as high as a third of the population of the colonies, only a small fraction actually went to Canada. The great majority made their peace and returned home, or settled elsewhere in the new republic. Many of the wealthy and the well-connected found more attractive opportunities in Britain or in the West Indies. Thus frontier conditions in Canada and the Maritimes operated selectively, and in a liberal direction, in attracting immigrants. They also exerted a powerful leveling force upon those who did come. Even the well-educated, the cultivated, and the well-to-do learned unforgettably the meaning of equality as they faced the untamed wilderness. Though the social composition of the Maritime migration might be more varied than its Upper Canadian counterpart, neither offered promising foundations for an aristocratic tradition.

Indeed the American Loyalist undoubtedly never understood his own basic liberalism until the circumstances of his exile thrust it upon his consciousness with unmistakable clarity. Those who went to Upper Canada made the discovery most dramatically, for here they found their new townships still part of the old province of Quebec, administered according to the Quebec Act. During the first few critical years, the absence of a legislative assembly and of English common law did not greatly bother them, for of what use was either in the midst of the wilderness? But they found the feudal tenure of their lands more than a little disquieting, since in law each township was a seigneury under the direct lordship of the Crown. They then discovered, with mounting anger, that the Crown proposed to alienate the milling *banalités* as monopolies to private individuals, with reversion of the mills to the Crown after fifteen years. When rumors began to circulate that the half-pay officers were planning to perpetuate the feudal system and to make themselves seigneurs, grumbling unrest flared into hysterical resentment and near-rebellion.[13] The settlers called unequivocally for freehold tenure and "the British constitution." But this storm passed quickly, and their aspirations for liberal institutions were satisfied by the separation of Upper and Lower Canada in 1791.

Those Loyalists who went to Britain discovered their American liberal heritage rather differently. Their case is interesting, for here we have a rare actual example of the transfer, after more than a century, of part of the colonial fragment back to the mother country. Several thousand Americans went to Britain during the war years, and in their impressions of the mother country we see a reverse image of themselves. To their friends in North America they wrote first of all of immense wealth on all sides; of luxury, corruption, and sloth; of universal condescension toward the colonies; of the aloofness and arrogance of the gentry; of brutality among the lower orders; of the strange rigidity of the class structure. Above all, many found England narrow, confining, and they longed for the lost freedom of America. Benjamin Marston gladly accepted a post in West Africa as "a door to escape out of England, the worst prison I ever was in," and there died of fever before the year was out. Others, in despair, returned to their native land.[14] The American exiles were often embittered, disillusioned, and querulous, but very few turned reactionary. Even in adversity they reveal their liberal heritage.

If the American Loyalists who came to Canada were representative of their fellow-Americans in social background and social outlook, this is not to say that they were exactly like them in all their convictions. For a second process of fragmentation or quasi-fragmentation is at work here, and the principle of selectivity in the composition of the fragment has served to differentiate the English-Canadian tradition from the American in certain subtle, minor ways from the very beginning.

Most Loyalists believed fervently in monarchy and in Empire unity. Indeed, this belief was the principal cause of their vicissitudes, and its influence can be traced extensively in Canadian history. In the War of 1812 it proved an important and perhaps decisive factor in stiffening the wavering loyalty of the Upper Canadian population under American attack. In 1837 it seems to have deterred many Reformers from following William Lyon Mackenzie all the way into overt rebellion, although characteristically, and in keeping with their liberal heritage, we find just as many Loyalists and sons of Loyalists among the Reformers as on the government side in the Legislative Assembly of 1835. In the longer run it is difficult not to attribute to the Loyalist tradition much of that hyperloyalism to Britain, Crown, and Empire which has exacerbated French-English relations in Canada.* In summary, while loyalism is a differentiating quality that distinguishes the Canadian fragment from its American origins, for many historians it has obscured the all-important parental relationship between them.

But there are other, more subtle differences. The American opponents of the Revolution, though they often disapproved strongly of imperial policy, had been advocates of moderation, gradualism, compromise, and preservation of the existing political order. They had a faith in the rule of law that amounted almost to a passion, and in many these beliefs were fortified by years of military discipline. It is not difficult to show that these qualities passed into Canada, where they became elements in the English-Canadian tradition. Among other effects, they frustrated the Upper Canadian rebellion of 1837, dominated the struggle for responsible government, and even influenced the pattern of westward expansion. There is an instructive contrast between

---

* Yet this hyperloyalism should not be overestimated. It would appear to be far more deeply if less belligerently felt in the single-fragment societies of Australia and New Zealand.

the informal folk law of the American frontier and the federal criminal law imposed by the North-West Mounted Police on the Canadian prairies, between the tumultuous rush to the California gold fields and the curiously regulated race to the Klondike.

Even here the differentiation does not end, and to trace all its ramifications would be an exacting task. It is worth noting that the Canadian Loyalist fragment is a defeated fragment, which is not precisely the same as an escaped one, for it carries with it the memory of shattered hopes. In its depths it can harbor dark resentments and anguished self-contradictions of a complexity unknown to more favored societies. Where American liberalism is dogmatic and self-confident, Canadian Loyalist liberalism becomes doubt-ridden—perhaps even guilt-ridden—in defeat. And thus when the imperial authorities attribute the loss of the first Empire to an excess of liberalism and attempt to preserve the second by systematically restraining the powers of colonial assemblies, Loyalist liberalism finds itself in no position to fight back. But neither does it die. Instead, it retreats underground for almost a generation while the work of taming the wilderness pushes forward, to emerge under more favorable circumstances in the decades following the Napoleonic wars.

In the meanwhile government had to be carried on. The period down to the eighteen-forties was marked in all the British North American colonies by the rule of small, tightly knit colonial oligarchies, to which Canadian history has applied the vivid but somewhat misleading term Family Compacts. It is not too difficult to explain the emergence of oligarchic control. The demands of the frontier left little time or energy for participation in politics, and the desperate lack of educational facilities was soon reflected in a lack of effective leadership. In the beginning the Family Compacts simply filled a political vacuum.

Their composition was extremely varied. In New Brunswick the ruling group were cultivated Loyalists, who preserved, more than in any other colony, an aura of patrician gentility. In Nova Scotia the Loyalists were initially outsiders, and the oligarchy consisted in leading Halifax families established before the Revolution, as well as British career officials. Upper Canada reflected its raw frontier condition in the variegated quality of its elite. Fewer than a third were original Loyalists, although a few of the latecomers were from New Brunswick Loyalist families. If the Upper Canada Compact was a rather nondescript group in its origins, there was no very broad social basis from which to select it. Even Lower Canada had its oligarchy, although by a reversal of its earlier history it was the representatives of the English minority that surrounded and influenced the governor from the seventeen-nineties onward.

To understand the significance of these Family Compacts is by no means a simple task. The complexity begins even in describing them. To risk a broad generalization for a fifty year interval, they include, characteristically, the heads of departments in the colonial administration, judges, most barristers, and the bishop or ranking churchman of the Church of England. But this is not all, for closely associated with this official oligarchy we find the leaders of the commercial and banking community. In the microcosm of colonial society there is no clear differentiation between the political and the economic elite.[15] And frequently it made for a strange amalgam, compounded of patrician principles and self-made men, of Old World polish and frontier crudity, of public spirit and naked greed.

In British North America the Family Compacts developed no appreciable interest in landed estates. There is no parallel in Canadian history to the pastoral ascendancy in Australia. Though they might speculate in unimproved land, the Compacts showed no inclination to retain and develop it. And this was just as well, for there could be no rural tenantry in a land where freehold farms could be had almost for the asking. But it was left to the unsuspecting English gentleman immigrant to make this discovery; the Family Compacts never made the experiment. Their interests were overwhelmingly in the commercial and governmental activities of the emerging cities.

Contemporary observers perceived the commercial role of

the Compacts, but they did not always correctly assess its significance. They merely cited this aspect to illustrate how ridiculous were their aristocratic pretensions. Judge Thorpe, one of the earliest critics, wrote scornfully in 1806 of a "Shopkeeper Aristocracy" of "scotch Pedlars . . . there is a chain of them linked from Halifax to Quebec, Montreal, Kingston, York, Niagara and so on to Detroit." [16] Lord Durham noted in 1839 that the Upper Canada Compact practically monopolized banking and owned much of the undeveloped land of the province. Even Sir Francis Head, replying to Lord Durham's criticisms, defended rule by a small group "who by their own industry and intelligence, have amassed wealth." There is little flavor of Old World aristocracy here. The much-traveled Mrs. Jameson, who certainly could tell a true aristocracy from a false one, referred to the Upper Canada group as "a petty colonial oligarchy, a self-constituted aristocracy, based upon nothing real, nor even upon anything imaginary." [17] For in European eyes a mercantile aristocracy is no aristocracy at all. The trouble is that the Family Compacts of British North America have been judged—and found ridiculous—in the light of what, in their most imaginative moments, they aspired to become. But it is far more realistic to assess them in the light of what they actually were: ambitious mercantile oligarchies that were not above using whatever measure of privilege they could get to perpetuate their position.

If we pursue this point a bit further, we find illuminating parallels. The first and most obvious is the substantial similarity between the Family Compacts and the American colonial oligarchies before the Revolution. But this parallel, while useful in many respects, is incomplete in that it ignores the crucial fact of the Revolution that separates the First and Second Empires. British North America, it has been suggested, was constructed out of the reaction to the American Revolution; it is therefore the land par excellence of the counterrevolution. There is truth in this view, provided it is properly understood. But if, as we have already noted, the American Revolution was a mere political revolution executed within a social framework already basically liberal, what sort of reaction would it engender? If the American reaction at its height could only produce a Whig-Girondin type of liberalism in the shape of the Federalists,[18] is it any wonder that the more primitive societies of British North America could scarcely do more? Neither the original European inheritance nor the North American environment would permit the successful planting of anything genuinely aristocratic. It is true that sustained attempts were made in all the colonies to establish the Church of England, and for Upper and Lower Canada the Constitution of 1791 even visualized for a fleeting moment a prospect of hereditary aristocracy, but these measures remained hopelessly unattainable. In the North American setting the blackest sort of reaction possible was commercial oligarchy, and the petty religious, educational, and social privileges to which these groups clung so desperately serve only to underline the essentially nonaristocratic nature of their ascendancy.[19]

When we understand this basic nature of the Family Compacts, we begin to discover the clues to their prolonged success. As miniature aristocracies modeled on the Old World, they would be inexplicable. But as mercantile oligarchies of ability and drive in colonies where these qualities were in short supply, they provided the banking and commercial facilities necessary to economic progress. As groups substantially involved in the economic development of their own province, they were often the most articulate spokesmen for provincial interests on the broad imperial stage. Finally, and simply because of their position as oligarchies, they soon found a profitable role for themselves in saving the colonial masses from the specter of republicanism and democracy.

Here a second parallel comes into view which may be even more revealing. It is the fate of their American contemporaries, the Federalists and Whigs. Because the latter found it impossible to impress the American masses with the dangers of democracy, they went down helplessly before the onslaughts of the Jeffersonians and Jacksonians. But the insoluble problem of the American Whigs proved the salvation of the Family Compacts. For in British North America democracy still held many terrors. Nothing was easier than to cry up the perils of demagoguery, lawlessness, and Yankee republicanism. In Loyalist tradition the memory of these persisted from Revolutionary days and had been rekindled by the War of 1812. This deep, unreasoning fear of unqualified democracy, carefully nurtured by the ruling groups, was the weakest link in the armor of the Loyalist liberal, and it led him to acquiesce uncertainly in the many inconveniences of oligarchical government rather than to run the risk of mob rule.[20]

Thus while the Federalists and Whigs were tasting the bitterness of defeat, the Family Compacts, operating on very similar social premises, were enjoying an unbroken ascendancy that lasted half a century. And luck was with them, at least for a time. For when a combination of official intransigence and temperamental instability led Mackenzie and Papineau into rebellion in 1837, did this not show that all the direst warnings of the Compacts had come true? Their luck ran out, however, when the Reform leadership passed into the hands of moderates like Baldwin and Howe, for then their claim to a monopoly on loyalism was patently ridiculous and their defeat became inevitable.

And yet, except in a narrow political sense, there was no complete repudiation of the Compacts and what they stood for, no flight of exiles to other lands, no real revolution at their overthrow. When responsible government came, members of the oligarchy simply adapted themselves to the new rules of democratic politics and in time found other means to return to power. The transition has a Hegelian flavor, sustaining and preserving something of the old order even while superseding it. And in New Brunswick, the purest example of the Loyalist mentality, the change was so smooth as to be difficult to date.

The British North America poised on the threshold of self-government in 1850 is not the same British North America whose foundations we have traced down to the War of 1812. One factor that greatly helped to overthrow oligarchic rule was the dramatic growth of the society by immigration.

If the first wave of English-speaking settlement in modern Canada was American in origin, the second stemmed from the great outpouring of population from the British Isles after 1815. Between 1815 and 1850 almost a million immigrants left Britain for British North America.[21] Their impact on the new society was far-reaching indeed. An English fragment of perhaps 350,000 in 1815 was more than doubled in twenty years, tripled in thirty, more than quadrupled in forty.[22] Nor was the rate of growth equal in all colonies. The populations of Nova Scotia and New Brunswick almost quadrupled between 1815 and 1851, but that of Upper Canada increased tenfold, from an estimated 95,000 in 1814 to 952,000 in 1851. This poses an interesting problem. What will be the fate of the original fragment when exposed to such conditions? Upper Canada, born of American liberalism, isolated from the rest of British America, and flooded by a tidal wave of almost wholly British migration, offers almost a classic testing ground for the survival of an original fragment in a rapidly growing society.

The social background of this wave of immigration is significant. The records of arrivals at Quebec and Montreal during the early eighteen-fifties provide a valuable picture of male occupations. Approximately half are designated simply as laborers, and the proportion was probably higher during the worst famine years of the eighteen-forties. Roughly thirty per cent are listed as farmers and farm servants, and practically all the rest are skilled artisans. The middle and professional classes are virtually unrepresented.[23] Thus while the British middle classes figured largely in the colonies' literary and cultural development down to the eighteen-fifties, they were statistically insignificant, and their supposed influence on social development may well have been considerably overestimated.

Down to the eighteen-fifties Upper Canadian society was overwhelmingly rural. The agricultural frontier dominated. And yet upon this simple foundation arose a social pattern of bewildering complexity. Settlement of the land was tried in almost every conceivable form. Direct grants, land companies, paternalistic despotism, and even squatting, all made their appearance. The census figures of 1851 and 1861 show that more than half of the British-born population were of Irish stock, the balance being fairly evenly divided between English and Scots. In many areas immigrant groups homogeneous in religion and ethnic origin created distinctive pockets of rural settlement whose imprint remains clearly visible today. The new arrivals brought with them all their clannishness and native animosities, most notably the deep-rooted antagonism between Irish Catholics and Ulster Orangemen. In the Canadian setting such a struggle was highly inflammatory, and it spread like a forest fire to non-Irish groups.

It would be inaccurate to say that this wave of migration was absorbed into the original fragment; an influx of these proportions does not permit of simple assimilation. And yet the original North American liberal heritage was working with irresistible force upon it in at least two basic respects. The first was the universal urge to own property. Though raised in a society where property belonged to the few, the vast majority of immigrants gravitated to the land—to their own land—at the earliest possible opportunity.[24] The second influence of the liberal heritage lay in the immigrants' discovery of the classlessness of North American society. For the first time in their lives they experienced a feeling of freedom, of independence, of camaraderie, of escape from a system of class differences. All too frequently they abused their new-found freedom. The accounts of English travelers are full of the swaggering impertinence of their ex-compatriots as they indulged in what they imagined to be Yankee manners. However, offensive or not, this behavior is the answer to our emerging question: the immigrant, despite his overwhelming numbers, quickly forgets his old notions of social hierarchy and becomes an egalitarian.

Landed property and equal social condition, the two key elements of the North American liberal tradition: though they may have been unfamiliar at first, it was inevitable that the British immigrant should embrace them both without reservation. For in their discovery he fulfilled in full measure the very hopes of bettering his condition that had first sent him in trembling anticipation to the New World.

Despite the flood tide of immigration, then, the original liberal inheritance of English-speaking Canada survived and dominated. Though the society had become more complex, its spirit was unchanged. The phenomenal growth down to 1850 showed that the liberal tradition could be diversified without being deflected from its course. After mid-century the rate of immigration fell off sharply, and for a generation English Canada had the same chance to harden and consolidate its tradition that French Canada had had following the Treaty of Utrecht. More challenges lay ahead: further waves of immigration, which would include new ethnic groups bringing with them alien traditions; the rise of industrial society; some epic battles with French Canada. The English fragment could look on all these issues with a confidence that bordered on complacency, for it was now ready to confront any challenge from a well-established position of its own.

3   Toward a Dual Society

The slow and often painful search for a *modus vivendi* between the French and English fragments encompasses most of Canadian domestic history, particularly during the nineteenth century. The journey has been at many points a tempestuous one, rocked by violent storms and bitter setbacks. Recent years have seen perceptibly improved relations between the two fragments, but even today the passage is made more difficult by a heavy burden of past animosities, and not all the portents for the future are favorable. To trace this relationship through all its intricate crosscurrents is clearly beyond the scope of this essay. Yet it is difficult to understand with any clarity the position of the French and English fragments in Canada without at least a general survey of their interaction.

We have already noted the first clash between the two cultures in the years following the Cession, and its resolution in favor of French Canada by the Quebec Act. The Loyalist influx strengthened the English fragment and created an ir-

247

resistible demand for English institutions, which were granted by dividing the old province of Quebec into Upper and Lower Canada by the Constitutional Act of 1791. But this measure also gave representative government for the first time to French Canada, which rapidly learned how to use parliamentary institutions for its own cultural survival. The War of 1812, unlike the American Revolution, found French Canada uniformly loyal to the British connection, more so indeed than the heavily Americanized population of Upper Canada. For French Canada, Napoleonic France had singularly little appeal. The war thus proved a unifying influence of considerable importance, but passions were soon violently inflamed again by an abortive attempt of the Lower Canada English to promote the union of the two provinces in order to establish an English ascendancy.

In both Upper and Lower Canada the protracted struggle to win emancipation from imperial control and local oligarchic rule flared briefly into armed revolt in 1837 and 1838. If we view the Lower Canada struggle solely as—in Lord Durham's famous phrase—"two nations warring in the bosom of a single state," we shall not fully understand it, and the revolt in Upper Canada will have to be explained in completely different terms. Deep ethnic cleavage and the memory of past grievances did serve to embitter and magnify the conflict in Lower Canada, but its origins were more complex. Indeed, several of the *Patriote* leaders were of English or Irish extraction, while many of the French Catholic clergy strongly condemned the drift to open hostilities. Moreover, if the uprisings in the two provinces were scarcely co-ordinated in any precise military sense, there was at least considerable liaison, co-operation, and sympathy between the *Patriote* and Reform movements.

To a degree the two movements shared a common outlook. Both opposed bitterly the aims and the privileged position of the ruling oligarchies. Both represented the revolt of the countryside against the metropolis, of an egalitarian social order against vested interests. Both idealized a stable agrarian society, while both found some of their support among the emerging labor force of the cities. Both looked for inspiration

248

and guidance to triumphant Jacksonian democracy across the border. But beyond this point the difference between the two fragments asserts itself and interposes differences. The agrarian ideal of Upper Canada was individualist frontier democracy of a familiar North American type. A few of the more radical Lower Canadian leaders shared the same vision, but undoubtedly the majority of the *Patriotes* were inclined to retain most of the traditional social structure of French Canada. Papineau himself, strong republican and anticlerical though he was, nevertheless was seigneur of Montebello and a firm upholder of existing rights of property. Imbued with a Jeffersonian concept of simple agrarian democracy, he saw in seigneurialism and French customary law a useful barrier against excesses of the mercantile spirit, which had been all too successful in defeating Jeffersonianism in the United States. But these agrarian dreams were to remain unfulfilled, shattered by the collapse of the rebellions.

In longer perspective, the rebellions were an unparalleled success, for they set in motion a direct chain of events that sent Lord Durham to the Canadas as governor, called forth his farsighted *Report on the Affairs of British North America*, and opened the way to self-government within a decade. English Canadians have viewed the Durham *Report* as a sort of colonial Magna Charta, and they are somewhat taken aback when they find that French Canadians do not share their enthusiasm. The reasons on both sides are easily evident from Durham's principal recommendations. Against the misrule of the oligarchies he boldly prescribed, in terms strikingly similar to those of the moderate Reformers of Upper Canada, full executive responsibility to the colonial legislatures on local matters. But he was unwilling to apply this formula to the French majority in Lower Canada. As a radical English Whig he could see in French Canada nothing but "an old and stationary society, in a new and progressive world," which was doomed sooner or later to be swamped by the triumph of the more dynamic English civilization throughout North America. Since assimilation was inevitable in the long run, he proposed to accomplish it quickly and humanely by reuniting Upper and Lower Canada. This recommendation was im-

249

plemented almost at once by the Act of Union of 1840, which also made English the sole language of record in the legislature of the united province. With complete assimilation plainly stated as the goal of British policy, the bitterness of French-Canadian reaction to the *Report* and the Union may easily be surmised.

But matters did not work out as planned. Imperial policy was to implement Durham's proposed Union and to defer responsible government. Within a few years the forces of Canadian politics had won responsible government while virtually nullifying the intended effects of the Union. The key to the change is to be found in 1839. Within weeks of the appearance of the Durham *Report,* the Reform leaders had begun to construct, patiently but persistently, a political alliance between Upper Canada Reformers and Lower Canada French to press for Durham's proposal of responsible government. Though the Colonial Office and three successive governors fought hard to avoid recognizing the new principle, the work of the Reform alliance was crowned with success in 1848.[25]

In addition to its achievement of responsible government, the Reform ministry established another principle of possibly greater significance. It established the convention that national political parties in Canada do not—and must not—divide along ethnic lines. To put this in a more practical way, the road to office for any Canadian political party lies in winning the support of a substantial section of French Canada. For more than a century this rule has suffered no exceptions of any significant duration, and even short-term lapses have been highly unusual. The association of the two fragments in the major political parties—indeed, this is one of the criteria of a major party—is one of the principal foundations of Canadian dualism.

The broad coalition which had won responsible government disintegrated shortly after its objective was gained. Its elements were too diverse to co-operate for very long. The bulk of the French representatives were socially conservative, and they found it increasingly difficult to work with Reformers from Canada West. Increasingly the ministries of the eighteen-fifties came to depend upon collaboration of most of the French Canadians with the conservative mercantile interests of Montreal and Toronto, who now accepted responsible government and turned it to their advantage. The bulk of the members from Canada West, still true to their agrarian radical tradition, drifted gradually into opposition, where they found an uneasy alliance with the Rouge minority of Canada East. But despite the imbalance in each region, the over-all balance of forces for the combined province was a fine one, and the system labored under increasing difficulty. Though the Act of Union was in force for only twenty-seven years, it saw no fewer than eighteen ministries in office.

To make matters inextricably difficult, convention perpetuated the very line of division that the Act of Union had sought to erase. Even while denying its constitutional validity, ministry after ministry soon found itself politically tied to the principle of the double majority, which called for all government measures to be approved by a majority of members from each of the two sections of the united province. The ministries and most of the departments show the same tendency, portfolios, personnel, and departmental organization being duplicated for Canada East and Canada West. Against all intentions, Canada had developed a practice strikingly similar to Calhoun's doctrine of the concurrent majority. Convention now proclaimed what the constitution of 1840 had explicitly denied, and the two fragments acknowledged the gulf between them by a tacit federalism. The trouble was that within a unitary legislature the double-majority principle could only spell legislative paralysis and chronic deadlock.

As an additional difficulty, parliamentary representation in the united province became increasingly unrealistic. The Act of Union, despite Lower Canada's considerably larger population, had granted equal representation to the two sections with the deliberate aim of reducing French-Canadian influence. But by 1851 Canada West had a slightly larger population, and by 1861 the disparity was very marked. Upper Canadian agrarians, condemned to opposition and increasingly anti-French and anti-Catholic as their political strength increased, repudiated equality and demanded representation by population. Lower Canada remained equally insistent on equality rather than English domination.

By the late eighteen-fifties it was clear that the Act of Union was no longer a workable constitution, and that a more explicit recognition of federalism was the only alternative to legislative paralysis. The only serious issue was a choice between federation of the two Canadas and a wider federation involving the other colonies of British North America. The factors on either side were complex, but the eventual outcome was a victory for the principle of wider federation. After three conferences and considerable pressure from the imperial authorities, a British statute of 1867 gave a new federal constitution to the Canadas (which were now repartitioned into Ontario and Quebec along the old boundary of 1791), Nova Scotia, and New Brunswick. The same act provided for the possible future admission into the federation of Newfoundland, Prince Edward Island, British Columbia, Rupert's Land, and the Northwest Territory.

The federal constitution inaugurated in 1867 was a highly centralized one, so much so that in certain respects it falls short of the accepted criteria of federalism. In the circumstances it could hardly have done otherwise. Meeting in the shadow of the American Civil War, with its eloquent testimony to the fate of a looser federation, the British North American delegates who hammered out the broad principles of the new constitution were fully agreed on the need for a strong central authority. To it they gave what they felt to be "all the great subjects of legislation" as well as any residual powers not specifically assigned to the provinces. The provinces were assigned some sixteen enumerated powers, supposedly of local importance only, which were however felt to be broad enough in scope to embrace and protect the distinctive social institutions of French Canada. The federal government was also given certain direct controls over the provinces. It was to appoint the provincial lieutenant-governors, who were empowered to refuse assent to provincial bills or to reserve them for consideration by the federal cabinet. It could even disallow provincial statutes within one year of their enactment. In strict constitutional law, therefore, Canada has something less than a federal constitution, though the near-obsolescence of these overriding federal powers in recent years has brought it much closer to other federal constitutions in practice.

In the midst of this general tendency to centralization the 1867 Constitution offered a few slender guarantees for minority rights. The equality of the English and French languages was secured in the federal Parliament, in the Quebec Legislature, and in federal and Quebec courts. Education was entrusted basically to the provinces, but denominational schools, including the schools of the Protestant minority in Quebec, were protected by a right of appeal to the federal authorities against detrimental provincial legislation. The French civil law of Quebec was protected by assigning legislative authority over the critical field of property and civil rights to the provinces and by requiring that Quebec judges be selected exclusively from the bar of that province.[26]

Since these guarantees are neither very extensive nor very explicit, it may be wondered why the representatives of French Canada were willing to enter a larger union upon such restrictive and uncertain terms.[27] Probably the principal reason was that now, for the first time in history, the way seemed open for the French Canadians to be masters within their own house. If the degree of provincial autonomy was limited, the constitutions of 1840 and 1791 and even the Quebec Act of 1774 had been far less promising. Moreover, Confederation was backed by the high prestige and the disciplined followers of George Etienne Cartier, who epitomized the outlook of the developing French-Canadian urban middle class, expansionist, Hamiltonian, acquiescent in economic centralization but strongly traditionalist in cultural matters. The core of French opposition to federation was the Rouge minority, who vigorously denounced the scheme as ruinous to French-Canadian institutions, but their past revolutionary record made it difficult for them to pose now as sincere champions of traditionalism. In the Canadas the cabinet prudently avoided taking the issue to the electorate and it is doubtful whether a majority favorable to federation could have been obtained. Throughout the negotiations much attention was devoted to the powerful and vociferous English minority in Quebec, but the substantial French minorities in the other provinces went virtually unnoticed.* Their position had never been enviable, and they gained nothing now.

In the last analysis it was the prospect of provincial autonomy for Quebec that made Confederation palatable to the French-Canadian fragment. For if co-operation between the fragments in biracial political parties is the first foundation stone of dualism in Canada, the second is assuredly the principle of federalism. In the long run this principle has proved by far the most dependable constitutional guarantee of French-Canadian cultural survival. Since 1867 the original distribution of provincial and federal powers has been greatly modified by judicial interpretation, by the rise of the welfare state, and by Canada's enhanced international position, but the federal principle itself is established beyond serious challenge. Quebec is by no means the only province to uphold provincial rights jealously, but it has a compelling ethnic reason for doing so that is shared by no other province. And while federalism may have made Quebec less sensitive to the problems of French Canadians living outside its boundaries, it is possible that this insularity was an essential condition for the very survival of the minority fragment. Had federalism been absent, the French Canadians might have succumbed to outside pressures as completely as did the Dutch, Spanish, and French cultures in the United States.

The union achieved in 1867 was far from complete in a territorial sense. The prospect of uniting all the British North American territories under a single authority had been one of the most powerful factors predisposing the English fragment in the Canadas toward union. Upper Canadians, seeing

* At the 1871 census, the minority of British extraction in Quebec made up twenty per cent of the population, while the French minorities elsewhere amounted to sixteen per cent in New Brunswick, eight per cent in Nova Scotia, and five per cent in Ontario. For the provinces that entered the federation shortly afterward, the 1881 census showed French minorities of sixteen per cent in Manitoba, ten per cent in Prince Edward Island, two per cent in British Columbia.

their own good agricultural lands substantially filled, turned to the West as a natural hinterland for expansion. Montreal already had long-standing ties with the West through the vanishing fur trade, and its financial and railway interests could visualize their city as the metropolis for a new western empire. Westward expansion could unite the diverse interests of the English fragment in the Canadas as few other issues could, and the need for decisive action was imperative, for already the American frontier of settlement was reaching out to touch the international border.

Astride the Canadian path to the Pacific lay the Red River settlement, fashioned of diverse ingredients and yet strangely united in outlook. Here in what later became southern Manitoba was a remote and isolated society, unique in North America, whose total existence revolved around the needs and techniques of the fur trade. Ethnically the colony was a mixture. The English and Scottish personnel of the Hudson's Bay Company and the predominantly French-Canadian employees of the Montreal interests, long locked in bitter commercial rivalry, had learned to co-operate after the merger of the companies in 1821. Both groups had intermarried for generations with Indian women, to produce the only sizable mestizo, or *métis*, population to appear in Canadian history. Alongside the fur-trading groups lived the descendants of the Scottish highlanders of Lord Selkirk's colony, established in 1812. The latter, as agricultural colonists, had faced at first a bitter struggle for survival against determined opposition from the traders, but in time a substantial identity of interest emerged. When new settlers arriving from the East during the eighteen-fifties began to urge annexation to the Canadas, the Selkirk colonists remained aloof. But it was the *métis*, the "New Nation," culturally more Indian than European, credulous, easily aroused, yet superbly disciplined by the skill and co-ordination required for the annual buffalo hunt, that dominated the colony by their own numbers and by their hegemony over the Indian population of the plains.[28]

In the transition from a hunting to an agricultural society some clash of values was inevitable, and indeed it had begun as early as the arrival of the Selkirk settlers. But the ethnic

255

tensions that surrounded the birth of Manitoba were largely imported from outside the Red River colony, and their worst manifestations were displayed on the far-off stage of Canadian politics. From the beginning the *métis* of both groups had been substantially insulated from the acerbities of French-English differences by their Indian heritage, and a policy of equal rights for the French and English groups preserved harmony down to the eighteen-fifties. It was the arrival of new settlers from Ontario, militantly Protestant and backed by the strident voice of the Ontario press, that destroyed the balance. "We hope," proclaimed the Toronto *Globe* on June 2, 1869, "to see a new Upper Canada in the North-West Territory—in its well-regulated society and government, in its education, morality and religion." [29] In short, the colony had to be refashioned closer to the English Protestant ideal.

Against this inflexible attitude there could be only one possible answer: armed insurrection on behalf of the *métis* majority. Led by Louis Riel—whose destiny it was to become perhaps the most controversial figure in Canadian history—the *métis* took control of the colony, formed a provisional government with the support of all but the Canadian party, and forced the federal government at Ottawa to consider their claims. In the short run at least, the rebellion was conspicuously successful. Its direct result was the entry of the colony into confederation with full provincial status and constitutional guarantees of the rights of its heterogeneous population.

The Manitoba Act of 1870 created a miniature Quebec along the banks of the Red River, a second province within the federal union founded on the principle of cultural dualism. The French and English languages were granted equal status in the provincial legislature and in the courts. Denominational schools were protected against provincial infringement by a right of appeal to the federal government, as in the 1867 Constitution. As a further protection for minorities the legislature was made bicameral, with a small appointive Legislative Council. Finally, in recognition of the rights of the Indians and *métis,* land reserves of 1.4 million

256

acres were to be set aside as compensation for the loss of Indian title over the remainder of the province.[30]

During the eighteen-seventies and eighteen-eighties, however, the tide of settlement ran strongly from Ontario, and constitutional dualism did not long outlast the emergence of a strong Protestant majority. The Legislative Council, which had been inaugurated with a half-breed majority, was the first to go, as an economy measure, as early as 1876. The land claims of the *métis* were paid in negotiable scrip, which was quickly alienated at a fraction of its value, while they themselves, defeated and pushed aside by an unfamiliar civilization, retreated westward before the advancing frontier to the valley of the Saskatchewan. In 1890 a provincial statute wiped out overnight the equal status of the French language in the legislature and in provincial courts and made English the sole official language. At the same session the legislature abolished the dual school system for a single, English-speaking, nondenominational one, leaving to Catholics only the alternative of establishing their own parochial schools without state support.

This measure initiated a prolonged constitutional controversy, culminating in an attempt to invoke the educational guarantees of the federal Constitution. But the Conservative government at Ottawa was defeated in its bid to obtain remedial legislation, and in 1896 the issue was adjusted by a compromise which reflected the vastly unequal bargaining strength of the parties. The uniform system remained, religious teaching was permitted at the end of the school day, and under certain conditions elementary teaching was to be permitted in a language—any language—other than English. By this arrangement French was given the same status as Ukrainian or Icelandic or any of the other tongues of the immigrant groups now arriving from Europe in ever larger numbers. When this system broke down in chaos, all bilingual teaching, including that in French, was abolished in 1916. In less than half a century Manitoba, the little Quebec on the Red River, had been remade in the image of Ontario. But like many a colony, this new Ontario was even more orthodox than the old, for it lacked even the publicly supported Catholic separate school system that had been entrenched in Ontario by the federal Constitution of 1867.

By a strange fatality the harsh drama of the Red River settlement was re-enacted, with changes more in detail than in substance, on the prairie lands to the west. The *métis* and Indians along the Saskatchewan River joined forces in a second Northwest Rebellion in 1885, a final, hopeless stand against the relentless advance of the agricultural economy. Again they found a leader in Louis Riel, summoned from across the border in Montana. Under a full-scale military assault the revolt collapsed, and Riel was sentenced—by an English-speaking judge and jury—to hang. The rebellion had already ranged the two fragments against each other, and passions on both sides mounted to a white heat as Quebec opinion clamored for a reprieve for Riel while Ontario insisted perhaps even more hysterically on his execution. In the end the government gave in to Ontario, and Riel went to the gallows, a victim of political expediency.

Just as in Manitoba, the territories that later became Alberta and Saskatchewan first recognized the principle of dualism in their institutions, and then witnessed a gradual erosion of the rights of the French minority. A federal act of 1877 applied the language guarantees of the federal constitution to the Territories, thus giving equal status to French and English in the legislature and courts. But when in 1891 the federal government conceded to the territorial legislature the power to determine its own language policy, the legislature immediately designated English as its sole language of record. The first regular school system of the Territories, established in 1885, followed the dual Quebec pattern of separate Protestant and Catholic boards. In time this was changed to a public school system which retained rather narrowly circumscribed denominational schools but failed to provide a corresponding guarantee for language, with the result that teaching in French was eventually restricted to the primary grades in Alberta and all but banished in Saskatchewan.

If the most significant battles for a dualist society beyond the boundaries of Quebec were fought over the shaping of

Kenneth D. McRae

the West, some bitter struggles have also arisen in Ontario and the Maritime provinces, particularly on educational questions. To any dispassionate observer it must be evident that throughout Canadian history the English fragment everywhere has shown itself coldly unreceptive to the idea of dualism outside Quebec and often violently hostile to the values of the French fragment. Yet some twenty-three per cent of Canadians of French origin, or roughly 1.3 million persons, now live outside the province of Quebec, many of them scattered thinly through a preponderantly English-speaking culture. In such a setting powerful forces of assimilation take a heavy toll. In every province except Quebec a significant proportion of Canadians of French origin no longer understand French, and some, though not as many, have given up Catholicism as well.* Thus the outlook for the French fragment outside Quebec is at best a somber one. Mere survival on the cultural plane has demanded continuous, uphill struggle against crushing odds. Only in New Brunswick, with its over-all Catholic majority and its strong (thirty-nine per cent) French minority, is dualism holding its own. Even in Quebec itself, under conditions far more favorable, the drive for *survivance* has for two centuries been almost an obsession that has required the diversion of much intellectual effort from other channels.

Yet the significant fact is that the French fragment has survived, however precariously, in every province of Canada and in the northern territories. For this feat of heroic endurance much of the credit must go to the devotion of the French-Canadian clergy, to lay associations working to preserve French culture, and to support from Quebec for French-Canadian communities in other provinces. Something is owed to the French-language press outside Quebec, which is, however, demonstrably weak.[31] More important in recent

* The 1961 census showed that those French by origin who could not speak French ranged from a low of ten per cent in New Brunswick and thirty per cent in Manitoba up to sixty-two per cent in British Columbia and eighty-two per cent in Newfoundland. On a countrywide basis the proportion was nine per cent, but if Quebec is excluded this figure rises to thirty-four per cent for the other provinces. Those not Catholic ranged from three per cent in New Brunswick to twenty-four per cent in Alberta and thirty-eight per cent in British Columbia.

years have been the expanding French-language radio and television networks of the Canadian Broadcasting Corporation, the cultural activities supported by the Canada Council, and the work of the National Film Board. There is more than a touch of irony here, for these federal agencies which are contributing markedly to French survival outside Quebec are themselves viewed with deep suspicion by some groups within Quebec as a dangerously liberal influence subversive of traditional French-Canadian values.

In any attempt to assess the extent of dualism in contemporary Canadian society, it is clear from the start that the two fragments are far from a footing of equality, even in a strictly legal or constitutional sense. In the first place there is an imbalance of numbers. Psychologically, a beleaguered minority faces a more relaxed majority that has only at rare intervals been conscious of the other fragment. Even more important, there is a serious imbalance of economic power that has come more and more to the forefront in recent years as the principal grievance of French Canadians' within Quebec.

Yet with all the limitations, dualism has been attained to a substantial degree in constitutional law and custom. It is to be seen in the structure of political parties, and in their leadership;[32] in the formation of cabinets, which invariably provide appropriate representation for each fragment; in the publication of parliamentary debates and government documents in both official languages; in the alternation of appointments to the governor-generalship, and to the speakership of the House of Commons; in the close attention paid to the proportion between the two cultures in the federal civil service;[33] in the special protection of Quebec civil law at the federal level;[34] and in the appointment in July, 1963, of a federal Royal Commission to investigate existing French-English relations and to recommend measures for achieving an "equal partnership" between the two cultures.

Dualism may also be recognized in certain areas of disagreement and deadlock: in the failure of Parliament to agree upon an official Canadian flag; in a tendency to accord equal status to two competing national anthems; in the prolonged but as yet unsuccessful search for a satisfactory method of constitutional amendment.[35] On all these questions the deadlock stems ultimately from basic differences between the fragments, but the very willingness to wait for a solution acceptable to both is further testimony to the acceptance of dualism.

More important than the constitutional framework, however, is the range of current popular attitudes toward dualism. Within the French fragment two main points of view stand out. One segment of opinion rejects dualism in any form and pursues a rigid nationalism that envisages the secession of Quebec and the establishment of an independent Laurentian state.[36] On the other hand, a substantial majority of French Canadians accept the principle of a dual society while deploring the inferior status accorded their own culture and urging a greater degree of equality for it. There is no segment of French Canada that is basically content with the existing situation, unless one counts those who have surrendered unconditionally to the assimilative pressures around them. This last group, however, must be considered to have crossed the line between the cultures and joined the English fragment.

The English fragment reveals three distinct points of view. There still exists a minority who reject even the present imperfect degree of dualism in favor of a more uncompromising policy of assimilation. The majority of the English fragment seemingly accept the existing system but tend to oppose, in varying degrees, its extension. Probably most individuals in this group lean, consciously or not, toward an ultimate assimilationism which they define and justify in their own minds as a uniform Canadianism, but in the interest of harmonious relations they are content not to force the pace. The third point of view, and the most hopeful for the future of French-English relations, is that of a small but perceptible minority of the English fragment, particularly in eastern Canada, who accept dualism and who are prepared to see its extension in provinces where it now scarcely exists. Some see this extension as a matter of simple justice, but others find it a useful means of defining the Canadian identity more sharply against its similarly colored American background.

Though the edifice may be far from complete, dualism in Canada has become an established fact. Even though its current application finds French-Canadian pressures for reform sharply at odds with English-Canadian passivity on the question, the principle itself has been accepted, if not fervently embraced, by a very considerable majority in each fragment —the double-majority principle once again. In times of stress between the fragments the forces on either side that reject a dualist compromise invariably increase, but so far the two cultures have been able to resolve even the most intractable problems without mass violence, through the machinery of constitutionalism and party politics. The way has not been an easy one, and the tangible and hidden costs on both sides have been high, but the costs of following a more extremist course are virtually incalculable. Perhaps the cardinal fact of Canadian history is an event that did not happen, a potential conflict that was damped down, a Boer War that never came.

4 Canadian History: Some Wider Vistas

The preceding sections of this essay have described the two fragments in Canada and the relationship between them. It now remains to indicate in barest outline the impact in Canada of some of the broad forces that have helped to shape the other new societies. It will be seen that the response in the two fragments may in some cases be broadly similar; in others, markedly different; and sometimes these forces have become a source of acute antagonism between them.

The issues of slavery and of relations with the indigenous populations, which have often played so large a part elsewhere, have had a minimal impact upon Canada. Today it is almost forgotten that slavery existed under both the French and early British regimes and that it involved both Negroes and North American Indians. The essential point is that the institution of slavery had a tenuous existence and disap-

262

peared without a struggle.[37] Since it fulfilled no obvious need in the colonial economy, it collapsed without resistance with the first moves for abolition. Its last vestiges disappeared unobtrusively shortly after 1800, apparently well before its formal suppression by the Imperial statute of 1833. Thus it was possible in the eighteen-fifties for Canadians to respond warmly to American abolitionism and to provide asylum for escaped American slaves. But sympathy for the antislavery cause was more pronounced in the English fragment than in the French, which could not easily overlook the fact that the American South was a coerced minority like itself.

Similarly, contacts with the Indian and Eskimo populations have played a negligible part in shaping either fragment. Unlike the Spaniards, or the Dutch in South Africa, the French and English in North America faced indigenous populations that were sparse in numbers, simple in culture, and relatively decentralized in tribal organization.[38] Though the French in North America made strenuous efforts to Christianize the Indians, the work of the far-flung Jesuit missions had little effect on the settlements. Within the colony minor experiments were made in the seventeenth century with *francisation* and conversion of Indian children, but without marked success. Intermarriage between French and Indians was rare, and closely regulated. Thus the principal influence of the Indian culture on New France—apart from the early Iroquois military threat—was its tendency, already noted above, to lure away the discontented from the settlements and soften the impact of the authoritarian ideology.

The English fragment, founded from the start upon an agrarian democracy of relatively small holdings, was not influenced in any discernible way by Indian culture. As agricultural settlement advanced the Indians drew back, retaining their hunting and fishing economy. In eastern Canada the history is one of coexistence without friction, indeed with a minimum of contact. On the western plains, where the picture was complicated by the emergence of the *métis* "New Nation" prior to general agricultural settlement, the ultimate result was basically the same: the organized agrarianism of the English fragment thrust all opposition aside and re-fused any form of accommodation with an alien way of life. Throughout the formative years of the English fragment this attitude was reflected in official policy, which until very recent times condemned the Indian and the *métis* to a non-competitive, sheltered, subsidized, but essentially neglected and uneducated existence on reservations of his own. In the most immediate sense this policy stemmed from a simple demand for economy in governmental expenditure, but it also seems to reflect the underlying propensity of the English fragment to shrink from closer contact.

Immigration, as a factor that tends to change the ethnic composition of any society, will inevitably be a sensitive topic in any dualist society. In Canada it was massive immigration from Britain for a generation after 1815 that established the preponderance of the English fragment. A second major wave broke in the opening years of the twentieth century, but this influx was far more varied in ethnic origin. Since then polyethnicity has been a continuing characteristic of Canadian society, to the extent that by 1961 some twenty-five per cent of the population were of non-British, non-French immigrant stock.

The evidence suggests that a very large proportion of these immigrants gravitates toward the English fragment. The 1961 census shows that the total of those speaking French, including those bilingual in French and English, is only thirty-one and four-tenths per cent of the total population, a bare one per cent above the population of French origin. Thus, even by counting all those bilingual in French and English as members of the French fragment—an extreme assumption—the gains to the French fragment from the immigrant and British stocks combined are, at most, barely sufficient to offset the losses of French Canadians assimilated into an English-speaking milieu. The acculturation of immigrants toward the English fragment in the provinces other than Quebec is very nearly universal. Even within Quebec the tendency has been evident enough to cause grave concern in French-Canadian circles. The figures for children attending the Montreal Catholic schools are significant. There, in a city where the two fragments have perhaps the greatest degree of equality in Canada, the preference for English Catholic schools over French Catholic schools in 1959 was in the ratio of eight to one among the Polish group, eleven to one among the Ukrainians, and more than two to one even among Italians, Spanish, and Portuguese, the groups that might be expected to show the strongest leaning toward a Latin culture.[39]

Behind this strong preference for English undoubtedly stands the compelling practical consideration that it is the dominant language of North America. But it is only sensible to give due weight to the fundamental difference between the two cultures. The English fragment in Canada is a liberal fragment of the American type, immensely attractive to immigrants of every ethnic origin. Indeed, the liberal fragment in Canada, like its American counterpart, expects the immigrant to embrace its values and even harbors a visible resentment against the rare immigrant groups such as Doukhobors, Mennonites, and Hutterites that for religious reasons choose not to be integrated into the wider liberal society. On the other hand, the Italian or even the French immigrant soon discovers a great gulf between his own culture and that of French Canada, a gulf representing the French Revolution and the entire development of European society in the nineteenth century toward liberalism, socialism, and industrialism. Canadian experience suggests that ideological factors may be even more powerful than language in determining the cultural allegiance of the immigrant.

Thus if the percentage of British stock has decreased steadily in Canada, the relative proportion of the two fragments, as was suggested at the beginning of this essay, has remained remarkably constant.[40] It is scarcely surprising that on the whole the French fragment has always shown a cooler attitude toward immigration than the English one, or that its more extreme elements have viewed immigration darkly as an Anglo-Saxon conspiracy to offset the demographic effects of differential birth rates.

The receptivity of the English fragment to immigration

265

also had its limits, however, as it discovered when confronted with substantial non-European immigration. Canada's infinitesimal Negro population (0.18 per cent in 1961) has never been a source of tension, but in the early years of the twentieth century the West Coast faced a rapidly mounting wave of migrants from China, Japan, and India, chiefly male workers brought in by industries facing a shortage of labor. By 1907 it was officially estimated that one in four of the adult males in British Columbia was of Asiatic origin. The economic effects were soon felt in the displacement of Canadian labor, lower wages, and deterioration of working conditions. The local reaction was abrupt. Beginning as a protest by organized labor, it quickly took on ugly overtones of rioting and violence. The provincial legislature intervened, and in the end the federal government was forced to adopt a restrictive immigration policy.[41] Thus if the problem of interracial tension has found a relatively peaceful solution in Canada, this has been achieved only at the cost of stringent limits on the entry of non-European immigrants.

The nature of Canada's dualism has significantly affected the shape of its external alignments. The English fragment, as a liberal fragment of the American type, retains ideological affinities with the rest of the English-speaking world. Its sense of nationality, which began to emerge from the eighteen-seventies onward, has always labored under a handicap on account of this kinship. The French fragment, whose corresponding bond was severed forever by the French Revolution, has possessed since the eighteenth century a far clearer sense of its own identity.

Toward the United States, English Canada has a strangely ambivalent relationship. Born of American liberalism and in many essential respects closely similar to contemporary American society, the English fragment is nevertheless founded upon a rejection of the American Revolution, and it faces a constant need to justify to itself the continuing separate existence of Canada. Since the price of political independence is felt in a lower standard of living, English Canadians must find some satisfactory rationalization for their position.

266

This rationalization is achieved by a number of different lines of argument, some purely emotional, others based on careful thought. Perhaps the most common is that which emphasizes the value of Canada's membership in the Commonwealth. But the Commonwealth connection, like the imperial tutelage that preceded it, has for Canada a rather special function. It serves primarily as a political counterweight to an American influence which is so strong in the economic, military, and cultural fields as to endanger her political independence. Somewhat paradoxically, Canada has clung to the Commonwealth idea as a means of protecting her own independence, and hence for four decades her influence within the Commonwealth was aimed at minimizing the notion of collective responsibility and enlarging the sphere of independent action of member states.

Yet it would be a mistake to underrate the emotional attachment that many Canadians of British birth or parentage still feel for British institutions. The continuing diversity of Canadian society, its failure to develop a sharp focus of loyalty within itself, and the gradualness of Canada's separation from Britain—all these factors make it easy for English Canadians to cap the foundations of their North American liberal social ethos with a superstructure embodying elements of the wider British political heritage.

French Canadians look askance at these divided loyalties. Many of them still find in the Commonwealth connection merely a hurtful reminder of an era of subjugation. They perceive, far more clearly than the English Canadians, the affinity of the English fragment with American liberalism, and they know that their struggle for cultural survival must be carried on against both. Indeed, the more massive and more serious threat to French-Canadian values is that from across the border.

French Canada is naturally isolated in the world, but much intellectual effort has been expended in an attempt to bridge the chasm and to find some counterweight to the Anglo-American pressures that so largely shape Canada's foreign policy. With modern France any real *rapprochement* has been very slow to develop. In recent years French-Canadian intellectuals and the Quebec government have worked hard to rebuild cultural ties, but the modesty of the results to date serves to emphasize the intrinsic difficulty of the problem.[42] Nor is there any closer relationship with more strongly Catholic countries such as Italy or Spain. For a long time French Canada's most important link with the outside world was the Papacy itself, though diplomatic representation was blocked by the hypersensitive Protestantism of English Canada. Some writers in both fragments have tried to demonstrate affinities between Latin America and Latin Canada, but this comparison, even if ideologically sound in general terms, has not been productive of real contact. The fact is that the more one seeks for the natural counterparts of French Canada abroad, the more is the essential uniqueness of its tradition laid bare.

These differences in attitudes toward the external world have given rise in the past to major internal stresses. The Boer War found English Canada more unanimously imperialist than Britain herself, but French Canada was just as firmly uninterested in imperialist wars and even inclined to sympathize with the Boer cause. Both the World Wars provoked crises of the first magnitude over military conscription, and only the most delicate handling of an explosive situation in 1944 brought the country through the Second World War without a deep and bitter cleavage such as had lingered long after the First. Similar differences in outlook blocked Canada's support of League of Nations sanctions against Italy during the Ethiopian crisis, and both the Spanish Civil War and the French Vichy regime found Canadian opinion divided roughly along the fragment lines.

One of the modest, minor blessings of the Cold War has been its tendency to heal this rift. For Marxian communism, unlike Catholic-based authoritarianism of the interwar period, is an ideology to which both fragments find themselves intrinsically opposed, and the traditional isolationist tendency of French Canada is neatly offset by the greater hostility of Catholicism toward the Communist system. Canada played a substantial part in the formation of the North Atlantic Treaty Organization, and its present adherence to that alliance, if not exactly marked by public enthusiasm, is at least passively accepted by both the French and English fragments.

Perhaps the most interesting question of all remains to be explored: the impact of industrialization. For if agriculture and rural life played a primary role in shaping both fragments, Canadian society today is predominantly urban and industrial.[43] To what extent, then, has this fundamental change in the economy affected the underlying ethos of the fragments?

As with many other issues, the impact on English Canada may be read in larger and clearer characters in American experience, where industrialization began earlier and went further than in Canada. The significant point is that the American liberal fragment developed an industrial economy and a powerful labor movement without being significantly attracted to socialism.[44] In broad terms, Canada has done the same, and in world perspective the English-Canadian labor movement closely reflects its American counterpart in spirit and structure. But there is a complicating factor. Since 1944 the province of Saskatchewan has had the only avowedly socialist government in North America, and the political party behind it, the Cooperative Commonwealth Federation, or C.C.F., has formed the official opposition in three other provinces and become a moderately successful minor party at the federal level. Is there, then, some basic difference here between the English-Canadian and American fragments?

The background of the C.C.F. is the same setting of agrarian discontent that had earlier produced a whole succession of frontier protest movements on both sides of the border. But in this instance certain extreme conditions of world depression and severe drought combined to produce a setting favorable to a more radical political ideology. In addition, the Canadian Prairies, settled several decades later than the American Midwest, were generously sprinkled with British immigrants already familiar with Fabian socialism. The first C.C.F. convention at Regina in 1933 formally inaugurated an alliance between western agrarian radicalism and

269

the small socialist wing of the Canadian labor movement, an alliance dedicated to the eradication of capitalism.

The depression and war years saw some modest successes, the chief of which was the Saskatchewan electoral victory of 1944, but by the nineteen-fifties the advance ceased and the movement was becalmed, having failed to make any further headway among urban industrial workers. In an effort to enlarge the base of support the C.C.F. was refounded in 1961 as the New Democratic Party, another party of the left based on the same aims of farmer-worker alliance as its predecessor. Significantly, however, the new party has deliberately set out to create for itself a new and broader liberal image that will appeal to all progressive opinion in the community.[45] The lessons of C.C.F. experience seem clear enough. In its success in Saskatchewan the party represents a continuation of an agrarian radicalism that is fairly general in the history of North America. In its failure elsewhere it demonstrates once more the difficulty of building in North America a politically conscious socialist movement of the sort that emerged in Europe. To win mass support in the industrial provinces, parties of the left must, for the near future at least, operate within the limits imposed by the liberal social framework of English Canada.*

The impact of industrialization upon the French fragment is not so easily described. In the first place, industry in Quebec has been financed chiefly by non-French capital, controlled either by Americans or by English Canadians, a fact which has created a vast gulf between labor and management and added highly volatile fuel to the fires of nationalism. On the other hand industrialization and urbanization have taken

* The limits, however, are fairly broad. It is relevant that the issue of private enterprise versus state activity has always been decided upon pragmatic rather than ideological grounds in Canada. A small, struggling community under the shadow of a giant neighbor can scarcely afford the luxury of fixed principles on an issue of this kind. Hence even nonsocialist governments in Canada have subsidized and built canals, subsidized and nationalized railways, and established varying degrees of public ownership in air transport, radio and television broadcasting, hydroelectric power, and telephones, all without seriously incurring the charge of subverting the liberal way of life. Where improvisation of this type is possible, the appeal of doctrinal socialism may be significantly lessened.

place without seriously modifying the traditional emphasis on family and parish as the twin foundations of French-Canadian social structure, so that the French-Canadian worker has by no means become a proletarian in the classical Marxian sense.

Outside of metropolitan Montreal, where international unionism has made considerable headway, French Canada has developed its own characteristic Catholic trade-union movement, the Confederation of National Trade Unions. In its initial years this movement was organized and guided by the clergy, that is, by a sector of the traditional elite of French Canada, closely allied with the government and the middle classes. Under the circumstances it is scarcely surprising that in the nineteen-twenties and nineteen-thirties the leadership was far too weak and conciliatory, too willing to sacrifice the worker's interest to the cause of social and industrial peace. But in time this mildness produced a vigorous, anticlerical reaction, and the postwar period has seen the emergence of a strong lay leadership in the Catholic unions that has increasingly found common ground with the more militant sectors of the labor movement of English Canada.

On the ideological plane, French Canada has not yet come to terms with the new industrial society. Its electorate has shown no interest in socialism, which has been strongly and rather indiscriminately condemned by the church. Even the C.C.F., which repudiated all anticlerical tendencies, was long opposed by the Catholic clergy and made no headway at all in French Canada. Yet the church which accepted the principles of the encyclical *Rerum novarum,* with its insistence upon the just rights of labor, could not be enamored of unrestrained capitalism either. While the Catholic union movement tried to reconcile in some practical way the urgent need for vastly improved working conditions with the church's call for social harmony between classes, nationalist intellectuals during the nineteen-thirties toyed with theories of Catholic corporatism and even Italian fascism. But this proved a false trail, flatly unacceptable to the rank and file and impossible of application in a North American setting. Thus the rise of industrialism left the French fragment lost in an ideological

271

wilderness, conscious only of its inferior role in an unfamiliar economic system that forced the two fragments into closer and closer collaboration.

The English liberal fragment can adjust fairly easily to a solution of the labor question through collective bargaining between the parties concerned, with the state defining the rules and seldom intervening directly, but the French fragment, with its strongly organic view of society, has had difficulty in accepting a notion so alien to its own tradition. For a long time the ruling elite, composed of a loose alliance of the higher clergy, the professional classes, and the political and administrative leaders, was visibly reluctant to recognize either the claims of the worker or the existence of the labor movement. But the movement has emerged anyway and has found increasing support among sympathetic intellectuals. Within the last few years it has grown so strong as to constitute the only alternative center of power to the traditional elite, the only potential challenge to the authoritarian tradition. In the process of readjustment to industrial society that now faces French Canada organized labor is likely to play a decisive role, but what the ultimate pattern of adjustment will be is still far from clear.

This essay has ranged widely over many topics. It is time now to assess the prospects for Canadian society. As a starting point, the existence of the two fragments seems established beyond dispute—even more firmly, perhaps, than Canadian unity itself.

The English fragment seems firmly and irremovably anchored to its liberal heritage. One might even argue that the liberal tradition in Canada is free from some of the strains that trouble its American equivalent. For if its domestic history has been less happy and less tolerant, it has also been more sheltered from external stresses. Because it is less burdened with world responsibilities than its American counterpart, it has shown none of the latter's recent tendencies to "liberal absolutism." [46] It is significant that English Canada, so close to the American political tradition in other respects, has developed no parallel to the American extreme right. But neither has industrialization brought deviation to the left: with the formation of the New Democratic Party in 1961 the last modest, half-realized elements of socialism represented in the C.C.F. party seem to have been reabsorbed into the liberal tradition.

Of the outlook for the French fragment it is at present far more difficult to speak. We have seen that French Canada, founded on seventeenth-century absolutism, found its original ethos of unity and centralized control strongly reinforced after the Cession by the need to combat the Anglicizing and assimilative pressures all around it. In recent years, however, the climate in Quebec has changed. The survival of French Canada is assured. Energies have been diversified, and narrow horizons have been enlarged. The role of the provincial government in economic development, education, and culture has expanded in unprecedented fashion. The electric-power industry has been nationalized. The teaching profession, long a preserve of the clergy, is being rapidly laicized. The arts flourish as never before. The death in 1959 of Premier Maurice Duplessis, perhaps the most authoritarian personality ever produced by French Canada, seemed to open the floodgates to a pent-up surge of reform.

However, the theoretical problem remains unsolved. Do these developments portend some basic change in the underlying tradition? Many observers, including quite a few from English Canada, believe that French Canada has entered upon its long-delayed liberal revolution. Others, including some French-Canadian intellectuals, feel that their society, betrayed by a liberal capitalism that has long excluded French Canadians from its prime rewards, will pass, by a curious instance of the theory of combined development, directly from its authoritarian heritage into some form of postliberal socialism. Still a third diagnosis—and not the least worthy of consideration—is that the traditional elite, which has proved discerningly flexible in the past, will somehow find the means of adapting itself to the new forces and will continue to fulfill a strong directive role as before. From French colonial authoritarianism to Catholic clerical authoritarianism to separatist-leaning, ultranationalist authoritarianism: in this view the core of the tradition would remain unaltered.

At a time of rapid social change it is clearly unwise to be dogmatic. The situation of French Canada today appears to be one of genuine indeterminacy, and it would be foolish to predict its future development from historical guidelines alone. Clearly the central enigma lies in the internal social evolution of the French fragment itself, and here English Canadians can only look on from the outside, like spectators on the shore who watch the agony of a ship caught in a raging sea. But the English fragment is not wholly absolved of responsibility, for the reaction of English Canada toward a changed Quebec may well tip the scales in the French fragment in favor of either extremism or compromise on the issue of future relations between the two communities. Thus in the last analysis both fragments may well have a voice in deciding whether and under what conditions the experiment in dualism shall go on.

Chapter Eight

The Radical Culture of Australia

by Richard N. Rosecrance

1 England and the Origin of Australia

There is a sense in which the frontier societies, populated from overseas by European migrants, fail to outgrow the conditions of their birth. The cultural fragment of British society implanted in Australian soil in the first half of the nineteenth century has retained a remarkable distinctness and fixity. Its lineaments are still discernible and its influence largely undiminished. Australian society today has umbilical connections with the egalitarianism of the gold camps, the struggles of exclusives and emancipists, and even the sullen resentments of the early convict settlements. More than other frontier countries, perhaps, Australia was isolated from the main streams of European culture; in consequence, it was destined to find its political and social tendencies immanent in the foundational population. Foundation, of course, was not a solitary act. The "founding" of Australia continued for three-quarters of a century, and the ethos of the population was not fully formed until after the gold rushes of the eighteen-fifties. But the Australian social adult of today is prefigured in the social embryo of yesteryear.

This is not to overstress heredity and neglect environment as a shaping influence. The outcomes of Australian social his-

275

tory cannot be explained without reference to the natural features of the Australian subcontinent—climate, soil, resources, and, above all, water. The founders had to contend with an intractable land mass, and much of what they did was largely determined by it. Tropical horticulture was ruled out for the bulk of Australian settlements, whatever their cultural background. But geographic determinism is not a sufficient explanation of Australian history, and the striking feature of that history is its British character. More than this, Australia's uniqueness is a result of settlement by a particular fraction of British society. For Australia was never a microcosm of Britain. The British aristocracy did not touch Australia, and even the substantial middle class did not find an important place in Australian development. At one extreme Australia was bourgeois; at the other, it was unrelievedly proletarian. Laboring classes have had a prominent role in Australian history, and the divisions in Australian society, important as they have been, have taken place within an overarching working context. Australia was and is a land of toilers, and even the graziers have not been notable exceptions to this rule.

Since it was the destiny of the human race that the commonest methods of bread-winning and production were to undergo changes incomparably more rapid than those of any previous age, there must in any case have been terrible suffering while the life of a whole people was being thus uprooted. But the misery in England, necessarily great, was increased by the political and intellectual atmosphere of the period in which change began. . . .[1]

The early populace of Australia emerged out of a heady brew of British social ferment. The enclosure movement during the eighteenth century and the factory system that began to develop at the end of the eighteenth and the beginning of the nineteenth combined to reorganize the pattern of social existence. Both forces drastically speeded up the process of urbanization, and for the first time British cities were crowded with the surplus population of village and town. The enclosure movement gradually dispossessed the

276

yeoman farmer. "Scientific agriculture" may have benefited from the consolidation of landholdings; the wealthy and aristocratic classes certainly did so. At the time, "land" was the foundation of social and political influence, and the acquisition of land was a fundamental means of preserving and extending social privilege. In England and Scotland where the land remained in the hands of indigenous owners conditions were bad enough. In Ireland the enclosures enhanced the position of foreign landlords, but manufacturing industry did not provide occupations for the expropriated peasantry. Instead, they continued to suffer under the tyranny of an external oligarchy.

The developing industrial system in England attracted a substantial number of Irish immigrants and gave employment to the surplus population of the countryside. At the same time, herding men, women, and children together to work in the filth and degradation of the factories and mines, it sapped personal independence and created powerful discontents. The regimen of manufacturing probably made the British working classes less amenable to other social controls.

The operation of the Poor Laws restricted the movement of labor and artifically depressed wage rates. Often the indigent were faced with the alternatives of starvation or work for subsistence wages. In order to reduce the poor rates, conscious attempts were made to hire workers at the lowest possible wage levels. As long as the conditions of employment were slightly better than those of the workhouse, the poverty-stricken would be discouraged from becoming a public charge; as long as wage rates were low, poor rates could be even lower. The economic plight of the lower classes inclined them to be disrespectful of property. It was an interesting paradox of the Industrial Revolution that the forces which elevated property and wealth to a high pinnacle of prestige and power among the higher fractions of society brought them into reproach and disrepute among the lower orders. Improvements in the position of one class took place at the expense of the position of the other. Nor did the reforming energies of "philosophical radicalism" ameliorate the conditions of the poor and disinherited. Malthus' theory of population was in fact a rationalization for continued indigence. Impersonal economic forces were aligned against social reform.

Simultaneously, the weight of the criminal law fell more heavily upon offenders. Crimes "without benefit of clergy" were extended during the eighteenth century, and new crimes were added to an already formidable list. Larceny above the value of one shilling was technically a capital offense, but judges often imposed transportation as a sentence. There were, in addition, a large number of specific felonies for which transportation was punishment. Because of the asperities of the law, juries sometimes refused to convict, and at the beginning of the nineteenth century the British penal system was characterized by unremitting severity in theory and a certain leniency in practice. Because of gaps in the law, certain crimes that should have been crimes were not; because of an outrageous schedule of sentences, punishment was sometimes too extreme to be inflicted. In the circumstances the legal order did not pose an effective deterrent to crime, while the economic order seemed to make it a necessity. Crime rates at the turn of the century were exceedingly high, and well-to-do citizens often had to carry cudgels to defend themselves from gangs and pickpockets.

The signal result of enclosures and the Industrial Revolution was the creation of a class which rejected the existing social order and which began to seek political remedies for its difficulties. The collection of dispossessed agriculturalists and industrial laborers in the great urban centers fostered common notions of reform and began to make possible common action. The failure of the French Revolution as a reformative influence and the consequent postponement of reform for more than a generation gave rise to new outcries against oppression. "The enforcement of Pitt's laws against incipient Trade Unionism pointed the working classes to the need of political action through Parliamentary Reform." [2]

In the cause of reform the working class had an important ally; the British middle classes were equally disfranchised by the old borough system, and their grievance against the land-

lords was also acute. When the Great Reform Bill of 1832
became law it was carried through by middle-class Radicals
as well as by the support of Cobbett and Place. Unqualified
middle-class suffrage was not established by the new electoral system. Rather, the Ten Pound suffrage enfranchised
half the middle class while prolonging the influence of the
Tory gentry, and country gentlemen faced each other across
the House of Commons for a generation after the Reform
Bill. But the workingmen supported the change as the first
step in a series of electoral reforms, leading to the enfranchisement of labor.

The victory of 1832, the reform of municipal government,
and the new factory act, however, did not satisfy the working
classes. And the Poor Law of 1834 which put an end to the
system of supplementing insufficient wages out of the poor
rates was a radical surgery for pauperism. It was one of the
curious tragedies of social history that brought a simultaneous
demand for bourgeois reform on the one hand and proletarian reform on the other. Because of the intervention of
the Napoleonic wars bourgeois reform was postponed, and
it was achieved finally only after the demands for more
favorable treatment of the working class had matured. In
the circumstances the temporary Whig-Liberal ascendancy
could not satisfy the lower orders of society, and the socialist
and trade-union militancy of the end of the nineteenth century was prefigured in the decade after the Reform Bill. It
was not accidental that Robert Owen had taken up the cause
of socialism before the liberal program had been even half
achieved. The liberal victories of 1832 to 1846, indeed, represented the triumph of a class hostile to the workingman. The
tenuous legality with which trade unions were endowed after
1824-25 did not prevent the "transportation of the 'Dor-
chester labourers' for attempting to form an agricultural
labourers' Union in which oaths were administered." [3]

And the failures of trade-unionism in this early period
engendered further attempts at political reform. An extension of the Reform Bill in the direction of manhood suffrage,
the ballot, equal electoral districts, payment of members of
Parliament, and abolition of the property qualification for

M.P.'s could facilitate the political realization of a working-class program, much as the act of 1832 had facilitated the triumph of the liberal program. But adherents of this People's Charter were not successful. Even the trade-unionists thought these political ambitions premature, and the liberals would not tolerate Chartist attempts to harry repeal of the Corn Laws. Chartism repudiated the older working-class alliance with the liberals and actually sought to enact a lower-class program in the heyday of middle-class reform. Though they could not win, the Chartists at least, re-emphasized the growing gulf between "two nations" in England, a gulf which mid-century liberalism served to widen.*

It was a fragment of this British society which lodged in Australia during the first six decades of the nineteenth century. The cultural sector of Britain which was abstracted during this period of settlement, however, was not a mere replica of British society. While it would be inaccurate to describe Australian settlers as "outpourings of the poor-houses and the unions of the United Kingdom," [4] there seems little doubt that they were largely a homogeneous group of city folk of humble economic and social origins. The convict chapter in Australian history was written by a group of paupers, political prisoners, and genuine criminals. Because of the severity of British sentences, convicts might be transported for seven years for committing the most minor offenses. Economic need was undoubtedly the prime explanation for the crimes of many transportees. After the French Revolution, Pitt's repression was partly reflected in the convicts transported to Australia, though the number of political criminals has undoubtedly been exaggerated. And yet, the leniency of English juries and the reduction of sentences by judges often meant that the convicts sent to Australia had been guilty of major crimes under English law. As the costs of transportation grew, moreover, the British Government

---

* Later in Australia it was this gulf which helped to explain acute class consciousness in the absence of real class differentiation. See Geoffrey Serle, *The Golden Age: A History of the Colony of Victoria, 1851-1861* (Melbourne, 1963), pp. 374-375.

inclined increasingly to send the major offenders and to keep those convicted of minor crimes in English jails.

In any event, the transportees were largely from a degraded and debased fraction of the British public. If we can place credence in the accounts of contemporary commentators, it must be concluded that they were an indolent lot. The enclosures of land and the Poor Laws of Britain had destroyed the independence of the laborer and lent incentives to pauperism, and the pauperism was but one stage removed from crime. It was not surprising that the convicts in Australia relied overmuch on authority and seemed incapable of thrift or industry.

The convict population of the Australian colonies was leavened by the assisted and other free immigrants of the period after 1820. And the officers and men assigned to guard the convicts established an important place for themselves in the economic and social life of the colonies. Between 1825 and 1830 the majority of people who emigrated to Australia were from the English middle class. And while the number of assisted immigrants between 1829 and 1851 was three times that of unassisted migrants, there were a number of years in which immigrants able to pay their own way predominated. By 1841 convicts, emancipists, and expirees in New South Wales were just a little over half the number born in the colony or arrived free.[5] Numerically speaking, the convict preponderance was over, and for the rest of the century a different kind of migrant made his way to Australian shores.

Even the free immigrants, however, were creatures of the British social and industrial system. They were eager to emigrate as a group, but Canada and America usually had the greatest attractions; Australia remained to take the residue who could not go to North America. Canada and the United States were not so distant that a land fund was needed to assist immigration; passage was not expensive. And "on the whole the American immigrants were men and women filled with the earnest desire to advance their economic status by hard work in the colonies."[6] Those who opted for Australia could often not afford even the modest cost of passage to America. They succeeded in escaping the British cul-de-sac, but they had no vision of a self-reliant life in Australia. Only with the gold rushes after 1851 did a more ambitious type seek his fortune in Australia, and then at a time when political and economic reform was coursing the globe. "Gold trebled the population in ten years . . ." [7] and much of the increment was energetic and hard-working. The "diggers" added a new strain to Australian blood, and the vast increase in population after 1851 helped further to submerge the convict compartment of Australian development. The Australian fragment was stretched and enlarged.

Of a higher economic stratum were the exclusives, the social elite of New South Wales. They included wealthy ex-members of the officer corps who had acquired great tracts of land, the substantial middle-class settlers of the twenties, and high civil officials. This group, of a rather different class background from the rest of Australian settlers, was primarily interested in protecting its economic position. This meant particularly a more secure position on the land. As the emancipists attained position as agriculturalists and won social recognition, they came to ally with the exclusives on the land question. Squatters of all social backgrounds had to find security of tenure; they could not allow themselves to be dispossessed by the emergent radical democracy.

Thus, the Australian settlers ranged in a gamut extending from the humble poor to the propertied middle class. But Dilke was wrong when he said Australian civilization was English "with the upper class left out." [8] More than the upper class was omitted from the fragment of British society which was Australia. The working classes predominated in its founding, and their attitudes were of a special character. Australia could not be described as a land in which Gladstonian liberalism would have no opponents. Gladstonian liberalism reflected essentially middle-class dominance, and in Australia the middle class was not as firmly entrenched as in Britain. The working segment was of greater importance, numerically and in terms of social ethos. And that ethos was affected by the specific motivations which brought immigration. The convicts were thrust into Australia: they had no vision of a better life in the colonial context; they could be expected to rely upon Australian officialdom as they had relied upon the poor rates. By and large they could not be counted on as either agents of reform or of an independent existence. Two of their major contributions to the Australian ethos, however, were hatred of the upper classes and an abiding love of leisure. The "philosophy of the alehouse bench" had some impact in Australia and with good reason: in the English context, providence and frugality brought no greater rewards to the indigent poor than indolence. As Arthur Young said: "If I am sober, shall I have land for a cow? If I am frugal, shall I have half an acre of potatoes? You offer no motives. Bring me another pot." [9]

But pauperism and lassitude were not the only importations from Britain. The trade-unionists and the working-class radicals who already rejected the full-blown apparatus of economic liberalism also had their impact. In the thirties and forties both convict and free migrants had grievances against the British social system, grievances which they sought to air in the colonies. Many of them repudiated liberal governance and the unregulated Industrial Revolution. Their attitudes on social questions were militant and relatively specific. Unlike American workers, they could not be dazzled by the Whig sleight of hand: they could never become proponents of Horatio Alger. The "rags-to-riches" transformation was illusory for the British proletariat, for the Industrial Revolution occurred in Britain at a time of considerable class differentiation. In America it occurred at a time of relative class fluidity.

The "gold-rush mentality" provided yet another strand. The migrants drawn to Australia by the lure of gold had still different social attitudes. They were independent seekers of fortune, animated by the desire to improve their condition and status. They may not have been stolid conservers of capital or patient toilers, but they were self-reliant and energetic. And their ambitions for self-improvement were tinctured with reformism. They could be expected to hazard their economic substance for an improbable gain or to lend their efforts to an assault on privilege. Madgwick probably puts the case too strongly when he says that the subservience of pre-1851 immigrants "to the will of the Government and their disinclination to combat the growing power of the great squatters and merchants seemed likely to produce a form of oligarchic or plutocratic Government; and in this connection it is well for Australia that the gold rush immigrants were fired by zeal for political and economic reform." [10] At the same time it was not altogether accidental that the first democratic triumphs in Australia were won when a persistent radicalism agitated the gold camps. The gold diggers were avowedly materialistic, but they were not servile, and they could be expected to act against the established order where other colonists had merely endured it. And the gold rushes probably helped to solidify the philosophy of practical materialism as an operative creed for future generations of Australians. It is not surprising that Australian elections have often been fought over questions of sheer pecuniary reward.

2 The Challenge of the Squattocracy

The colonial social hierarchy lacked the appearance of permanence that marked the old world. It carried no sanction of long and inherited custom, and change of status was a familiar colonial experience even before the rapid changes of fortune that marked the years of the gold discoveries. Therefore, social divisions were neither accepted as an inevitable part of the social order nor regarded as something which could be altered only by a radical subversion of the whole.[11]

In the latter half of the nineteenth century Australia emerged as a truncated version of Europe. Only a fragment of British society landed on Australian shores; the architectonic three-class structure typical of Europe was not imposed on Australia. In political terms Australia was the "radical" fragment of British society. A certain admixture of "philosophical radicalism" mitigated the working-class ethos of convicts, gold diggers, Chartists, and trade-unionists. At the same time Australia's political bias was already skeptical of the liberal position. Australian "radicalism" was in part a species of revolt against "philosophical radicalism." In any event, the relative social homogeneity of Australia as compared with the relative social heterogeneity of Britain made for a powerful unity on political questions. And this was true despite the obvious divisions between convicts, emancipists, expirees, and free settlers. Australians were conscious relatively early of the benefits of natural cultural relaxation in a context of a "radical" consensus. And the relaxation within the "radical" fragment was directly proportional to the tensions engendered outside it. Defectors from the radical myth were as heavily penalized as those who subscribed to it were rewarded.

This was the problem posed by the squatters. There was nothing intrinsic in their quasi-aristocratic pretensions. Some of them were of middle-class backgrounds and some acknowledged convict antecedents. Their opposition to the emergent radical democracy could not be explained by heredity or tradition. Rather, their unique position was to be explained by economic forces partly beyond their control. The land was the means of their existence. Because of the relatively sparse pasturage and the general aridity of the land, economic sheep and cattle runs had to be of large size. Thus, the geographic and economic imperatives of the Australian subcontinent imposed habits of life not altogether unlike those of the British gentry. It was not to be expected that even Wentworth would demur when aristocracy beckoned.

In this context the Australian frontier operated quite differently from the American. The American frontier consisted, with a few notable exceptions, of rich agricultural land; it was sufficiently productive to support an average family on a reasonably small plot. But Australian land was not uniformly free, nor was it unusually productive, and the result was the development of vast sheep and, to a lesser extent, cattle stations which led quite early to the occupation of a major portion of all economic lands and to the temporary end of the frontier in the American sense.

The political consequences of the development of what Brian Fitzpatrick has called the "Big Man's Frontier" were far-reaching.[12] The pastoral stations became rural capitalist enterprises, and in turn gave rise to a rural proletariat of shepherds, boundary riders, and shearers. In comparative terms Australia in 1840 could be likened to an America in which the agriculturalists were predominantly the great ranchers, and the conflict we find between the farmer and the cattleman in America is multiplied many times in the struggle between farmer and squatter in Australia.[13] The consequence was that while the American frontier was on balance an egalitarian force, the Australian frontier tended to foster conflict and social cleavage in Australian society. The antagonism of squatter and swagman, pastoralist and farmer is a striking characteristic of Australian history during the nineteenth century, and it prevails in diminished force even today.

But the pastoral way of life could not support a full-blown aristocracy. Despite the peculiar nature of the Australian frontier, the squattocracy provided no more than a rudimentary insight into the nature of traditional European conservatism. A fundamental point is that the victory over the pastoralists was won relatively early. If the graziers maintained their privileged political position into the eighteen-fifties and their absolute control of the land for a decade longer, they had so far fallen from their high estate by the eighteen-nineties that a national ethos could be created which smacked not of conservatism, but of militant radicalism.[14] This is not to say that wool has not remained the mainstay of the Australian economic system; it is simply to assert that the social and political significance of "wool" and the class which produces it has rapidly diminished.

There were substantial reasons for the early demise of the squatters' political pre-eminence. In the first place the squatters had intrinsic weaknesses as compared with the strengths of the old European society. Indeed, though their method of life seemed to link them with the landed interests of Europe, they were in fact rural capitalists, and their hirelings were not serfs, but rural proletarians.[15] Their political aims were similar to those of the European bourgeoisie: the furtherance of their own economic interests. When the British Colonial Office objected to the measures the squatters desired, it was eminent logic to take up the cry for self-government. It is not surprising to find Sir Keith Hancock remarking: "Wool made Australia a solvent nation, and, in the end, a free one." [16]

In the second place, the political character of the remainder of Australian society was very likely to put the squatter at a disadvantage. Australian settlements, as we have seen, had been formed out of the crucible of British social ferment. Australian colonization followed the Industrial Revolution in Britain and reflected many of the social innovations which it had made. The development of large-scale enterprise, the deplorable conditions of work in the factories and mines, and the high tariff on the import of grain had created a class which, if it did not fundamentally repudiate the liberal philosophy, at least desired a radical transformation of the theory of liberalism in the direction of greater social and political justice. It followed that the social ethos of a majority of Australians even at this early stage was in the direction of radicalism, not doctrinaire liberalism. The squatter, therefore, was confronted with an enemy not one, but two political jumps ahead of him. If he might have secured a workable compromise with a population which was largely bourgeois, he was overwhelmed by one which was further to the left. In any circumstances the radical segments of Australian society would harbor little good will for the squatter; for here, after all, were the English industrialists and the perpetrators of the Corn Laws rolled into one. If economic liberalism was not fully adequate as a social gospel, how much less tolerable would be the creation of a class which reeked of landed privilege? Indeed, many Australians qua Britons had had to fight the *ancien régime* before they arrived in Sydney; they were scarcely likely to put up with an Australian version of the old enemy.

In the third place, the Australian frontier, if it did not conduce to the development of an independent yeomanry, at least did not present a blank wall to the rural laborer.[17] The American safety valve in analytic terms was the presence of an escape hatch for potential fomenters of urban discontent. It undoubtedly ameliorated, if it did not prevent, conflicts between middle class and proletariat, but most important, it prevented the development of a feudalistic bourgeoisie on the land. In Australia, however, the land offered no escape from gentility. Indeed, the only avenue of escape for the rural Australian proletariat was an urban setting. Without the city as a haven for discontent on the stations, the development of a full-blown gentry would have been a possible result of rural capitalism. In fact, the rural capitalists themselves opened the escape hatch to shearers and shepherds. The booming wool trade, which constituted almost half of British wool imports by 1850, was the dominant economic fact in the colonies, and quite literally it financed the growth of secondary enterprise. The great agricultural industries, moreover, required only a small labor force and thus facilitated the movement toward the cities. Under the stimulus of pastoral industry the old administrative centers of the penal colonies became great trading centers and later financial and manufacturing hubs as well.

Of course, as must be obvious, the city is a unique kind of safety valve. Although it could absorb the rural proletariat cast up by the sheep stations, it could not provide the kind of independent existence found on the American agricultural frontier. Hence, while the American immigrant or farmer could make good his escape from the capitalist city and the bourgeois "boss," the Australian, as it were, merely escaped from the frying pan into the fire; he went, in a sense, from city (in the outback) to city (in the city), and though the ability to change masters was a real reinforcement of freedom, the master in each case was real enough. Thus Australia's peculiar safety valve strengthened Australian radicalism, for urban life is in a sense intrinsically radical.

But there was another outlet for the Australian laborer of the eighteen-fifties. The discovery of gold created a new mining frontier of a special kind. This frontier was not always on the fringe of settlement; indeed, in the cases of Ballarat and Bendigo, it was not far from the established center at Melbourne. But the gold rushes did bring hordes of Australians and others to new and unpopulated areas. In a decade the population of Australia increased threefold, and gold became the colonies' major export. For ten years and more, "gold" afforded a safety valve, an alternative to both city and station which had not been available before.

Fourthly, the squattocracy were by and large excluded from participation in the formation of a national myth. The carping against "moneygrubbing" and affluence was not to be taken as a serious indictment of practical materialism as a way of life. Rather, it was an implicit criticism of the pastoralists and the wealthy; for it was the well-to-do section of the Australian community that was least committed to a colonial existence. As against the settlers who considered Australia their only home, the upper orders were "temporary sojourners" who viewed Australia as an economic, not a national, enterprise. Once avarice had been gratified, the wealthy might return "home." And in thus viewing colonial life as an instrumental, not a final value, the affluent undermined their right to speak politically for the Australian colonies. Australia had no fully formed national traditions and would acquire them only much later; still, the rudimentary national consensus at least excluded those who would not accept the colonies as the primary national arena. Nadel says that "with the possible exception of the company settlements in South Australia and New Zealand and of the small groups of foreigners, there was little of a sense of mission to be found among the colonists. The desire to build a New Jerusalem, indeed the desire to build at all, was not a conspicuous motive." [18] And yet, those who were unwilling to commit their fortunes and descendants to the colonies violated a rudimentary commandment of emergent nationalism. Thus, "temporary sojourners" failed to exert an important cultural influence, and the standards of cultivation were left to be set by those who would make Australia an "unregenerate workingman's paradise."

In the final analysis the Australian pretenders to gentility were the inverse of the American South. They maintained their economic primacy, but had no lasting political persistence. The American South imposed political traditions which still endure, even though its economic predominance has been undermined. And the difference between the two

289

situations is instructive of an essential difference between Australia and America. The Australian pseudo-aristocracy was overwhelmed in a militantly working-class radical context; even their enormous economic resources could not (and cannot today) remedy their political obsolescence. If Marx was ever wrong, he was wrong in the Australian situation, because after the mid-nineteenth century, economic and political power do not go hand in hand; the second is most certainly not the derivative of the first. In America, conversely, the South shared in the shaping of the liberal myth, and its elemental persistence politically may be attributed partly to its acceptance of essential liberalism at the theoretical level. Who is to say that Calhoun was less garbed with political legitimacy than Jefferson? It was precisely because he distorted (but still shared) the liberal creed that he could not be condemned as a European oligarch and thereby dismissed. The Australian aristocratic pretenders did not have this signal advantage; they were excluded from participation in the creation of a foundational myth.

And in the end, the fall from power of the Australian pastoralists was rapid. As Manning Clark tells us, there were two bites at democracy during the nineteenth century, and the second, which saw the abolition of plural voting, the enfranchisement of women, payment of members of Parliament, and a modicum of social legislation, was perhaps as important as the first.[19] Yet what is amazing is not the triumphs of 1880 to 1900, but the early victories of 1856 to 1865. Few European aristocracies lost their political powers as rapidly as the Australian graziers at mid-century. In nine years' time responsible self-government had been largely established, and manhood suffrage, the secret ballot, the eight-hour day, and a degree of land reform had been achieved. Though these victories were incomplete, they represented democratic gains far in advance of those achieved in Britain. The social strife between pastoralists and the much more numerous radical democracy had to end in the triumph of the latter.

This result was testimony to the coercive power of the radical fragment which lodged in Australia. The radical ethos would not admit upper-class pretensions, and geographical and economic imperatives could not themselves create and sustain an aristocracy. Insofar as these factors imposed rural or agrarian capitalism upon the workingman, they tended to reinforce existing radical dispositions. The early establishment of an urban pattern in Australia served merely to remind the colonists of their urban backgrounds. Thus, perhaps surprisingly, the ultimate political and social ethos of Australians was remarkably unaffected by either doctrinaire liberal or aristocratic ideas. While the Civil War had to be fought in America to dispatch an alien way of life and while a civil war could not be fought in Canada, where divisions were too fundamental, in Australia the frustration of the cryptoaristocracy was easily accomplished, and it did not involve a resort to force. By no stretch of the imagination can the Eureka Stockade be viewed as a manifestation of civil war; it proved, rather, that it would be unnecessary.

3 Nationalism

Canberra, Australia's young capital city, has as yet only two statues. Neither commemorates a notable Australian.[20]

One of the strange outcomes of Australian history, however, is that social and political reform did not lead to the consolidation of a nation-state in mid-nineteenth century. The first blows of democracy did not forge the structure of Australian nationhood. Unlike the American and French examples, political and social cleavage did not lead to national unity. In the French and American cases nationalism and nationality, *inter alia,* were forces legitimizing the codicils of revolution. It was the common experience of revolution that was the touchstone of the nation, and, in both instances again, it was the common sacrifice borne and the common burdens imposed which distinguished nationality from foreignness. Those who had not shared or participated, those who had opposed or temporized—these could be initially excluded from the political General Will. Australia, on the other hand, won reform without nationality; social change without unity.

In the Australian case there were no traditional symbols which would differentiate the Australian from outsiders. The immemorial monuments of the Australian tradition were actually British. The Magna Charta and the Petition of Right linked Australians and Englishmen; they did not differentiate a uniquely Australian nationality. And in the traditional experience of Australia there were no events which fired the imagination and uplifted the heart. There was no glorious past to which Australian sons would wish to recur in memory and legend.[21] The founding of penal colonies in New South Wales and Van Diemen's Land was not memorable, though it might be remembered; it did not provide a hallmark of nationality which Australians would universally acknowledge. Much later it turned out that the rebellion at the Eureka Stockade was the first historic exploit which Australians could recall without mixed feelings; it thus became, finally, the legal tender of nationalism.

But the absence of a heroic past was not the only reason for the slow construction of Australian nationality. Another was the successful and beneficent policy carried on by the British Colonial Office. The reforms applied by Bathurst, Goulburn, and Stephen were progressive in spirit, and they operated to make another American Revolution an unlikely occurrence. The deductions from the American experience had been taken to heart, and Britain would ever afterward take a much more lenient attitude toward her colonial possessions.* And while it clearly overstates the point, there is something to be said for the view that Australian nationalism was unsuccessful because American nationalism had been victorious. The very resilience of colonial policy, the quick attention to colonial grievances, the willingness to reform over the protests of entrenched interests in the colonies—all these combined to make nationalism superfluous. Under the guiding hand of Grey, self-government was conceded to the colonies at a re-

* It should be noted, of course, that Canadians were also colonial pacemakers. The Canadian crises of the eighteen-thirties produced the Durham *Report* and a more conciliatory line in colonial policy.

markably early time. And governors of the stamp of Phillip, Macquarie, Bourke, and Gipps were remarkably able advocates of the colonial cause; they were no handmaidens of the privileged classes. In the result, it was the very conciliatory and enlightened tone of British policy toward the Australian colonies which helped to make political and social transitions easier. Since the Colonial Office was itself an agent of reform, there was no need for the consolidation of an Australian nationality to carry issues which Britain would not concede. In this manner Australia was deprived of Bunker Hill and Yorktown. London continued to be the common point of reference for Australians at least until the end of the century.

The absence of an external foe and the failure of the outside environment to force a national consolidation upon Australians led to a new type of nationality. Because of the beneficence of the external world the shibboleths of nationality could not distinguish in terms of geographic frontiers. Australia, in the first instance, therefore, was not a geographical expression. All those included within a given boundary were not nationals; all those outside it were not aliens. The Eureka Stockade, however, brought a new definition of the national bond. Unlike the end product of the French and American situations, this bond did not differentiate in territorial terms; it did, however, differentiate in social terms. And in this sense it had certain links with aspects of the French and American experience. "Dinkum" Australians were those who accepted and welcomed the democratic triumphs of the fifties and early sixties. Those who balked at those results were not genuine Australians.

Strangely enough, then, nationalism was first defined in the Australian context in social terms, only later in political and territorial terms. And the fact that one aspect of nationalism was given before the other was of great importance. In both the American and French cases the internal-external division eventually succeeded in legitimizing as members of the national body politic even those who had opposed the Revolution. The *émigrés* and the Tories were ostracized for a period, but they eventually were allowed the title of "citizen." They were, after all, united to the rest of society by the political boundary line and the fact of statehood. In the Australian case, however, there was no internal-external demarcation which could be used to legitimize the squatters and the higher orders. Australia was not a national state; Britain was not a foreign power. Geography could not be a factor for the settlement of the social issue on a national basis. And the fact that the squatters were "temporary sojourners" confirmed their ostracism. As Hancock writes:

Australian nationalism took definite form in the class struggle between the landless majority and the land-monopolising squatters. For the squatters and their allies were not like the great mass of immigrant settlers and their children, compelled by circumstances to break their connections with England and accept Australia as their only home. They went to and fro from one hemisphere to another; often they ended their days in England, and sometimes they sent their sons to Oxford or Cambridge. . . . Australian nationalism is the child of Australian democracy, and grew to be an untidy, vociferous urchin in that bitter period of democratic bluster and bungling over the land problem.[22]

In this situation Australian nationalism was a means of imposing radical social attitudes on a recalcitrant class. The squatters had no means of redeeming themselves or of proving their political loyalty, except that of submission to the radical myth. They were forced to abandon their social views before they would be allowed to enter the Australian nation. More than anything else, perhaps, the compulsive operations of early Australian nationalism are the real measure of the defeat of the squattocracy. Not only are they forced to concede politically; they are forced to give up their political views to earn the national imprimatur. In order to get back into national good graces, the squatters themselves must hum the radical tune.

Thus, the heroes of Australian nationalism are different from those found elsewhere. In many societies the national heroes are those who operate to create and reinforce the internal-external division in a territorial sense. The great military heroes of Britain and France, the leaders of the struggle for independence from Great Britain in the United States—these have been traditional myth creators. It is not accidental that Washington is called the Father of His Country while Benedict Arnold is deemed the embodiment of treason. One laid down, the other transgressed the internal-external division. America's national heroes are mostly of this sort, though the Civil War provided an opportunity for historic exploits on social grounds. In France the division is more equal; national heroes are both patriots and reformers. But in Australia patriots do not exist. The real nationalists are fighters of the social struggle. In this sense the gold diggers are the first nationalists, and Ned Kelly, the renowned bandit and bushranger, the only authentic folk hero. The swagman is to the bush what the digger is to the gold camp. And "Waltzing Matilda," a song which glorifies the theft of a sheep from a squatter, has become Australia's only truly national song. One American commentator notes that many Australian radio stations start daily broadcasting with the playing of "Waltzing Matilda" and asks: "How many American stations begin their broadcasting day with 'Casey Jones' or 'Hallelujah, I'm a Bum'?" [23] This oddity is just one more reflection of the fact that nationalism has been tied up with the social issue in Australia in a way that has never been true in the United States.

The later development of the Australian colonies confirmed this pattern. Despite the German occupation in New Guinea and the French position in the New Hebrides, Australia did not denounce Britain for having failed to protect its interests. It complained, it is true, but that led to no sentiment for separation from the parent. As Britain was so willing to concede self-government, federation, and *de facto* independence, there was no need to seek it *de jure*. As Hancock says: "Since the Mother-Country was so placid and so impotent, what occasion was there for that mutinous defiance proper to adolescent, independent daughters? The posture of rebellion would be ridiculous." [24] Federation was graciously conceded by Her Majesty's Government without conditions or controls.

And one of the surprising features of later history was that the presence of external challenges did not fundamentally alter the character of Australian nationalism. Perhaps Aus-

tralian national ties were solidified with the Gallipoli land-
ing of 1915 and with the New Guinea campaign of the Pacific
war; at the same time these historic exploits have not transformed Australian nationalism. The significant fact of present-day nationalism is its social character. Australian soldiers
of two world wars were called "diggers," the lineal descendants of gold-camp radicals, and the wars did not make heroes
of Generals Monash and Blamey. Even the creators of the
Australian Constitution are largely unmemorialized. Barton
and Deakin are not patriotic counterparts of Madison, Jay,
and Hamilton. When independence comes, it is untouted,
and the Statute of Westminster is only adopted by the Australian Parliament in 1942. In the end Australian nationalism did not begin to take on external significance until the
Second World War. Only the Pacific war and British weakness could underscore for Australians the need for separate
action in external relations. The internal-external barrier
could not be erected originally, but the steel for it was forged
in the Second World War.

The result is that Australians have come to have an instrumental view of the state. In the Australian case the nation
was given before the state, and nationalism could not be
used to define and limit the scope of the state. In the British
and American cases nationalism was always intrinsically connected with the political state. For Burke the utmost rever-
ence was due the British Constitution; for Americans the
same was due the product of the Philadelphia Convention.
Nationalism in both cases supported and legitimized a political product; to change the political organization, the constitution, would be to interfere with the charter of nationhood. In such a context, political change and reform have
always to be won through reinterpretation of the constitution; change has always depended upon exegesis of foundational documents. The political state has in this manner enjoyed historic sanction, and reform of the state has had to
contend with conservative nationalism.

In Australia the state has never in this sense represented a
"final value," nor has it enjoyed nationalist legitimacy. Because of the social basis of nationalism, the state has been

primarily instrumental in character. It was not the embodiment of the nation; it was the nation's tool. As a result, in Australia political arrangements are pragmatic contrivances more than elsewhere. The state cannot be employed as a conservative device. As Nadel says:

The very fact that the Australian's view of nationality is at its fundamental level ethical, so to speak, rather than political, makes it possible for him to lean more on the state than those who define their national membership largely in terms of the political state to which they belong. To the latter the state expresses perfectly or imperfectly the ideals to which they are committed, and hence its activities are more circumscribed by the traditions and habits from which these ideals are drawn.

The state to the Australian expresses no ideals in itself. It is an instrument to be used for the enforcement of an ulterior unity, one which owes nothing to the state but to which the state and those reluctantly entrusted with its guidance owe all.[25]

The deductions from the social basis of Australian nationalism are manifold. First, and most obviously, the state would not be as restricted in powers as traditional nationalist states. If the advancement of the social issue required greater governmental intervention into the economic system, that intervention could easily be sanctioned. On the other hand, a certain degree of intervention in the past did not legitimize intervention for all time to come; the state could be used for any number of different purposes. In the founding of colonies over great distances and where a considerable centralization was required, an expanding government would be a great aid; where government's presence was deemed to be neither necessary nor beneficial, its presence could be whittled down without trenching upon historic wont. In the latter event it is not surprising that the Australian Constitution has been interpreted in such a manner as to restrict governmental intervention in the economy.

A second deduction was that the squatters and higher orders would be forced to conform to the social bases of nationalism. To be an Australian was to adopt the radical myth. Thus the operations of Australian nationalism helped to create a socially unanimous society where one did not naturally exist. The victory over the squatter in political terms was in the end a victory in intellectual terms. But the radicalization of the squatters made for an essentially one-myth society. It did not, to be sure, level economic differences or make for uniform habits of life. Today the Australian industrial bourgeoisie and the graziers live much differently from the bulk of Australian citizens. But different habits of life have not meant fundamentally different class ideologies.* The radical fragment in Australia has had a coercive impact on those who presumed to set themselves outside it.

4 State and Native

What gave Australian nationalism its especial significance was that it embraced the definition of social values. Despite some dissent and widespread variety of interpretation, it is clear that the promise of a society essentially democratic in temper and action and in opportunities and rewards commanded the allegiance of the majority. Hostility to privilege, dislike of social gradations, hatred of economic exploitation and an abiding scepticism about the claims of those exalted over their fellows were powerful in shaping the sentiment. This levelling instinct of the Australian was grounded in experience.[26]

Of equal importance with the timing of the original fragment was its congealing. It cannot be denied that the shaping ethos of the settlers of Australia, convict or free, was that of the British lower class of mid-nineteenth century and earlier. But if this ethos had not rapidly congealed into a national myth largely immune to influence by latecomers, Australia would not be as it is today. If Australia had been colonized gradually over a considerable period of time, if settlers had arrived in driblets over the entire century, the process of mythmaking would have had to occur again and again. Myths would not have been fixed, and Australia would have remained in tune, *mutatis mutandis*, with the main

* Australian historians who have analyzed class solely in terms of income or mode of existence have persistently failed to grasp this fact. See note 19.

298

anthems of European development. Abstracting for a different class structure, Australia would simply have been a truncated version of Europe. But in actuality, this is not what happened. At a certain point the fragment of Europe which had been lodged in Australia congealed and became fixed, and continuing immigration after that point did not alter the Australian ethos; rather, it was altered by it. Until the eighteen-sixties, immigrants outnumbered those who had been born in the colonies; afterward, the immigrants had to contend with a majority indigenous fraction. We have various evidence of the process of myth-congealing and of the time periods between which it was accomplished. In 1850 an Irish laborer who decided on a new life had to choose between an America in which he would be regarded as a foreigner and an Australia in which he would share in the development of the national culture. In America the settled population and the suspicion of the newcomer developed in the Irish a racial consciousness which they have never quite lost. "In Australia, on the other hand, the Irish shared with the English and Scotch the task of opening up the country." [27] The gold digger helped to form the Australian ethos; he did not have to acclimatize himself to it.

Shortly after the gold rushes, however, the Australian fragment hardened. An an English observer could remark in 1878: "Five and twenty years ago nine-tenths of the European inhabitants of Australia regarded the country as a camping-ground for money-making purposes, but now nine-tenths of them think of it as their home." [28] In the intervening period a distinctively national ethos had been formed which would impose itself on new migrants. The shaping force of this early synthesis can be seen today when Australia has acquired more than a million "New Australians" since the Second World War. While this new wave of European settlement has influenced culinary habits, it has not changed the national myth. Like the Irish in America at mid-century, the New Australians have been forced to assimilate themselves to a pre-existing national ethos. In this sense even the vast wave of immigration since the Pacific war has not represented a new "fragmentation" of European society; it has had to come to terms with the settled population just as the late-nineteenth-century migrations to the United States had to come to terms with prior national myths.

The time of congealing was of great importance. Congealing took place before the "radical" views of the mid-nineteenth-century British working class could be transformed in a more doctrinaire direction. The Chartists and others were "class conscious," to be sure. They did not accept the full-blown liberal society which was then in process of establishment in Britain, and they did not rely merely on trade-union activity to improve their position. As political rights had been the means of winning reforms for the middle class in 1832, an extension of those rights might win reforms for the working segment. Political democracy and an extension of the franchise were prominent parts of the Australian creed. At the same time, the radicalism of Robert Owen, of the Chartists, of the trade-unionists, of the convicts and paupers —this was not doctrinaire socialism. It was radical reformism. The English industrial system was not rejected out of hand; nationalization of industry was not the only therapeutic measure. And if socialism did have its impact in Australia, it was predominantly socialism of the idealist, not of the "scientific" variety. Political good will of opposing classes was still a possibility; the state was not the only agent of the reform. Coercion of the bourgeoisie was not the sole means of ensuring general economic welfare. Thus, the early congealing of the fragment, its rapid consolidation and traditionalism, prevented the development of European socialism in the Australian context. Radicalism was the extent of Australian reform.

There was yet another aspect of Australian nationalism. It was not to be expected that the Australian ethos would brook challenge from the native population. In the beginnings of settlement the British Government enjoined a policy of "amity and kindness" toward the aborigines, and as late as 1825 a governor of New South Wales was directed to see that the natives were "protected in the full enjoyment of their possessions and preserved from violence and injustice." They were also to be "civilized." Yet, none of these humanitarian objectives was the result of settlement. Because colonial existence depended upon land, the nomadic aboriginal tribes could not be secured in possession of it. And as the frontiers of settlement expanded, the food-gathering area for aborigines was continuously reduced. "The aboriginee quickly realised what had occurred. To hunt and gather native foods over his tribal country became trespass; to hunt the white invader's animals or gather some of his crops was stealing and, indeed, was regarded as the predatory raid of an enemy. The alternative was to become a landless employee, a type of life which had no meaning for the aboriginee. His land had been more than a place of living and a source of food; it was the symbol of his spiritual life." [29] When the aboriginal reaction came, largely in the second half of the nineteenth century, it was severely dealt with. Isolated attacks by natives on Australian settlers led to the conviction that the natives "had to be taught a lesson," and punitive expeditions occurred in all the colonies.

In some instances at least, the justification for punitive measures was slight. Where differences in ways of life were made painfully apparent, repression often followed. The settler's attitude toward the native was conditioned by the combination of superiority and fear. Superiority justified repression; fear made it necessary. In this manner native policy had links with the compulsions of Australian nationalism. A fragment of European society bent on maintaining its homogeneity and willing to use nationalist pressures to enforce it would not hesitate to deal radically with the native problem. Unlike the graziers, the natives could not be assimilated to the cultural ethos, but they could be equally coerced. The graziers had to accept the radical egalitarian existence; the natives could not accept it. In consequence they had to be put down. After the Second World War about 50,000 of the estimated 350,000 full-blood aborigines of 1788 remained, and as late as 1930 "punitive expeditions" were still being undertaken. This is not to say that systematic repression was responsible for the decline in the aboriginal population; the mere interruption of native folkways, and the change in habits of life were massive assaults on the fragile aboriginal culture. The aborigines had difficulty accepting a place in the white man's society even when it was tendered, and that was not often enough. But withal, the very homogeneity of Australian society made real integration difficult if not impossible. In the long run it was believed that homogeneity could be protected only by undermining the aboriginal influence, and that was what happened.

White Australia showed the same factors at work. The importation of "Kanaka" labor from the New Hebrides, the Solomons, and New Guinea in the second half of the nineteenth century to work on the plantations of Queensland and the participation of Chinese in the gold rushes of the fifties and afterward represented a challenge to the Australian way of life. Like the aborigines, these denizens of Australia were not regarded as full participants in the new radical society. The Chinese, quite unjustly, were regarded as a threat to Australian labor in the gold fields and elsewhere, and in the eighteen-eighties and eighteen-nineties laws were adopted in all the colonies to prohibit or very severely to reduce Asian immigration. The Kanakas were indentured laborers brought into areas of labor shortage. In New South Wales the experiment failed, the "cool" climate being unfavorable to the natives. In Queensland, however, the scheme reaped economic rewards. The islanders "proved cheap, docile and relatively efficient workmen." [30] But the conditions of their transportation to Australia were deplorable, and atrocities were not infrequent. A growing abolitionist movement flowered briefly in the eighteen-eighties, but in the eighteen-nineties the Kanaka trade was reopened. Finally the labor movement and a group of "liberals" succeeded in writing exclusion into the statute books of the new Australian federation. Queensland plantation owners' objections were overcome by a high price for sugar. Labor interests in particular feared the undercutting of the working wage by indentured labor, and that was indeed the original aim of the introduction of islanders into the plantation economy.

In the long run humanitarian sentiment combined with the coercive operations of the radical fragment to force the White Australia Policy. *De facto*, the aboriginal natives had been excluded from the new radical society which was ninety-eight per cent of British origin. *De jure,* Asians were barred from access to the Australian way of life. Again, a homogeneous society, racially and socially, could not tolerate challenges to its purity. The pretenders to gentility had been "equalized" as a precondition to entry into Australian nationalism; tbey had to give up their social and political privileges before assimilation. The natives, on the other hand, could not really be assimilated; they had to be held apart or decimated as a social force. The Asians could not be made into "dinkum Aussies"; they could not participate in a social sense; hence, they were simply excluded in the most rigorous fashion. Undoubtedly, there were differences between the Australian and American cases in this respect. American society was more of a "melting pot." But even Americans returned to principles of Oriental exclusion and to an immigration system that would maintain the racial balance of American society. Too great a departure from the original "fragment" would alter the basis of American society. And from this point of view Australia's insistence upon racial homogeneity has perhaps received undue historical criticism. It may be necessary to change social bases for reasons which are essentially ethical, and the White Australia Policy undoubtedly is more absolute than would be required to protect original social foundations. But Australians grasped an important truth when they realized that the whole Australian tradition was at stake in the nature of immigration policy. If a new "fragment" of Europe or Asia had been imported, Australian development would have been decisively affected.

5 Capital, Labor, and the National Myth

Unlike England, where the Industrial Revolution was followed by the Democratic Revolution, Australia had achieved her democratic institutions before the onset of industrialism at the end of the century. Although the pastoral industry marked the beginnings of capitalism, Australia had a highly organized labor movement before it had organized industrial capital.[31]

One of the most fundamentally important facts of Australian development is that capitalism emerged in a society which had been "born radical." In this sense Australia never went through a period of full-blown liberalism analogous to that of England or the United States. The economic forces which might have sustained a liberal ethos were too long delayed. The radical myth had been implanted too deeply for it to be extirpated by the Industrial Revolution. And the odd result in the Australian context was that economic and industrial development took place under the auspices of militant radicalism. Capitalist institutions appeared; but there was no capitalist credo. From this point of view the "triumph of unreconstructed Whiggery" was unthinkable in the Australian context. In America the liberal ethos was such that it was amenable to the Horatio Alger myth. When the quasi-oligarchical shibboleths of Hamilton were abandoned, the American Whigs found that the American "petty bourgeois giant" could be won for capitalist development and the "pot o' gold." With capitalism rationalized·as democratic, it was entirely acceptable to American liberal society. In Australia, conversely, capitalist Whiggery could perform no such prestidigitation. Instead of allowing capitalism to capture the liberal myth, as happened in America, and keep it against attack until 1929, the Australian radical myth captured capitalism and never let it go. Australian industrialists, financiers, and magnates were, to a degree unknown in the United States, the domestics of the radical myth; Australian capitalism was "kept" by the radical ethos.

The very weakness of capital forced it into alliance with labor. While the graziers' political pre-eminence fell early from its high pedestal, their economic primacy continued. From the point of view of developing capitalism, the pastoral influence was restrictive. Generally speaking, primary producers wanted free trade; emergent manufacturers wanted protection. Like the plantation South, the agriculturalists looked toward the export market; their economic situation was quite different from that of the English landowners. With the rise of manufacturing after the gold rushes there came a new sentiment for protective tariffs. Protection of the domestic market against foreign competition would be necessary if industry were to be established. Again there was a difference from Britain. British industries did not need protection; they relied on free trade to hold down the price of raw materials and on comparative advantage to assure their penetration of world markets. But Australian manufacturers had no natural comparative advantage; they could not compete with the industries of developed countries. As one contemporary observer remarked:

The manufacturers and artisans of Australasia . . . look upon a different side of the question of Free Trade from that which was perceived in England. It is not with them a question of obtaining cheap raw materials—these they have always to their hands— but a question of establishing new industries. They desire to create while the Englishman desired to develop what was already created. Consequently the classes which in England encouraged the competition of foreigners, because only foreigners could offer them the necessary raw material, wish now in Australasia . . . to exclude the same competition, for fear it may destroy their infant industries.[32]

Thus the tariff was heralded as a device to maintain high wages and high profits. An alliance was forged between labor and capital against the great agriculturalists. But this alliance, similar in certain ways to that of business and labor in America in the second half of the nineteenth century, was actually quite different from its American counterpart. In the United States business captured labor and inculcated its free-enterprise ideology; in Australia labor captured the inchoate industrialists and secured their acceptance of the radical creed. Without the alliance of labor, which lasted until 1890, industry would hardly have been in a position to withstand the economic assaults of the graziers. Labor was the midwife of capitalism in the Australian context.

And in the long run the alliances of 1850 to 1890 have had a fundamental impact upon Australian politics. Just as today American labor is not an effective political force against petty bourgeois industrialism, so Australian capital is not an effective political force against working-class radicalism. In America labor was politically socialized by business; in

Australia business was politically socialized by labor. Thus, to take a present case, the Australian Liberal Party is not primarily a party of business leaders with a distinct liberal middle-class point of view to advance; it is, rather, a "party of resistance" animated by no particular political philosophy save that of opposition to the existent Labor Party program. Parties of resistance in the Australian context have been successful only when they could show that labor was weak on derivative issues of public policy; they have never been able to assault the fundamental radical-labor philosophy which has underlain that program. Business has been the gadfly of Australian politics in somewhat the same way in which labor has been the gadfly of American politics.

Thus, present-day political constellations in Australia are completely unlike those of Britain. It has often been remarked that Australia has never had a conservative class in the European sense or a Conservative Party to go with it; what is less often recognized is that Australia has not even had a liberal middle class in the European sense or a Liberal Party to go with it. Gladstonian Liberalism is just as alien to Australia as aristocratic toryism. As Sir Frederic Eggleston once wrote:

In Australia there is little respect for wealth as such and insufficient acknowledgment of the services rendered by businessmen to the organization of Australian industry. It is harder for an industrial magnate to enter politics than for a camel to pass through the eye of a needle. There are historical reasons for this. The wealthy classes have never provided leaders or shown the community any guidance in political matters. As political organizers, they are feeble. They rarely succeed as politicians. . . . The Victorian Liberal, George Higinbotham, coined the phrase "the wealthy lower orders" and it has stuck.[33]

But the influence was not only one way. The acceptance by business of the radical myth had an impact upon labor leaders. In particular it reinforced a radical as opposed to a doctrinaire socialist mode of thought. The Australian fragment was radical, not militantly socialist; industry acclimatized itself to that pattern and rendered unnecessary a further movement toward the left. And what emerged in Australia was one of the strangest labor movements in the Western tradition. In Europe nationalization was at one time or another a central intention of all socialist parties. In Australia, despite the program of 1921, nationalization has never been a central tenet of the Labor Party. And the reason for this important difference seems to be that Australia "naturally" enjoyed the benefits of socialism without nationalization. For after all, what was the *raison d'être* of nationalization? Nationalization assumed a recalcitrant bourgeoisie which would not "naturally" co-operate with labor to assure an equal division of the fruits of production, but one which would give up its "surplus capital" only through coercion by the "dictatorship of the proletariat." Since business was congenitally opposed to labor, labor would have to take power and use the instruments of the state against the capitalist. In the Australian context, however, this assumption was invalid. As long as business would co-operate "naturally," it did not have to be governmentally coerced. There was no need to use the government as an instrument of oppression of class by class. Many working people believed that the Australian employers would "see the light" and be "fair."

And what is prima facie surprising is that even after the period of industrial strife and depression of 1890 to 1893, labor was not disabused of the possibility of an accommodation with capital. This is the paradox of the compulsory arbitration schemes which emerge out of the industrial clashes of the early eighteen-nineties. To be sure, those disputes showed that the Australian employer would not always be "fair"; but what is amazing is the moderation of the deduction from this fact. As one writer notes:

For the labour movement as a whole the party policy on arbitration was of the utmost importance. It clearly indicated that the Labour Party was moving away from the concept of industrial struggles as the means by which the working class could obtain economic advantages. In place of industrial struggle they had put the idea of economic justice to be obtained by judicial procedures. The state was to intervene to redress the balance in favour of the workers.[34]

If the employers would not willingly meet with labor to discuss grievances, the state would force them to do so. But there were a number of revealing assumptions underlying the policy of compulsory arbitration. The first was that the state would be more sympathetic to labor interests than to the employers; the second was that coercion by nationalization was unnecessary. Compulsory arbitration, therefore, assumed the fundamental good will of the nonproletarian state. Victorian Liberals like Deakin could be trusted to protect labor interests. More than this, state intervention in the economic system did not have to go so far as nationalization. Both these assumptions were denied by doctrinaire continental socialists. So long as the state was dominated by the bourgeoisie, as important a power as compulsory arbitration could not be given to it. After the political triumph of the toilers, even more drastic medicine would be needed. Even a proletarian state would demand nationalization of the basic industries.

Thus, Australian labor's acceptance of compulsory arbitration was a measure of its distinctiveness. The nonlabor state could be trusted in a context of the overarching predominance of the radical myth. Because there was not an irreconcilable conflict between labor and the employers, coercion or destruction of the capitalist class was not necessary. And insofar as there was a labor theory, it was directed as much or more against the landowners as against capitalists. Henry George had much more impact in Australia than Marx, and he provided a doctrine which could be used par excellence against the graziers. And Edward Bellamy was the inspiration for Australian idealist socialism. Poverty could be eliminated by a vast expansion of the productive powers of society and an end to the waste of capitalism. With production and distribution planned by the state and a secure Christian moral foundation, class warfare would be unnecessary. People would naturally embrace socialism.

Even William Lane, in some ways the most doctrinaire of Australian socialists, had much more in common with Owen and the co-operative socialist projects of America than with the "scientific" socialism of Europe. In many instances also, political labor was far more pragmatic and conciliatory than even these theoretical strands. Gollan says:

Inevitably, because it was not directed by any coherent political theory, it became a party of practical politics, suspicious of theory and increasingly alienated from the militant trade unionism and idealist socialism that had given it birth. As its policy thus took shape there was a conflict within the party and between it and the industrial movement, but by 1910 the Labour Party had become firmly established as a party with a liberal rather than a socialist theory. The Labour Party grew out of a movement that was implicitly directed against the basis of the capitalist system, but it became a party whose function was to modify the capitalist system and make it acceptable to the movement of which it was a part.[35]

In Australia Horatio Alger is turned on his head. Instead of workers looking forward to a golden future as capitalists, capitalists look backward with nostalgia to their working days. And the ability of capital to stand against labor is drastically affected by capital's own social origin. The pervasive working-class ethos unites both sides of the Australian economic fence, and capital is deprived of intellectual credentials to advance against labor.

The Australian soldier has frequently been admired for his personal independence and individual initiative. The Australian voter has been continually blamed for his lack of initiative and for his excessive dependence upon the State.[36]

To the Australian, the State means collective power at the service of individualistic "rights." Therefore he sees no opposition between his individualism and his reliance upon Government.[37]

Sir Keith Hancock's paradox, stated in the first epigraph above, is only puzzling for societies which experienced the full-blown liberal society of the nineteenth century. Individualism is developed and succored by *laissez faire;* dependence upon the state, then, becomes its contrary. But the paradox does not really apply to Australia. For Australia did not experience the triumph of Gladstonian Liberalism; it was, as it were, "born modern." Australian society was built by those

309

who did not identify individualism with straitly limited government. Rather, as we have seen, the founders of Australia already believed that individual rights could only be defended by political action: the state had to act in support of private rights; those rights could not be sustained by individuals alone. Thus, there was no contradiction between Australian individualism and Australian reliance on government. Born modern, Australians believed that the state, far from encroaching upon individual rights, would be the most likely protector of rights against other agencies of social coercion. Unlike the doctrinaire liberals of Europe, Australians believed that the major constraints on individual liberty were not public, but private. The graziers and unregulated capitalists were the greatest threats to individualism; use of the state against these enemies was proper individualist doctrine for classes "born yesterday." "Liberalism" in the twentieth century had a very different meaning from "liberalism" in the nineteenth century. And in a sense Australian radicalism was very close to twentieth-century liberalism.

But there was a sense also in which the Australian approach to governmental power has been different from the American. With certain variations the Alger theme in American development runs until 1929. Aside from intermittent "trust busting" and the New Freedom, government intervention in the economic system was held to a minimum during the capture of the liberal ethos by expanding business enterprise. When the breakdown of 1929 occurred, therefore, it seemed to indicate the need for a redressing of the balance. Roosevelt was unhampered in "solving problems" under the New Deal in part because his business adversaries had held the stage so long. As the American liberal ethos was broad enough to accommodate Jay Gould as well as democratic reform, there was no problem in switching from one to the other.

In Australia, however, the radical ethos was more specific. While it did embrace partisans of different economic positions, after 1890 it did not permit extreme interpretations. There could be no important variation from Australia's upside-down version of Horatio Alger. Hence when an Australian Labor Government confronted the Great Depression, there was no way to turn. There was no balance to be redressed and no means of action, save that of traditional radicalism. There was nothing to do except what had already been done.

And in certain respects the amount of government intervention legitimized by the Australian radical myth was subject to debate. The interventionalist impulses carried from Britain actually had more application in Britain than in the Australian colonies. In Britain "radical" intervention was required to deal with the entrenched classes of resistance. Governmental action would force recalcitrants to do what they would not otherwise do. In a context of contending classes, then, government intervention made sense. In Australia, however, the radical fragment succeeded after 1850 in imposing a kind of uniform national ideology. Businessmen, even graziers, were compelled to accept a version of radical egalitarianism; the radicals' triumph at the ideological level seemed complete. But it was the very pervasiveness of radical success which brought into question the rationale of intervention. If other classes or groups accepted the notions of radicalism, to what purpose intervention? If the privileged did not oppose equalitarian schemes, government coercion would not be necessary. And this was one of the great problems of Australian development. Because of the very success of the radical fragment in imposing a conformitarian pattern, the opposition faded. To a degree the radicals could assume even after 1890 a kind of "natural" radical-socialist commonwealth. Governmental instruments would be superfluous in a context of political and social good faith.

What emerged in Australia, then, in one of the most remarkable paradoxes of industrial countries, was a type of "socialist" *laissez faire*. Since the Australian community was imbued with the radical myth, the co-operative commonwealth of social and economic progress naturally existed. Australia was merely New Lanark writ large. "Idealist socialism" was realized in practice. With this degree of natural radical-socialist success, the doctrines of Adam Smith were endowed with a validity which they could not find under the aegis of

European liberalism. Class conflict in the European arena entangled the "invisible hand" in numberless contradictions. Where social reformism was the order of the day, however, and class conflict confined, the invisible hand might produce a natural harmony of interests. Socialist *laissez faire* might exist. The benefits of socialism and co-operative reform could be won without substantial governmental intervention.

And what is noteworthy in Australia, of the modern welfare democracies, is not the panoply of governmental intervention, but its tenuousness. Where intervention was solemnized, it tended to have a politically impartial, administrative, or even judicial character. Governments, particularly the Federal Government, have not been able to exercise political control of quasi-judicial bodies and independent commissions. Thus two tendencies have proceeded simultaneously. On the one hand, there has been a surprising disinclination to involve government in the economic system. Section 92 of the Australian Constitution denies a certain range of intervention to both states and Federal Government. On the other hand, when intervention is undertaken, it has been usually carried on by some impartial body, thus depriving intervention of its political character. Both phases rest on the assumption of social good faith; impartiality is impossible in a context of social antagonism.

Until the Great Depression the tariff and the basic wage seemed sufficient policies. ". . . Australians generally were convinced that their country had already been made 'the workingman's paradise.' They claimed, rightly enough, that wealth was more evenly distributed in Australia and New Zealand than in other comparable countries, and they pointed with pride to the fact that, after New Zealand's theirs was the lowest death rate in the world." [38] When the Depression came, it caught the co-operative commonwealth off-guard; socialist *laissez faire* was found wanting. "There is, therefore, nothing surprising in the fact that Australia's various schemes for meeting the problems of the Great Depression were far less radical in relation to the social context in which they were evolved and applied than were the parallel policies of the New Deal in the American context. It is not unfair to say that the basic idea in Australian policy was to make the economy work profitably by an all-round reduction of costs to meet the lower prices the depression had brought about." [39] This species of classical economics was quite different from the consumptionist and quasi-Keynesian remedies employed in the United States.

Thus, the Depression showed the possibilities of economic maladjustments even in a context of social good will. An industrial system might go awry even with the best of intentions. Appropriate monetary and fiscal powers would be necessary to even out the swings of the business cycle. To a degree the lessons of the Depression have been taken to heart, and since then federal powers of industrial regulation, social services, and monetary controls, and certain fiscal controls have been strengthened. Yet one Australian observer can still comment:

The Commonwealth government is unique among the governments of capitalist countries in the degree to which it is tied down to the use of purely monetary controls—by constitutional limitations on power. It can intervene directly only in foreign trade; everywhere else it must proceed by financial inducement or verbal persuasion. Whilst the power of warnings or pleas to private interests to respect public ends should not be underestimated, the absence of effective sanctions severely limits the scope of public planning.[40]

From this point of view the 1945 White Paper on Full Employment must be read as pious hope as well as solemn intention. In the result, Section 92 of the Australian Constitution, which specifies that trade and commerce among the states shall be "absolutely free," limits Section 51 (1), which gives to the Commonwealth Government the power to make laws with respect to trade and commerce among the states. Now Section 51 (1) is used only for regulation of shipping, monopolies (ineffectively), and stevedoring. The "commerce power" in Australia would not now be elastic enough to accommodate nationalization of any substantial industry, and its scope in fact is measurably smaller than that of the "commerce power" in the United States. As Professor Greenwood comments: "The position, therefore, with regard to the sec-

tion [92] is wholly unsatisfactory, for it means that the totality of legislative power in both Commonwealth and states is
insufficient to establish whatever form of commercial regulation may be thought desirable." [41]

6 The Foreign Outlook

The pattern of Australian life is in many ways more rigid than
the pattern of British life. Independence of thought is not greatly
prized. In comparison with Britain, academic freedom has to be
fought for more vigorously; a considerable number of subjects
are difficult to discuss in the press and on the air. Such syndicates
as Chambers of Manufacturers, associations of doctors and lawyers, and trade unions, are jealous of their corporate unity and
bring heavy penalties to bear upon members who do not conform.
Solidarity under majority rule is the principle on which most
Australians work. . . . It runs through the whole texture of
Australian social life, and party solidarity is only one of its manifestations. John Stuart Mill might well argue that Australian life
presented a vindication of his fear of the tyranny of the majority.[42]

If the implantation of a radical fragment in Australia
meant freedom from the class oppressions of Europe and the
growth of natural cultural relaxation, it also had other implications. Good faith, good will, and "mateship" were possible where fundamental acceptance of the radical creed was
unquestioned. Where acceptance was in doubt, however, as
the coercion of the squatters demonstrated, the radical ethos
could become compulsive. Thus the degree of "relaxation"
depends entirely on whether one is within or without the
radical nation. Inside, relaxation and camaraderie hold forth;
outside, there is the compelling "tyranny of the majority." In
these circumstances much has tended to depend upon how
the radical ethos is construed.

At the end of 1950 both party and majority public opinion
apparently favored the dissolution of the Australian Communist Party. After a bill to that end had been declared invalid by the High Court and a constitutional amendment proposed to remedy the defect, the Australian public changed its

mind and rejected the new powers in a national referendum. At least one observer mentioned the possibility that the voters "did not reject the proposal to dissolve the Communist Party but merely the methods of achieving this end proposed by the Government." [43] Such imponderables would militate against the simple conclusion that civil liberties and a concern for minority rights had prevailed.[44] The repressive force of the national radical myth evidenced against the squatters might be seen elsewhere in Australian life.

But the internal aspects of coercive radicalism, the demand for solidarity—these were not the only manifestations of the power of the uniform radical fragment. In external relations as well, its crusading energy could be seen. There is something in the Australian tradition of the American oscillation between isolation and intervention, each founded on the premise of uniqueness and superiority. At the height of the Australianism of the eighteen-eighties divers trumpets sounded the call for nationhood. There was an emergent consciousness that Australia was not merely a social replication of Europe. Class cleavage and oppression were either submerged or absent in the Australian context. Possessing an enlightened liberty, Australians were ready to pass judgment upon those who had yet to attain it.

In the American case the adoption of a policy of isolation reflected the most pessimistic estimate of the prospects of European society. Ideally, Europe should be "Americanized," but it had so far fallen from grace that redemption was impossible. The other response was interventionist: make the world safe for American democracy, or, perhaps better, remake it according to American principles and in the American image. There are analogues in the Australian experience to this process. John Dunmore Lang was as jealous of Australian prerogatives in the Pacific as was Monroe of America's position in the Caribbean. Prime Minister "Billy" Hughes moved farther in the direction of Monroe when he established Australian hegemony in East New Guinea at the Versailles Conference, and if Woodrow Wilson lectured Europe on American principles, Dr. H. V. Evatt, in a more recent era, has been scarcely less hesitant in pointing out those instances in which nations have failed to live up to an Australian standard of conduct. Both statesmen presumed their countries could set a course for other states to follow.

Yet there were important differences between Australian and American patterns in foreign affairs. Australian nationalism, as we have seen, was bound up with the social issue; it was peculiarly silent on questions of the internal-external bond. It was appropriate to coerce the squatter, but could one dictate to the British Government? Clearly Australia did not possess the might to defend her isolation, to say nothing of carrying on a policy of intervention. But the question vis-à-vis Britain was not one of sheer power. The failure to consolidate Australia as a territorial entity, the very magnanimity of British colonial policy—these left Australians in a state of external ambivalence. How could the outside world be rejected? How could it be reformed? Australia was bound by an unsevered "silver cord" to her motherland, and would not cast it off. Thus a raucous national egalitarianism contended with indefeasible ties of sentiment. At once Australians have been the most defiant members of the community of nations and the most pliant servants of the Commonwealth bond. Australians still yearn for "home" while rejecting the social system on which it is based.

And the ambivalence of Australia's response to Britain has colored her perceptions of the rest of the world. The dependent role and the grateful regard for Britain have operated to create a species of diffidence toward the outside world which contrasts with the strand of bold assertiveness. The fact that Australia was rudely thrust into the external world with the Second World War has made her suspicious of outsiders and sorrowful for the passing of the traditional relationship with Britain. It still longs for the protective-security umbrella of yesteryear and is in one sense unready to face the outside world. Where confidence is lacking, fear appears in its stead. The Asian environment in which Australia is situated is made to appear more hostile by virtue of Australia's own uncertainty. And thus a real duality tinctures Australian attitudes toward Asia. On the one hand, by social standards Asia is clearly inferior, and is therefore a prime subject for

Australian moral imperialism; on the other hand, by psychological standards Asia is unfamiliar and perhaps malevolent. A nation which lacks psychological self-sufficiency tends to believe others harbor ill will. Intervention-isolation then is accompanied by suspicion and insecurity. Asia is a danger because it is a challenge to the radical way of life; it is even more to be feared because of Australia's uneasiness in the world environment. The correlate of the superiority premise socially is the inferiority premise internationally. In both cases an extreme reaction to the outside world is sanctioned. The oscillation between overconfidence and chronic diffidence, however, is not a satisfactory basis for policy.

In the final analysis there is at least the possibility that the external challenge will bring an internal reorientation of social attitudes. The coercive operations of the radical fragment in the Australian context were in part to be accounted to the isolation from European culture. A fragment of European society was lodged in Australia; in isolation from social and political movements elsewhere, it congealed. The traditionalism of the fragment enabled it to mold subsequent waves of immigration. Divorced from Europe, the new migrants had to conform to the social ethos of their new home. But international contacts held out the possibility of accomplishing what immigration could not. Immigration imposed no sanction on maintenance of the original character of the fragment. But international relations assessed penalties for traditional social attitudes. Isolation-intervention or intermittent timidity would hamper the national foreign policy.

As America can no longer afford to try to reshape the world on American principles, Australia cannot persist with the fear of contamination by Asia which the White Australia Policy represents. White Australia was an understandable reaction of a coercive radical society in the nineteenth century. Australia's society did indeed depend upon the purity and fixity of the abstraction from the British context. And if preservation of the foundational myth in its pristine form was necessary, immigration restriction would be required. Today, however, international position may be more important than absolute fidelity to the original ethos. It may be

317

more important to be an effective international competitor than to avoid the slightest derogation from traditional social bases. Just as Southern racialism can no longer be tolerated by America, White Australia is now a handicap to Australia. Both Australia and America seem to be discovering that feelings of uniqueness or superiority are simply untenable under the conditions of modern international relations.

Present world imperatives, then, hold the possibility of requiring both countries to transcend the social ethos underlying their policies, both domestic and external. If both countries are to meet the challenge of world events, political and social traditions in both nations may be altered. Here may lie the real answer to those who claim that a country cannot outgrow the conditions of its birth.

Notes

Chapter One

1 Cf. C. Jane, *Liberty and Despotism in Spanish America* (Oxford, 1929), pp. 20-27.
2 Cf. A. A. Phillips, *The Australian Tradition: Studies in a Colonial Culture* (Melbourne, 1958), pp. 37 ff.; R. N. Rosecrance, "The Radical Tradition in Australia: An Interpretation," *The Review of Politics*, XXII, 1 (Jan. 1960), 115-132, 124.
3 Cf. N. Legendre, *La Langue française* (Quebec, 1890), p. 7.
4 For a sensitive interpretation of the *criollo* and *mozambo* mentality, see V. Moog, *Bandierantes and Pioneers* (New York, 1964), pp. 102-110; for the movement of *indigenismo*, J. Comas, *Ensayos sobre indigenismo* (Mexico, 1953), especially pp. 261-272.
5 M. Wade, *The French Canadians, 1760-1945* (New York, 1955), p. 345.
6 G. M. Carter, *The Politics of Inequality: South Africa since 1948* (New York, 1958), pp. 60 ff.

Chapter Two

1 J. R. Commons, *Races and Immigrants in America* (New York, 1907), p. 97.
2 "L'État française et l'Amérique latine," *L'Action française* (Montreal), VII, 5 (May 1922), 258-274.
3 "Sociabilidad chilena" in *Obras completas*, P. P. Figueroa, ed. (Santiago, 1897), I, 19-50, 21.
4 M. Wade, *The French Canadians, 1760-1945* (New York, 1955), p. 144.
5 H. T. Manning, *The Revolt of French Canada, 1800-1835* (London, 1962), p. 366. See also E. Circé-Côté, *Papineau: son influence sur la pensée canadienne* (Montreal, 1924), esp. pp. ii-iii, 3-43.
6 Cf. F. García Calderón, *Latin America: Its Rise and Progress*, Bernard Miall, trans. (London, 1913), p. 88.
7 See C. O. Bunge, *Nuestra América* (Buenos Aires, 1918), pp. 226 ff.
8 H. F. Quinn, *The Union Nationale: A Study in Quebec Nationalism* (Toronto, 1963), p. 126.
9 Quoted in E. C. Hughes, *French Canada in Transition* (Chicago, 1963), p. 152.
10 Cf. M. Wade, "Social Change in French Canada" in *Tradition, Values, Socio-Economic Development*, Braibanti and Spengler, eds. (Durham, 1961), pp. 276-296, 290.
11 R. J. Alexander, *Labour Movements in Latin America* (London, 1947), pp. 15 ff.
12 Wade, *The French Canadians*, p. 837.
13 M. J. Boon, *The History of the Orange Free State* (London, 1885), p. 9.

319

14 E. Walker, *A History of South Africa* (London, 1928), p. 269. See *Select Constitutional Documents Illustrating South African History 1795-1910*, G. W. Eybers, M.A., ed. (London, 1918), pp. 287, 292.

15 *The Selected Writings of William Lyon MacKenzie, 1824-1837*, M. Fairley, ed. (Toronto, 1960), p. 311.

16 E. McInnis, *Canada: A Political and Social History* (New York, 1947), pp. 211, 282-283, 435.

17 Cf. S. Jamieson, "Labour Unity in Quebec," in *Canadian Dualism: Studies of French-English Relations*, Mason Wade, ed. (Toronto, 1960), pp. 290-308.

18 A. Dunham, *Political Unrest in Upper Canada, 1815-1836* (London, 1927), especially pp. 142 ff.

19 Cf. Rosecrance, "The Radical Tradition in Australia," p. 120.

20 See M. Cresswell, *An Epoch of the Political History of South Africa* (Capetown, n.d.), *passim*.

21 J. Bryce, *Impressions of South Africa* (New York, 1898), pp. 411-412.

22 I. Edwards, *The 1820 Settlers in South Africa* (London, 1934), *passim*.

23 F. W. Eggleston, *Reflections of an Australian Liberal* (Melbourne, 1953), p. 63.

24 Cf. L. Webb, *Communism and Democracy in Australia: A Survey of the 1951 Referendum* (New York, 1955).

25 W. K. Hancock, *Australia* (London, 1930), p. 222.

Chapter Three

1 S. Zavala, *De encomiendas y propiedad territorial en algunas regiones de la América española* (Mexico, 1940), p. 9.

2 J. T. Lang, *I Remember* (Sydney, 1950), p. 32.

3 F. Tannenbaum, *Slave and Citizen: The Negro in the Americas* (New York, 1947), p. 48.

4 G. Freyre, *Brazil: An Interpretation* (New York, 1945), p. 2; *The Masters and the Slaves* (New York, 1946), p. 201.

5 Quoted in W. R. Crawford, *A Century of Latin-American Thought* (Cambridge, 1944), p. 173.

6 For the Spanish pattern see Raúl Carrancá y Trujillo, "El estatuto juridico do los esclavos en las postrimerias de la colonizacion española," in *Revista de historia de América*, No. 3 (1938) , pp. 20-59.

7 Tannenbaum, *ibid.*, pp. 53 ff.

8 See M. W. Williams, "The Treatment of Negro Slaves in the Brazilian Empire: A Comparison with the United States of America," *Revista do instituto histórico e geographico brasileiro*, I (1922), Tomo especial, 274-292, 287; K. M. Stampp, *The Peculiar Institution* (New York, 1963), pp. 215-217.

9 See L. Hanke, *Aristotle and the American Indians* (London, 1959).

10 Cf. M. Picon-Salas, *Pedro Claver, el santo de los esclavos* (Mexico, 1950), *passim*.

11 C. H. Haring, *Empire in Brazil* (Cambridge, 1958), pp. 94-95.

12 Quoted in P. A. Martin, "Slavery and Abolition in Brazil," *Hispanic American Historical Review*, XII, 2 (1933), pp. 151-196, 178.

13 See M. de O. Lima, *The Evolution of Brazil* (Palo Alto, 1914), p. 23.

14 C. W. De Kiewiet, *A History of South Africa* (London, 1941), p. 193.

15 See my *The Liberal Tradition in America*, Chs. VI-VII.

16 H. R. Helper, *The Impending Crisis of the South: How to Meet It* (New York, 1857), p. 43.
17 L. M. Thompson, *The Unification of South Africa* (Oxford, 1960), pp. 11-12.
18 G. Myrdal, *An American Dilemma* (New York, 1944), I, pp. 3-25.

Chapter Four

1 See R. G. Adams, *Political Ideas of the American Revolution* (Durham, 1922), *passim.*
2 Cf. E. Scott, *A Short History of Australia* (Melbourne, 1947), p. 40.
3 B. Mitre, *Ensayos históricos* (Buenos Aires, 1918), p. 121.
4 See B. F. Wright, Jr. "The Early History of Written Constitutions in America," in *Essays in History and Political Theory in Honor of Charles Howard McIlwain* (Cambridge, Mass., 1936), pp. 344 ff.
5 Cf. M. de O. Lima, *The Evolution of Brazil*, p. 26.
6 Quoted in the Introduction by Lewis Hanke, *Do the Americas Have a Common History?*, L. Hanke, ed. (New York, 1964), p. 5.
7 L. B. Dunbar, *A Study of "Monarchical" Tendencies in the United States, from 1776 to 1801* (Urbana, 1922), *passim.* On this whole problem see the excellent discussion of A. P. Whitaker, "The Americas in the Atlantic Triangle," in *Do the Americas Have a Common History?*, pp. 141-164.
8 M. Farrand, *Records of the Federal Convention* (New Haven, 1911-1937), I, p. 227.
9 *Fragments From an XVIIIth Century Diary: The Travels and Adventures of Don Francisco de Miranda*, J. H. Stabler, comp. and trans. (Caracas, 1931), p. 59.
10 *The Works of Alexander Hamilton*, H. C. Lodge, ed. (New York, 1886), IX, p. 251.
11 I have discussed this issue from the angle of Europe in "The Rise of the Democratic Idea," in *Paths of American Thought*, A. Schlesinger, Jr., and M. White, eds. (Boston, 1953), pp. 37-51.
12 W. E. Binkley, *American Political Parties* (New York, 1958), pp. 130 ff.
13 Cf. F. Byrdsall, *The History of the Loco-Foco, or Equal Rights Party* (New York, 1842), pp. 92-93.
14 H. D. Sheldon, *The History and Pedagogy of American Student Societies* (New York, 1901), p. 162.
15 R. M. Hartwell, "The Pastoral Ascendancy, 1820-50" in *Australia, a Social and Political History*, G. Greenwood, ed. (Sydney, 1955), pp. 46-97, 55.
16 C. W. De Kiewiet, *A History of South Africa*, p. 48.
17 G. Freyre, *The Masters and the Slaves*, pp. 188 ff.
18 (New York, 1881), especially Ch. I.
19 Quoted in W. T. Hagan, *American Indians* (Chicago, 1961), p. 140.
20 Quoted in *ibid.*, p. 156.
21 Quoted in V. Moog, *Bandeirantes and Pioneers*, p. 38.
22 *Ibid.*, p. 43.
23 Quoted in M. Wade, "Social Change in French Canada" in *Tradition, Values, and Socio-Economic Development*, Braibanti and Spengler, eds. (Durham, 1961), p. 286.
24 S. G. Hansen, *Economic Development in Latin America* (Washington, 1959), p. 185.
25 Cf. *Triumphant Democracy* (New York, 1893), *passim.*

26 Hansen, *op. cit.*, pp. 183-184.
27 Cf. R. Ward, *The Australian Legend* (Melbourne, 1958), p. 197.
28 See *The Challenge to Liberty* (New York, 1935).
29 Cf. *The Public Papers and Addresses of Franklin D. Roosevelt* (New York, 1932), II, pp. 3-16.
30 See W. G. Carleton, *The Revolution in American Foreign Policy* (New York, 1963), pp. 477 ff.

Chapter Five

1 O. Nogueira, "Preconceito racial de marca e preconceito racial de origem" in R. Bastide and F. Fernandes, *Relações raciais entre negros e brancos em São Paulo* (São Paulo, 1955), p. 552.
2 The inquisitors in Cartagena complained in 1619 that Negro slaves about to be flogged by their masters would cry out, "I renounce God!" On the spot they became subject to inquisitorial trial and the flogging had to stop. After a juridicial formality they would be scolded and released, a process which might be indefinitely repeated. H. C. Lea, *The Inquisition in the Spanish Dependencies* (New York, 1922), pp. 465-466.
3 J. M. Ots Capdequí, *Manual de historia del derecho español en las Indias* (Buenos Aires, 1945), p. 191.
4 G. Céspedes del Castillo, "La sociedad colonial americana en los siglos XVI y XVII" in J. Vicens Vives, ed., *Historia social y económica de España y América* (4 vols., Barcelona, 1957-59), III, 395-396.
5 R. Guerra y Sánchez, *Sugar and Society in the Caribbean* (New Haven, 1964), pp. 9-57.
6 E. R. Wolf, *Sons of the Shaking Earth* (Chicago, 1959), pp. 235-242.
7 F. Tannenbaum, *Slave and Citizen: The Negro in the Americas* (New York, 1947).
8 E. Williams, *Capitalism and Slavery* (Chapel Hill, 1944); see also his "Race Relations in Caribbean Society" with "Discussion" by Tannenbaum in V. Rubin, ed., *Caribbean Studies: A Symposium* (Kingston, 1957), pp. 54-66. A review article by S. W. Mintz in *American Anthropologist*, 63, 3 (June 1961), 579-587, is a good conspectus of the problem.
9 H. Hoetink, " 'Colonial Psychology' and Race," *The Journal of Economic History*, XXI, 4 (Dec. 1961), 629-640.
10 M. Góngora, *El estado en el derecho indiano, época de fundación (1492-1570)* (Santiago, 1951), p. 300.
11 *Ibid.*, p. 301.
12 *Ibid.*, p. 303.
13 J. M. Ots Capdequí, *Instituciones* (Barcelona, 1959), p. 8.
14 Góngora, *op. cit.*, pp. 178-179, 183.
15 C. Sánchez-Albornoz, *España, un enigma histórico* (2 vols., Buenos Aires, 1956), II, 7-103. Also, M. Bloch, *Feudal Society* (London, 1961), pp. 186-187.
16 See R. M. Morse, "Some Characteristics of Latin American Urban History," *The American Historical Review*, LXVII, 2 (Jan. 1962), 317-338.
17 Góngora, *op. cit.*, pp. 184-185.
18 Wolf, *op. cit.*, p. 204.
19 K. Burke, *Attitudes toward History* (2 vols., New York, 1937), I, 176-177.
20 The Argentine historian Ricardo Levene even proposed that the preindependence era of his country no longer be called the "colonial period"

and that, instead, the phrase "period of Spanish domination and civilization" be employed. *Las Indias no eran colonias* (Buenos Aires, 1951), pp. 161-165.

21 F. Morales Padrón, *Fisonomía de la conquista indiana* (Seville, 1955), pp. 43-47.

22 Interestingly enough, the word "conquest," or the Spanish *conquista*, derives from the Latin *con-quaerere*, which means to "seek out" or "bring together" without the intimation of aggrandizement.

23 See R. M. Morse, "Toward a Theory of Spanish American Government," *Journal of the History of Ideas*, XV, 1 (Jan. 1954), 71-77.

24 Notably M. Giménez Fernández, *Las doctrinas populistas en la independencia de Hispano-América* (Seville, 1947).

25 For an off-target exchange on this subject see C. W. Arnade and B. W. Diffie in "Causes of Spanish-American Wars of Independence," *Journal of Inter-American Studies*, II, 2 (April 1960), 130-131, 141-144; also C. C. Griffin, "The Enlightenment and Latin American Independence" in A. P. Whitaker, ed., *Latin America and the Enlightenment* (2nd ed.; Ithaca, 1961), pp. 124-125.

26 P. Janet, *Histoire de la science politique dans ses rapports avec la morale* (3rd ed.; 2 vols., Paris, 1887), II, 76.

27 E. Troeltsch, *The Social Teachings of the Christian Churches* (2 vols., New York, 1960), I, 280-328.

28 *Ibid.*, I, 314, 318.

29 M. Weber, *The Theory of Social and Economic Organization* (New York, 1947), pp. 341-358, 373-381. Also R. Bendix, *Max Weber: An Intellectual Portrait* (New York, 1962), pp. 334-369.

30 The exercise of arbitrary free will at the expense of limiting traditions gives rise to what Weber calls "sultanism."

31 L. Machado Ribas, *Movimientos revolucionarios en las colonias españolas de América* (Montevideo, 1940), p. 23.

32 Sometimes called the Diocletian of the Spanish empire.

33 The thesis that Bolívar's political thought was cast along Thomist lines is advanced in J. Estrada Monsalve, "El sistema político de Bolívar en la doctrina tomista," *Bolívar* 13 (Sept. 1952), 463-474.

34 J. Sanín Echeverri, "Los Estados Unidos y los estados desunidos de América Latina," *Revista de la Universidad de Antioquia*, 149 (April-June 1962), 393-411.

35 L. Villoro, *La revolución de independencia* (Mexico City, 1953), p. 194.

36 *Ibid.*, p. 207.

37 This argument is developed in M. Giménez Fernández, *Hernán Cortés y su revolución comunera en la Nueva España* (Seville, 1948).

38 O. Paz, *op. cit.*, p. 117.

39 E. Arcila Farías, *El siglo ilustrado en América* (Caracas, 1955), pp. 255 ff.

40 J. Lynch, *Spanish Colonial Administration, 1782-1810* (London, 1958), pp. 279-289.

41 L. Zea, *The Latin-American Mind* (Norman, 1963), pp. xv-xvi and *passim*.

42 *Ibid.*, pp. 9-10.

43 T. Parsons, *The Social System* (Glencoe, 1951), pp. 198-199.

44 O. Gierke, *Political Theories of the Middle Age* (Boston, 1958), p. 35.

45 For the natural-law revival in modern Latin-American legal philosophy see J. L. Kunz, *La filosofía del derecho latinoamericana en el siglo XX* (Buenos Aires, 1951), pp. 49-71.

Chapter Six

1 G. M. Theal, *History of Africa South of the Zambesi from 1505 to 1795,* 3 vols. (London, 1897), II, 370, III, 353.
2 O. F. Mentzel, *A Geographical and Topographical Description of the Cape of Good Hope,* English edition, 3 vols., translated by H. J. Mandelbrote (Van Riebeeck Society, Cape Town, 1921, 1924, 1944), II, 21.
3 *Journal of Jan van Riebeeck,* English edition, 3 vols., edited by H. B. Thom, translated by J. Smuts *et al.* (Van Riebeeck Society, 1952, 1954, 1958), II, 401.
4 On primitive Calvinism, see E. Troeltsch, *The Social Teaching of the Christian Churches,* 2 vols. (New York, 1931), II, 546 ff.
5 *Journal of Jan van Riebeeck,* II, 394.
6 Mentzel, *op. cit.,* III, 105.
7 H. Lichtenstein, *Travels in Southern Africa in the Years 1803, 1804, 1805 and 1806,* English edition, 2 vols., translated by A. Plumptre (Van Riebeeck Society, 1928, 1929), I, 116.
8 Theal, *op. cit.,* II, 497, III, 35, 262-263.
9 W. Blommaert and J. A. Wiid (editors) *Die Joernaal van Dirk Gysbert van Reenen, 1803* (Van Riebeeck Society, 1937), pp. 1-8.
10 J. S. Marais, *Maynier and the First Boer Republic* (Cape Town, n.d. [1944]).
11 E. G. J. Barrow, *Travels into the Interior of Southern Africa,* 2 vols. (second edition, London, 1806).
12 Mentzel, *op. cit.,* III, 120.
13 P. J. van der Merwe, *Die Trekboer in die Geskiedenis van die Kaapkolonie* (Cape Town, 1938), p. 242; I. D. MacCrone, *Race Attitudes in South Africa* (Johannesburg, 1937), pp. 116-117.
14 Lichtenstein, *op. cit.,* I, 464.
15 I. Firenczi and W. F. Willcox, *International Migrations,* 2 vols. (New York, 1929), I, 627-630, give tables showing that 43,695 people migrated from the British Isles to South Africa between 1821 and 1870. A considerable but unknown number of these people did not settle permanently in South Africa.
16 H. E. Hockly, *The Story of the British Settlers of 1820 in South Africa* (Cape Town, 1948), p. 18, suggests that there were "about 4,000" British settlers in South Africa before 1820. This is probably too large a number.
17 A. F. Hattersley, *The British Settlement of Natal* (Cambridge, 1950).
18 Hockly, *op. cit.,* p. 34.
19 J. Bond, *They Were South Africans* (London, 1956).
20 In 1951 fifty-seven per cent of the white people of South Africa spoke Afrikaans at home, thirty-nine per cent spoke English, and one per cent spoke both. *Union Statistics for Fifty Years* (Pretoria, 1960), Tables A 18 and 19. The percentage who speak Afrikaans at home is now larger.
21 The following is a select list of books in English on South Africa in the nineteenth and twentieth centuries: G. M. Carter, *The Politics of Inequality* (London, 1958); C. W. de Kiewiet, *British Colonial Policy and the South African Republics, 1848-1872* (London, 1929), *The Imperial Factor in South Africa* (London, 1937), *A History of South Africa, Social and Economic* (Oxford, 1941); G. W. Eybers, *Select Constitutional Documents Illustrating South African History, 1795-1910* (London, 1918); J. S. Gal-

braith, *Reluctant Empire: British Policy on the South African Frontier, 1834-1854* (California, 1963); H. R. Hahlo and E. Kahn, *The Union of South Africa: The Development of Its Laws and Constitution* (London, 1960); W. K. Hancock, *Survey of British Commonwealth Affairs*, 2 vols. in 3 (London, 1937, 1940, 1942); D. W. Krüger, *The Age of the Generals* (Cape Town, 1958), *South African Parties and Policies, 1910-1960* (Cape Town, 1960); N. Mansergh, *Survey of British Commonwealth Affairs, 1931-1952*, 2 vols. (London, 1953); J. S. Marais, *The Fall of Kruger's Republic* (Oxford, 1961); L. Marquard, *The Peoples and Policies of South Africa* (Second Edition, London, 1960); A. P. Newton *et al.*, eds., *The Cambridge History of the British Empire*, Vol. VIII (Cambridge, 1936); S. Patterson, *The Last Trek: A Study of the Boer People and the Afrikaner Nation* (London, 1937); G. B. Pyrah, *Imperial Policy and South Africa, 1902-10* (Oxford, 1955); M. Roberts and A. E. G. Trollip, *The South African Opposition, 1939-45* (London, 1947); H. M. Robertson, *South Africa: Economic and Political Aspects* (Durham, N.C., 1957); L. M. Thompson, *The Unification of South Africa, 1902-1910* (Oxford, 1960); J. van der Poel, *The Jameson Raid* (London, 1951); E. A. Walker, *The Great Trek* (London, 1938), *A History of Southern Africa* (Third Edition, London, 1957). For a discussion of historical writing in Afrikaans see L. M. Thompson, "Afrikaner Nationalist Historiography and the Policy of Apartheid," *Journal of African History*, III, i (1962), 125-141. See also footnote 22 below.

22 For books in English on the history of relations between white and non-white people in South Africa, see those listed in footnote 21 above and also: J. A. I. Agar-Hamilton, *The Native Policy of the Voortrekkers* (Cape Town, 1928); M. Benson, *The African Patriots* (London, 1963); E. H. Brookes and J. B. Macaulay, *Civil Liberty in South Africa* (Cape Town, 1958); C. W. de Kiewiet, *The Anatomy of South African Misery* (London, 1956); E. Feit, *South Africa: The Dynamics of the African National Congress* (London, 1962); E. Hellman, ed., *Handbook on Race Relations in South Africa* (Cape Town, 1949); R. F. A. Hoernlé, *South African Native Policy and the Liberal Spirit* (Johannesburg, 1945); D. H. Houghton, ed., *Economic Development in a Plural Society* (Cape Town, 1960); M. Hunter, *Reaction to Conquest* (London, 1936); L. Kuper, *Passive Resistance in South Africa* (London, 1956); A. Luthuli, *Let My People Go* (London, 1962); I. D. MacCrone, *Race Attitudes in South Africa* (Johannesburg, 1937); W. M. MacMillan, *The Cape Colour Question* (London, 1927), *Bantu, Boer and Briton* (London, 1929); J. S. Marais, *The Cape Coloured People, 1652-1937* (London, 1939); S. Pienaar and A. Sampson, *South Africa: Two Views of Separate Development* (London, 1960); N. J. Rhoodie and H. J. Venter, *Apartheid* (Cape Town, 1959); E. Roux, *Time Longer than Rope* (London, 1948); I. Schapera, ed., *The Bantu-speaking Tribes of South Africa* (London, 1937); South African Institute of Race Relations, *A Survey of Race Relations in South Africa*, compiled by M. Horrell, (Johannesburg, annually, 1949 ff.); L. M. Thompson, *The Cape Coloured Franchise* (Johannesburg, 1949); S. T. van der Horst, *Native Labour in South Africa* (London, 1942).

23 Compiled from data in *A Survey of Race Relations in South Africa, 1962* (Johannesburg, 1963), pp. 64-65, and *A Survey of Race Relations in South Africa, 1963* (Johannesburg, 1964), pp. 74-75.

24 Article 9 of the Grondwet of the South African Republic. *South African Archival Records, Transvaal No. 3* (Cape Town, n.d. [1951]), p. 497.

25 The theory was most fully developed in the following works by Professor G. Cronjé: *'n Tuiste vir die Nageslag—die Blywende Oplossing van Suid Afrika se Rassevraagstukke* (A Home for Posterity—the Lasting Solution of South Africa's Racial Problems) (1945), *Afrika sonder die Asiaat* (Africa without the Asian) (1946), *Regverdige Rasse-Apartheid* (Just Racial Separation) (in co-operation with Dr. W. Nicol and Prof. E. P. Groenewald, 1947), and *Voogdyskap en Apartheid* (Trusteeship and Apartheid) (1948).

26 *Transkei Constitution Act*, 1963.

Chapter Seven

1 L. Hartz, *The Liberal Tradition in America*, p. 3.

2 It was Francis Parkman who first analyzed absolutism in French Canada and contrasted the colony in vivid terms with liberal New England. See in particular his résumé of the system in *The Parkman Reader*, S. E. Morison, ed., ch. 17. Parkman's thesis is modified by Guy Frégault in his *Civilisation de la Nouvelle France, 1713-1744*. Frégault concludes: "The French monarchy assumes a character more paternalistic than absolutist" (p. 134). It was "absolutist in theory, paternalistic in fact" (p. 137). But there is no contradiction here. French rule in Canada was paternalistic *and* absolutist. It might on occasion be misguided, vacillating, inefficient, or even neglectful, but it was not despotic or arbitrary.

3 W. A. Riddell, *The Rise of Ecclesiastical Control in Quebec* (New York, 1916), pp. 70-76.

4 *Quebec Statutes*, 25-26 George V, ch. 82, as amended in 1940 by 4 George VI, ch. 25.

5 Tithes, originally fixed at one-thirteenth, were reduced after protests to one-twenty-sixth, and were limited by the Sovereign Council to grain only.

6 Of the 10,000 immigrants, it is estimated that some 3,900 arrived as *engagés*, or indentured servants, 3,500 as soldiers who remained to settle, 1,100 as *filles du roi*, 1,000 as deportees (mainly prisoners but including some deported by *lettre de cachet* at the request of their own families), and only 500 as immigrants at their own expense. See A. R. M. Lower, *Canadians in the Making* (Toronto, 1958), p. 34.

7 The importance of the bourgeoisie during the French regime is a topic of current debate among Canadian historians. See, for example, G. Frégault, *Canadian Society in the French Regime* (Ottawa, 1954), and M. Brunet, "La Conquête anglaise et la déchéance de la bourgeoisie canadienne (1760-1793)" in *Amérique française*, XIII (1955), 19-84, and reprinted in Brunet, *La Présence anglaise et les Canadiens* (Montreal, 1958), pp. 49-112.

8 Quoted in Frégault, *La Civilisation de la Nouvelle France* (Montreal, 1944), p. 165.

9 M. Wade, *The French Canadians, 1760-1945* (Toronto, 1956), p. 50.

10 See above, Ch. IV, and also Hartz, *The Liberal Tradition in America*, Part II.

11 This view is not the traditional one, but see the impressive evidence in its support in E. C. Wright, *The Loyalists of New Brunswick* (Fredericton, 1955), ch. 8.

12 Ontario. Bureau of Archives. *Second Report*, 1904, p. 22. Dundas to Cornwallis, Oct. 3, 1787.

13 A. L. Burt, *The Old Province of Quebec* (Toronto and Minneapolis, 1933), pp. 384-390.
14 G. M. Wrong, *Canada and the American Revolution* (Toronto, 1935), pp. 401-407. The subject cries out for a full-length study.
15 There is a possible exception in New Brunswick, where Fredericton officialdom seems to have shunned commerce and looked down upon the mercantile interests of St. John.
16 Quoted in Lower, *Canadians in the Making*, p. 159.
17 A. Jameson, *Winter Studies and Summer Rambles in Canada* (Toronto, 1943), p. 30.
18 Hartz, *The Liberal Tradition in America*, pp. 67-70.
19 Indeed, in New Brunswick, where the commercial element was lacking, the Compact's lack of a suitable economic basis contributed directly to its disintegration. See Wright, *The Loyalists of New Brunswick*, pp. 239-240.
20 In Lower Canada, moreover, majority rule spelled French Catholic supremacy.
21 Actually, some 960,000. Some died on the voyage, and some re-emigrated to the United States, but it is worth noting that from 1815 until the famine years of the mid-eighteen-forties more British emigrants went to British North America than to the United States.
22 In 1806 it was estimated that the British North American colonies had a population of 460,000, and by 1815 this figure had probably reached 600,000, of whom about 250,000 belonged to the French fragment. By 1851 the same colonies had grown to 2.4 million, of whom perhaps slightly less than a third were of French origin.
23 See the figures in H. I. Cowan, *British Emigration to British North America: The First Hundred Years* (Toronto, 1961), p. 304. If it is frustrating that "farmers and farm servants" were grouped together on these lists, was it not entirely realistic in the light of New World agriculture? For a similar United Kingdom list, see W. S. Shepperson, *British Emigration to North America* (Minneapolis, 1957), pp. 262-265, where the middle and professional classes account for one per cent of adult males, and farmers (as distinct from farm laborers) thirteen per cent.
24 The one significant exception was the Irish Catholic peasant of the eighteen-forties, who clung to wage employment, but his influence was not decisive.
25 Responsible government was conceded almost simultaneously in Nova Scotia, and it spread rapidly to other British colonies throughout the world.
26 See the British North America Act, 1867, sections 92, 93, 98, 133.
27 When the Resolutions of the Quebec Conference were debated in the Legislature of the Province of Canada in 1865, the French members endorsed the draft scheme by 27 to 21 in the Assembly, and by 14 to 6 in the Legislative Council.
28 A census made in 1870 recorded 1,565 whites, 5,757 French-speaking *métis*, 4,083 English-speaking *métis*. Of the white population, just under half had been born in the Northwest.
29 Quoted in F. H. Underhill, "Political Ideas of the Upper Canada Reformers, 1867-78," *Canadian Historical Association Report*, 1942, p. 109.
30 *Canadian Statutes*, 33 Victoria c.3, sections 9-13, 22, 23, 31.
31 In 1961 there were two daily and thirteen weekly or semiweekly publications, but they accounted for only six per cent and one and four-tenths

per cent respectively of total French-language newspaper circulation. See *Canada Year Book*, 1962, p. 865.

32 The Liberals have chosen their leaders alternately from the French and English groups since 1880. Other parties, if less successful in its practice, nevertheless recognize dualism in principle, and parties formed on religious or racial lines have had no impact on federal politics.

33 Despite serious efforts, a balanced civil service has not been achieved. Strong complaints have been voiced against English-Canadian preponderance in the upper echelons.

34 To ensure familiarity with the Quebec Civil Code, the Supreme Court Act specifies that three of the nine justices must be drawn from the Quebec bar, and convention requires at least two to be French Canadians.

35 Since the Statute of Westminster in 1931, the original method of amendment by forwarding a Canadian request to the British Parliament has been an irritating anachronism, but the problem of devising a new method has been to reconcile Quebec's concern to safeguard her special position within the federation with the desire of other provinces for greater federal powers over fiscal policy and economic development.

36 For a recent survey of the strength of separatist opinion, see *Maclean's Magazine,* November 2, 1963, pp. 13-18.

37 The numbers involved in French Canada over a period of some one hundred and twenty-five years have been estimated at roughly 4,000, of whom rather less than one-third were Negroes. See M. Trudel, *L'Esclavage au Canada français* (Quebec, 1960), ch. 3.

38 For present Canadian territories the Indians are thought to have numbered about 200,000 at the time of the first European discoveries, and the numbers are roughly the same today, or one per cent of the total population. The Eskimos are so few (11,000) and so remote that contact with settled areas has been virtually nonexistent until very recently.

39 The figures are from a paper by Professor Michael Oliver on "Political Problems of Poly-Ethnic Countries—Canada," presented to the Fifth Congress of the International Political Science Association at Paris, September 26-30, 1961.

40 See above, p. 220. The "English" fragment is, of course, being slowly transformed in its cultural values by polyethnic immigration, but its central liberal ethos seems to be untouched as yet.

41 See M. F. Timlin, "Canada's Immigration Policy, 1896-1910," *Canadian Journal of Economics and Political Science*, XXVI (1960), especially 523-532.

42 On the difficulties, see P. Mélèse, "France Looks at French Canada," *University of Toronto Quarterly*, XXX (1960-1961), 367-378.

43 The 1961 census showed that seventy-one per cent of the population is urban, and that only one Canadian in eight actually lives on a farm. In 1901 the population was sixty-three-per-cent rural.

44 See above, pp. 107-113.

45 There is some evidence that it has done so. Opinion surveys suggest that the New Democratic Party attracts modest support from all occupational levels, but the problem of mass industrial support remains, for in trade-union households, as among other groups, it is still outdistanced by both the Liberal and the Conservative parties.

46 For a discussion of this development, see Hartz, *The Liberal Tradition in America*, ch. 11.

Chapter Eight

1 G. M. Trevelyan, *British History in the Nineteenth Century and After, 1782-1919* (London, 1937), p. 142.
2 *Ibid.*, p. 61.
3 *Ibid.*, pp. 251-252.
4 I. D. McNaughtan, "Colonial Liberalism, 1851-92," in Gordon Greenwood, ed., *Australia: A Social and Political History* (Sydney, 1955), p. 103.
5 R. B. Madgwick, *Immigration into Eastern Australia, 1788-1851* (London, 1937), p. 231.
6 *Ibid.*, p. 248.
7 McNaughtan, *loc. cit.*, p. 99.
8 Quoted in *ibid.*, p. 111.
9 Quoted in Trevelyan, *op. cit.*, p. 149.
10 Madgwick, *op. cit.*, p. 251. See also Geoffrey Serle, *The Golden Age: A History of the Colony of Victoria, 1851-1861* (Melbourne, 1963), pp. 371-372.
11 R. M. Crawford, *Australia* (London, 1952), p. 107.
12 B. Fitzpatrick, *The Australian People, 1788-1945* (Melbourne, 1946), ch. 18.
13 N. D. Harper, "Turner the Historian: 'Hypothesis' or 'Process'?" *University of Kansas City Review*, 18, No. 1 (Autumn, 1951), 79-80.
14 See C. S. Blackton, *Australian Nationality and Nationalism: The Imperial Federationist Interlude, 1885-1901, Historical Studies, Australia and New Zealand*, 7, No. 25 (November, 1955), 14.
15 See F. Alexander, *Moving Frontiers* (Melbourne, 1947), p. 33, n. 51.
16 W. K. Hancock, *Australia* (London, 1945), p. 12.
17 See Harper, *loc. cit.*, p. 84.
18 G. Nadel, *Australia's Colonial Culture* (Melbourne, 1957), p. 30.
19 C. M. H. Clark, *Select Documents in Australian History, 1851-1900* (Sydney, 1955), p. xii. This argument is amplified in his recent *A Short History of Australia* (Sydney, 1963), particularly Chapter Eight. As enlightening as this work is, it still seeks to interpret Australian development in terms of European categories. The urban mercantile classes are no more to be denominated a European "bourgeoisie" than are the squatters to be deemed an "aristocracy."
20 D. C. Gordon, "The Heroes of Australia," *Best Articles & Stories*, 4, No. 8 (October, 1960), 38.
21 As Russel Ward has pointed out, the only acceptable folk myth was the legend of "the bush." *The Australian Legend* (Melbourne, 1958).
22 Hancock, *op. cit.*, pp. 52-53.
23 Gordon, *loc. cit.*, p. 39.
24 Hancock, *op. cit.*, p. 56.
25 Nadel, *op. cit.*, p. 273.
26 G. Greenwood, "National Development and Social Experimentation, 1901-14," in Greenwood, ed., *op. cit.*, p. 205.
27 Madgwick, *op. cit.*, p. 236.
28 Quoted in Hancock, *op. cit.*, p. 53.
29 A. P. Elkin, "Native Peoples," in C. Hartley Grattan, ed., *Australia* (Los Angeles, 1947), p. 360.
30 McNaughtan, *loc. cit.*, p. 125.
31 J. G. Murtagh, *Australia: The Catholic Chapter* (Sydney, 1959), p. xiv.

32 B. R. Wise, *Industrial Freedom: A Study in Politics* (London, 1892), quoted in Clark, *op. cit.*, p. 272.
33 F. W. Eggleston, "The Australian Nation," in George Caiger, ed., *The Australian Way of Life* (Melbourne, 1953), p. 11.
34 R. Gollan, *Radical and Working Class Politics: A Study of Eastern Australia, 1850-1910* (Melbourne, 1960), pp. 188-189.
35 *Ibid.*, p. 153.
36 Hancock, *op. cit.*, p. 59.
37 *Ibid.*, p. 62.
38 A. C. Garnett, *Freedom and Planning in Australia* (Madison, Wis., 1949), p. 81.
39 C. H. Grattan, *Introducing Australia* (New York, 1942), p. 55.
40 A. F. Davies, *Australian Democracy* (London, 1958), p. 11.
41 G. Greenwood, *The Future of Australian Federalism* (Melbourne, 1946), p. 155.
42 J. B. D. Miller, *Australian Government and Politics* (London, 1954), p. 93.
43 L. Webb, *Communism and Democracy in Australia* (Melbourne, 1954), p. 176.
44 See *ibid.*, pp. 175-176.

Index

Index

333

Index